THE
CHINA EXECUTIVE

Marrying Western and Chinese Strengths to Generate Profitability from Your Investment in China

WEI WANG

2W
PUBLISHING

First published in Great Britain in 2006 by
2W PUBLISHING LTD
20 Brailsford Close
Bretton
Peterborough PE3 9JU
www.2wpublishing.com

Printed and bound in Hong Kong by Regal Printing

British Library Cataloguing in Publication Data
A catalogue record for this book is available from the British Library.

ISBN 0-9551636-0-9

For my family,
which makes my world
meaningful

CONTENTS

PROLOGUE

THE IDEA OF WRITING A BOOK like the one you are holding was born more than a decade ago, when I was a part-time MBA student at a leading business school in the UK in 1991. I consciously invested in my personal development to prepare myself for a China-related business career. As I read management guru Tom Peters' *In Search of Excellence*, I thought that maybe one day I could write its China version. However, the experiences I gained at a British-based multinational not only illuminated the limitations of Tom Peters' research-based approach; they also helped me develop the *feel* for the *whole* nature of business, which has served as the foundation of this book.

The multinational I joined in January 1995 was a food conglomerate (FC) with an annual turnover of about £4 billion, 55,000 employees, and businesses in Europe, Australia and North America. Although publicly traded, over 60% of the multinational was owned by a billionaire family, the head of which had been chairman and CEO of FC for twenty-five years and nicknamed "the Boss". Recognising the economic potential in Asia, he set the grand vision of "building another FC in Asia within ten years" and gave the spearheading task to the CEO of his leading British company (BC), which contributed half of FC's profits. In late 1994, the CEO appointed Tony, his former director of research and development, as Asian director to set up an office in Hong Kong.

I was appointed as business development executive, assisting directors at the "nerve centre" of BC to make China-related investment decisions. On my first day at BC, the CEO personally came down to the "nerve centre", introduced himself and welcomed me by shaking my hand. I felt very warm. But soon, I discovered that what drove the corporate behaviour of BC was one word: "logic". The directors seemed to be in debates about everything, yet they acted co-operatively once decisions were made. One such decision was to develop BC's struggling starch subsidiary in the Chinese context through forming a joint venture with a local partner. It was an "investment logic" that convinced everybody at BC because, using the joint venture as a foothold, the starch subsidiary would have access to a market that could be predicted only to grow. It was also the norm for junior staff to challenge senior staff – even the secretary challenged the directors when the former had a piece of truth or logic in hand. In short, it was logic that made BC an organised entity and ensured everyone's efficiency.

In China, however, the biggest lesson I learnt was that, for better or for worse, it is people who are central to everything. As such, the China investment challenge is a **people challenge** in nature, as demonstrated by my experience of being at the heart of developing and running one of BC's multimillion-dollar joint ventures.

People's disruption of the logic based on which an investment decision should be made. As published data on the China starch industry were extremely scarce, BC's director of starch development and I had to rely on *guanxi* (i.e. people one already knows), including a German equipment supplier and my personal friends in China to arrange visits for us in China. But logic did have a place – I spotted a potential partner in a Chinese statistics book, a Chinese company (CC) that was China's largest producer of a flavour ingredient from starch. In March 1995, we visited a few ministry officials, and some major starch producers and users. Located in rural central China, CC was state-owned. Its chairman Mr Chen told us that CC had just imported equipment for a new starch plant, which could be built and run jointly by BC and CC, with BC contributing know-how and CC buying the produced starch. Upon hearing our report back in the UK, BC decided to pursue Mr Chen's proposal.

The following eight months saw streams of BC staff travelling to CC for visits and discussions, during which, while BC strove to check every technical detail, Mr Chen wanted to get on with making the decision to establish the relationship. Then the dire prediction by Lester Brown of the Worldwatch Institute that China was to have problems with feeding its growing population caused "the Boss" concern over investing in China starch. My on-the-ground investigations, however, showed that the plant would have a secure maize supply. Of course, central to all these activities had been the effort of a BC accountant to assemble a financial model based on local operating conditions, but he had no way to verify the reliability of the data provided by CC staff.

In November, Mr Chen visited BC in the UK. We also took him to see "the Boss" in London. I was struck by the very plain style of the billionaire's dress and office, which was in sharp contrast to the extravagant style of many newly rich Chinese I had encountered. "The Boss" first asked Mr Chen about the ownership of CC, showing concern that as CC was owned by the state Mr Chen might not be CC's chairman in a few years' time. Mr Chen answered that that was true in theory but in the Chinese reality his job was almost guaranteed for the rest of his life. Satisfied by Mr Chen's answer on ownership, "the Boss" then advised that as "competition" would soon erode margins in starch production, it might be worth BC and CC considering an integrated starch and derivative facility. Mr Chen said that CC had achieved its success through "rolling a snowball", but accepted his logic. Following further discussions, BC and CC agreed to target a starch derivative (SD) that was being produced by just one Chinese state-owned enterprise using technology and equipment imported from Europe.

A technical expert and I were given two weeks to complete the market research, which confirmed the potential of SD, but we also pointed out that the key success factor was to build a marketing capability because neither BC nor CC had any. Upon returning to the UK, we found that it was up to John, director of overseas operations, to read our report due to a reshuffle. As John had rarely been involved in starch, he relied on his director of sales and marketing to digest our report. With neither direct experience in the sales of SD nor first-hand feel for the China market for SD, he only asked us a few questions of a logical nature.

BC's engineers, meanwhile, negotiated with a Danish equipment supplier (ES) on the supply of technology and equipment for the SD business, and agreed with CC's technical team, led by Mr Zhang, that

BC was to supply some refurbished centrifuges through ES to reduce capital expenditure. Then came the Chinese government announcement to abolish import duty exemption for foreign investments approved from 1 April 1996 and to require any import to be completed by the end of 1996. This meant that, to import the required equipment free of duty, which was 25–30% of US$9 million, CC and BC had to sign the supply contract with ES before forming their joint venture! As there was always the possibility that the joint venture might fail to be established, BC and CC shared the contract cancellation charges according to a 51:49 equity structure by facsimileing ES jointly signed memorandums.

Meanwhile, we struggled to assemble a satisfactory financial model for the CEO, who wanted it to show a return-on-investment (ROI) of over 20% by the fifth year before presenting it to "the Boss". The biggest uncertainty was with the forecast of sales volume because nobody had any SD sales experience while CC maintained that they could sell any volume of SD. BC and CC also struggled to agree on the transfer prices of starch by-products the joint venture would have to sell to CC. To break the negotiation deadlock while realising the vision of "the Boss" to target added-value starch business, John saw that the "most logical thing" to do was to take the starch plant out of the joint venture proposition. He consulted the CEO, whose view was that it was not until one left the negotiation table that one was able to find the bottom line of one's opponent. John then instructed Tony to tell CC that BC only wanted to work with CC on the SD business and that if CC did not accept this new position there would be no joint venture. He also added: "This should hurt them." Mr Chen then accepted the former.

As if this wasn't enough, the ROI figure of the financial model for the SD business was still less than satisfactory. John then asked us to "improve" it, so technical staff scaled down the scope of imported equipment while Tony raised the forecast sales prices.

There was one more hurdle: project cost stood at US$18 million, exceeding the US$10 million provincial approval limit, but we had no hope of obtaining central approval before 1 April. Backed by its legal advisor, BC accepted CC's idea of dividing the joint venture into two and seeking provincial approvals. Due to Mr Chen's *guanxi* in the province, it took only three days for CC to secure all the approvals, with the joint ventures obtaining the business licences on 27 March 1996.

People's disruption of the logic based on which the invested venture should be operated. At the first board meeting of the CC–BC joint venture on 15 May 1996, Mr Chen, Mr Zhang, John, Tony and I became directors of the joint venture with Mr Chen and Tony approved as the chairman and the deputy chairman. We also approved CC's nominations of Mr Zhang as the deputy general manager, and Mr Yu as CC's financial representative who, Mr Chen proudly explained, would work part-time for the joint venture because he was also a deputy chief of the local tax bureau. However, Tony's hiring advertisement in Hong Kong had so far only led to the appointment of Victor as the financial controller due to the lack of applicants for the general manager job.

Victor was Canadian-born, Cantonese/English-speaking. After establishing himself at a hotel owned by CC, he reported to Tony in Hong Kong that CC had transferred some employees to the joint venture without consulting BC. Tony did not arrive at the CC hotel until 6 August because, on completing the formation of the CC–BC joint venture, he had been asked by BC's headquarters to develop a new business in Indonesia. At his meeting with Mr Chen, Tony frankly pointed out that according to the joint venture contract, the joint venture would publicly recruit employees, and that he expected the two parties to discuss matters before taking any action. Mr Chen said CC could not afford not to do anything until BC's technical team arrived. He also added that Victor's Cantonese was not helpful in local communication.

On 12 August, BC's technical team – made of one and a half engineers because one of them also worked on the Indonesian project – arrived in Guangzhou for the first technical meeting. In contrast, Mr Zhang brought an interpreter and nine people to the meeting. When BC's engineers asked Mr Zhang about CC's plan for the starch plant that was to supply the feedstock to the SD plant, Mr Zhang emotionally replied, "This is not your business" – after all, CC had kept its expensive, imported equipment packed for over eight months in vain.

Back in the UK, John got very uneasy about the situation. Following internal discussions, BC decided to nominate me as the general manager of the joint venture, supported by an on-site technical specialist.

John wanted me to relocate my family to a local city close to the joint venture, but with a newly born son I could only rely on intensive trips between the UK and China and constant telephone calls and faxes to run the business. Tony also withdrew Victor so that I could appoint a young, Mandarin/English-speaking financial controller from Shanghai.

My new financial controller's first discovery was that as a way of contributing its 49% equity, CC had used BC's injected cash as the deed of security to open a letter of credit (LOC) to pay for the imported equipment from ES. Everybody at BC got very nervous about it but Mr Chen explained that it was "very normal" in China. This was resolved by Mr Chen, Tony and me signing a memorandum for the local bank spelling out CC's sole responsibility for the LOC. Later on, Mr Chen complained to me: "You British are doctrinaires."

Civil construction had been in good progress but problems in purchase seemed to be endless. Too many electrical cables had been ordered, while the diameters of flanges differed from those of pipe work. An assistant cook told me that he suffered from hepatitis and should work in purchase, but my investigations showed that kickbacks were the real reason. I thus decided to review the budget and established a reforecast of US$20.5 million, which included both missing items and import items previously regarded as local. I then obtained board approval for a document specifying purchase procedures and approval limits, and persuaded Mr Chen to replace dominant deputy general manager Mr Zhang with co-operative Mr Huang. I also began to build a marketing team. As the sales person Mr Chen recommended even struggled to make a phone call to potential customers, I recruited a bright marketing manager, Mr Deng, from another joint venture in the northeast.

Then came the commodity inspection bureau's declaration that the imported five centrifuges and several other items were not allowed to be used because of defects. At the third board meeting, Mr Huang said that the five centrifuges were industrial waste, while Mr Chen explained that the incident had adversely affected CC's reputation. They even brought a lawyer to advise on any legal action against ES. John's new finance director, who attended the meeting with his proxy, said nothing while Tony and I had to pretend to be angry. The resolution was for me to lead a team to negotiate with ES. On 1 April 1997, we reached an agreement for ES to repair the items in its workshop in Shanghai.

In early May, ES completed its repair work, but while I was away to relocate my family base to Shanghai, Mr Huang overstepped his authority by signing a contract worth RMB5 million with a local tank fabricator nobody had even visited. Mr Yu refused to reimburse some business trip expenses of Mr Deng's because I had refused to authorise the reimbursement of some of his personal expenses at local restaurants. When I saw Mr Chen, he said that it was time for the joint venture to take legal action against ES, and that he trusted Mr Huang and his fabrication contract because BC's technical specialist always wanted to use expensive contractors. He also complained about my recruiting sales people from other provinces on the grounds that they cost too much, even though I told him that the local sales person he recommended was incompetent. On hearing my report, John advised that BC was to send a panel of directors to review the SD project and I could discuss these issues with them. Given the pressure I was under, the review panel later decided to let Tony take over my job.

The tank fabrication contract had indeed been a disaster. Tony resolved the issue by re-importing stainless steel from Europe and choosing a fabricator in Shanghai to do the job. Following intervention from the provincial governor who met the CEO during an official trade mission in the UK, the inspection bureau declared the repaired items qualified for use on 1 April 1998, but CC did not pay the last LOC instalment. In August 1998, the police arrested Mr Huang for soliciting bribery – one piece of evidence was that he had used the joint venture's civil contractors to build two new houses for his family as side deals.

Entering 1999, the plant was commissioned as ES had promised in its contract with the joint venture but the joint venture had no working capital to keep the plant running. With little hope to obtain any bank loan and CC refusing to increase its equity, BC had no choice but to increase its equity share to 57% by injecting an additional US$2.5 million. Then, after expatriate Tony was replaced by a local director of another state-owned enterprise on cost grounds, Mr Deng left because he felt the company was no longer a joint venture under the new general manager. In 2000, following the sale of its UK starch subsidiary, BC sought to sell its stake in the joint venture to CC, but Mr Chen offered an unacceptable price. Following consultation with a consulting firm, BC decided to withdraw all its personnel from the site, provide the joint venture with a shareholder's loan, and leave its operation to CC.

Being a China executive as a personal challenge. During four years of hard work to develop new businesses in China, I worked with people ranging from the once fourth richest person in the UK to peasants in the poorest regions in China. I made over forty return journeys between the UK and China, and covered much of China. After transferring my job to Tony in late 1997, I moved on to co-ordinate the establishment of BC's second food ingredient joint venture in Southern China and steer its management development work, with my family base changed to Hong Kong. One day, I was knocked down by carbon monoxide from an inferior gas-fired shower unit when I was having a shower in an expatriate flat on the joint venture site and only regained consciousness two hours later after being taken to a distant hospital.

Yet, along with many of my colleagues, I could not escape the irony of our initial "investment logic". In March 1998, FC announced that its annual turnover had dropped by 5.5% and its annual operating profit by 7.6% for the first time in the 1990s. Its joint venture in Indonesia had to be mothballed because of the financial meltdown in the country. In China, the food ingredient joint venture established in May 1995 had also suffered from an oversupply in the market. "The Boss" thus decided not to make further investments in Asia, but to consolidate the ones already made. This meant redundancies, and I became a candidate at the end of 1998. BC's personnel director flew to Hong Kong and offered me a choice between a redundancy package and a new start back in the UK through retraining. On deep reflection, I decided to choose the former: I remained convinced that making an investment in China was the most challenging business task in the world, and that no real effort had ever been made by anyone to tackle it. I strongly felt that I should be the one to play this role.

Will what follows in this book help the CC–BC joint venture (and, indeed, many other foreign investment ventures in China) find a way forward, and millions of existing and potential China executives rise to the China investment challenge?

INTRODUCTION
Rising to the China Investment Challenge

Today businesses grow through alliances, all kinds of dangerous liaisons and joint ventures, which, by the way, very few people understand.

PETER F. DRUCKER, FATHER OF MODERN MANAGEMENT, 1995

OF ALL BUSINESS ARRANGEMENTS, joint ventures are the most complex and challenging due to the dilemma between the maximum synergy that is needed to bind two partners into one and the maximum conflict that can result from the two partners' natural differences in interests and views. Of all joint ventures, Sino-Western joint ventures are the most complex and challenging because, as it will be shown, they are in a sense an engagement of 2,500 years of almost oppositely developed Chinese and Western civilisations.

The purpose of this book is **to define the essential qualities and skills required of the China executive in forming and running a successful Sino-Western joint venture**.

From my own experience of developing and running a number of such ventures, and my examination of both Chinese and Western civilisations, I found that a Sino-Western joint venture is rather like a family where the two partners are very different and yet have to live together. I also found that just like the making of a successful family, the making of a successful Sino-Western joint venture requires both finding a suitable partner, and having an effective approach to the "family" life.

To find a suitable business partner in China – which, when overlooked, often plants the seeds of problems and troubles for the family life of a joint venture – requires four critical skills. The first is the general approach to finding one's way around in the connections-based Chinese society, which is in contrast to a rules-based Western society. The second is to correctly read the dynamics of the China market through the use of a combination of analysis- and intuition-based methods so that the right business opportunity is identified. The third is to approach, assess and select a partner, emphasising the significance of strategic location and the necessity of considering both quantitative and qualitative factors in the taking of that life decision. The fourth is to effectively negotiate with a potential partner through thorough preparations, taking account of Chinese negotiating philosophy so that the right business deal is structured.

The aim of an effective approach to the "family" life of a Sino-Western joint venture is to achieve both successful results and harmonious relationships, which requires four key skills. The first is to undertake effective communication. Many communication gaps can exist in such a venture, including the clash between Western contract and Chinese relationship orientations, cultural barriers between Westerners and local staff, and the communication gap between expatriates and their headquarters. The second is to explore effective ways of training the Chinese in face of the human resource challenge in China, appreciating the importance of evolving from expatriate support to localisation. The third is to learn to lead the Chinese the Chinese way, given the Chinese criterion for human relationships, i.e., feelings, reasons and rules, in that order, and to manage oneself in the uncertain China business environment. The fourth is to drop the myth of Western management techniques' inapplicability to China and learn to balance managing and leading according to particular circumstances.

Apart from the above skills, Western executives will need to broaden their horizon of thinking to ensure success in China. First, they need to expand their strategic thinking from economic analysis and the pursuit of competitive advantage to one that is holistic, covering business purpose, business climate, business location, business organisation and business leader, and pursues strategic advantage that involves both creation and competition. Second and most profoundly, they need to establish a strong belief in a broadly based winning approach that seeks to combine Western and Chinese strengths, including combining a Western things-oriented, divided worldview and a Chinese human-centred, integrated worldview, and modern Western management excellence and ancient Chinese leadership wisdom.

In a broad sense, *The China Executive* thus defines the qualities and skills of a new generation of executives against the "effective" executives whom Peter Drucker defined half a century ago and who have since been at the core of Western modernisation. Despite recognising others' work in motivation, Drucker has, most of all, emphasised the effectiveness of managers, in the sense of their ability to organise resources in order to achieve the satisfactory performance of an enterprise. Managers, says Drucker, must in the end be measured by their economic performance, and management by objectives (MBO) is the key to this. In fact, MBO – *dividing* corporate goals into objectives and assigning them to units and individuals – was identified by Drucker as the first of seven primary tasks of management in his book *The Practice of Management* (1955), which established his reputation as a management guru.

As such, *The China Executive* represents an expansion of the "results" orientation to one based on both "results" and "relationships", or an expansion of the pure "economic" perspective to one that encompasses both "economic" and "social" facets, reflecting the reality of today's world of business where command-and-control is giving way to co-operation, goodwill and trust. It is characterised by *integration*: integration of theory and practice, integration of analysis and intuition – integration, in other words, of all major concepts and ideas related to business. These include history, society, politics, economics and culture; management and leadership; operation, personnel, finance and marketing; organisation, market, industry and strategy; and human being, philosophy and humour.

In short, against the "management theory industry" in the West, *The China Executive* is immediately refreshing because it not only integrates all major theories but also brings to light the highest essence of any business. It does not use jargon to confuse the reader but plain words to convey wisdom that works. It does not use long checklists that do not apply to every circumstance but simple pictures to focus the reader's mind on the essentials. It rises to the China investment challenge and draws a coherent road map of how to succeed in China, when most authors either talk up or despair.

Investing in China: From "Love Affair" to "Family Life"

China has been very successful in absorbing foreign direct investment (FDI) since Deng Xiaoping opened its door to the outside world in 1979. During the twenty years from 1979 to 1999, China absorbed over US$300 billion in FDI, second only to the US. Yet, surveys of various sources had consistently indicated that while a quarter of foreign investments had exceeded their initial expectations, over half had taken longer than forecast to achieve profitability or performed worse than expected. There had been instances of success but most foreign investors involved had simply been lucky because they hit the right thing at the right time. A survey conducted by the Economist Intelligence Unit in 1999 estimated that more than one fifth of all foreign invested companies had actually pulled out of at least one loss-making venture. Many had also reported that the return on their investments in China had been lower than in other Asian countries.

Most Western executives would quickly point to many reasons, of a Chinese nature, why their investments had under-performed in China, such as smaller-than-expected market size, poor joint venture partners and lack of qualified local staff. But underlying all these reasons is the fact that, between 1979 and 1999, Western investors had been conducting a "love affair" with China, where Western executives' trained tough-mindedness and scepticism gave way to the attraction of "1.2 billion shoppers". Although the CC–BC joint venture described in the Prologue is only one of hundreds of thousands of Sino-foreign joint ventures, the lessons it demonstrates, on the part of multinationals, are typical, with most knowing very little about what it takes to make a successful investment in China.

By the late 1990s, foreign investors' "love affair" with China had, in many ways, come to an end: they began consolidating and reflecting, with FDI in China falling to US$40 billion both in 1999 and 2000 from 1998's US$45.6 billion. On the other hand, they were now in a good position to live a "family life" with China because they could not only draw on the hard lessons learnt but also operate under the rules increasingly set by the World Trade Organisation (WTO), which China joined on 11 December 2001.

The WTO is a rules-based organisation, and China's entry means that the world's seventh largest economy and the ninth largest trading nation will be obliged to abide by a set of international rules that are binding, comprehensive and detailed. These rules, which are enforceable through the dispute settlement procedures of the WTO, guarantee that all members are equal in their rights and obligations. As such, foreign investors will enjoy freer operating conditions. There will be greater clarity and transparency in the rules, regulations, and procedures for doing business in China and in the awarding of contracts and licences, whilst the scope for discrimination will decrease. There will also be better protection for intellectual property rights given that China has agreed to implement the Trade-Related Intellectual Property Agreement of the WTO.

Many other operating conditions in China should improve too. Changes to the restrictions on trading rights will enable companies operating in China to import manufactured goods from outside the country, and will also allow them to export raw materials to overseas markets as part of global sourcing arrangements. The cost of sourcing raw materials for manufacturing operations in China will come down as tariffs come down or are phased out completely. China's agreement to open up its banking industry will improve local currency financing and make credit facilities much more accessible. Amendments to the regulations on market research will enable companies to conduct market research with greater confidence and help them respond more effectively to the needs of customers. Changes to the rules on foreign insurance, legal and accounting services should make them more accessible to foreign investors. Liberalisation in the telecom arena should help to make telecommunication services more efficient for all companies. Relaxation of restrictions on establishing their own distribution networks will provide foreign investors with greater certainty in managing their own business operations. Retail distribution should be improved by China's agreement to lift the joint venture restrictions on large retail stores and chains of more than thirty outlets. In the auto sector, foreign companies will be allowed to provide auto financing in China; all restrictions on the types and models of vehicles produced by joint venture manufacturers will be lifted. China's commitments to remove a number of onerous requirements on foreign investors, such as export performance, local content and technology transfer, are also welcome news.

Of course, unprecedented investment opportunities will also arise from China's opening of its highly protected markets, including telecommunications, banking, insurance, distribution, legal services, accountancy, architecture, tourism, construction and market research. China's WTO accession should, therefore, lead to a significant increase in FDI in the country. Evidence is already abundant. On 11 December 2001, the day China acceded to the WTO, New York Life received approval to establish a joint venture insurance company in China. Two weeks later, it announced the selection of Haier Group, China's leading home electric appliance producer, as its partner because "Haier knows China and we know insurance. Coming together, we make a strong company which knows both insurance and China." Twelve months later, the Shanghai-based joint venture sold its first policy in China.

In 2001, FDI in China began climbing again and reached US$46.8 billion, and in 2002, 2003 and 2004, the figure reached US$52.7 billion, US$53.5 billion (this was achieved despite the negative impact of SARS) and US$60.6 billion respectively. And when all this takes off, coupled with their existing strong presence in China, foreign investors will be in a position not only to respond to forces in the China business environment but also to weave the threads that will make its future.

Relevance to You

Despite the brief, coastal encounters between Chinese and Western cultures in history, China had largely been a mystery to Westerners. Even after two decades of interactions since 1979, China remains a "puzzle" to most Westerners. Because of its history, China is unique – "Nowhere quite like it, old boy." "It is totally different from anywhere else, opaque where others can be more readily understood," as Chris Patten, the last governor of Hong Kong, famously reflected in his book *East and West* (1998). Most Western publications on doing business in China thus overload the reader with things Chinese and encourage the reader to bridge the cultural gulf through learning "the Chinese way" (see Ming-Jer Chen's highly publicised *Inside Chinese Business* published by the prominent Harvard Business School Press in 2001, for example).

But is there a limit to such learning, and where can Westerners stand? Can everything the Chinese do be the right thing, and can the Chinese way of doing things always be the right one? By examining the present and the history of both China and the West, this book demonstrates that there is a limit to learning the Chinese way. There are things that you need to go about the Chinese way but there are also things that you definitely need to go about the Western way – otherwise, you lose the purpose of going there in the first place.

While this book focuses on Sino-Western joint ventures, the principles of finding worthwhile business opportunities and suitable partners to work with, as well as the principles of networking, negotiating, communicating, training, managing and leading developed here apply equally to other forms of commercial endeavour in China. Whatever happens, in China the Chinese are your partner, whether as employees, customers, suppliers, officials or even competitors. This book is therefore immediately beneficial to a wide spectrum of people directly related to doing business in China, including directors, managers, sales people, engineers, accountants, and IT specialists working in joint ventures and wholly foreign-owned businesses in China. Successful investment in China also requires the understanding and support of colleagues at headquarters in the West. In general, they need to be educated about the China business reality and be made fully aware of what it means to invest in China. This book can therefore also serve as a China education book for the Western business community at large.

With the end of the Cold War, developing countries have joined the

West in the pursuit of progress in all aspects of life, and there is huge potential for wealth to be created through the joint effort of people from different cultures. Through examining the most complex business arrangement, i.e. Sino-Western joint ventures involving two contrasting cultures, *The China Executive* develops concepts and principles, such as principle-centred adaptation, partner selection, negotiation and management-leadership unity, which are equally applicable to business arrangements involving more similar cultures. For example, the culture of Eastern European countries and Russia is closer to the Western counterpart; although the culture of East Asian countries, such as Japan and the "Four Dragons", originated from Chinese culture, it has been influenced on a vast scale by Western culture. As such, conducting business across these cultures is less challenging. This book therefore offers Western executives a way to deal with the challenge of today's ever-growing globalisation of business activities.

Even when operating in their homeland, Western executives will benefit from reading this book. Using China as a reference point, the book pinpoints a direction for the evolution of business management and leadership in the West. It demonstrates that there is a limit on operational excellence achieved through management tools, and that business success is the result of organically balancing managing and leading. In addition, it shows that there is substantial scope for Western executives to learn from ancient Chinese leadership and strategic wisdom because effective organisational change and new business growth will increasingly be the result of leadership skills and strategy.

Last but perhaps more profoundly, this book challenges the conventional thinking of Western business schools, which in my view concentrates far too much on sophisticated analytical techniques and touches little on what business really is and how it can be successfully done. Thus, business school students, in particular MBA students around the world, should benefit from reading this book, which provides a practical, highly integrated view of business.

I hope you enjoy using what you learn from *The China Executive* and that, as a result, you will enjoy healthier, happier and more effective working lives in China, in the West and elsewhere in the world.

PART I

FINDING A
SUITABLE PARTNER

Men are from Mars, women are from Venus.
DR JOHN GRAY, AUTHOR OF
TWENTY MILLION COPY BEST-SELLER

STEPPING INTO THE
NETWORKED SOCIETY

If you enter a region, ask what its prohibitions are; if you visit a
country, ask what its customs are; if you cross a family's threshold,
ask what its taboos are.

CONFUCIUS, *THE BOOK OF RITES*

It is not what you know but who you know that is the most important factor in doing business in China.

ANONYMOUS WESTERN BUSINESSMAN

HAVING LIVED AND WORKED IN THE WEST, what will Western executives experience when they step into Chinese society and seek to
do business with the Chinese? "Culture shock" has been the stereotype
answer, which is caused by differences in "the way things are done",
according to most culture experts. However, given the historical gulf
between the West and China, such cultural differences are endless and
exist in virtually every aspect of life. As a result, a lot of these cultural
analyses tend to overload Western executives because it is simply un-
realistic for them to immediately unlearn what they have learned over
decades in the West, and equip themselves with everything Chinese.
What they need is a "handle" on China to enable them to get started, so

they can learn and pick up the details as they go along. The purpose of this first chapter is to present such a "handle" to the reader.

Rules-Based West versus Connections-Based China

China cannot thoroughly be understood from either a Western or a Chinese viewpoint. To grasp its nature requires an orbital, historical view of both the West and China.

The Myth of the Collectivism of the Chinese

Seeing the Chinese inter-connected in various ways in society, and having been influenced by the conclusion of the leading culture expert Geert Hofstede's "monumental work" *Culture's Consequences* in 1980, most Westerners now hold the view that, in contrast to their own individualism, the Chinese are collectivist. They therefore assume that the prime motivation of the Chinese is towards the common objectives of the group. But in my years of experience in both the West and China, I have realised that, although Chinese individuals have a strong tendency to relate to each other, they do not necessarily work together towards a shared goal. In fact, on the contrary, the Chinese are much less collective than Westerners. For instance, inside Sino-Western joint ventures, I have found that, while Westerners debate vigorously among themselves about the best way to get something done, local employees neither communicate well with Western personnel nor discuss business issues adequately among themselves. When they do talk among themselves, they talk a lot about personal matters, and when they act, they tend to follow their own rules rather than those of the group.

Critics of the Chinese in history have made the following observations:

The Chinese cannot have a group of more than three people, and cannot have an enthusiasm lasting for more than five minutes.

The Chinese are like a pile of loose sand.

One Chinese is equal to intelligence, but two Chinese together are equal to stupidity.

Liu Chuanzhi, president of the then Legend Group, the leading Chinese computer giant with revenues of RMB17 billion in 1998, made the following comments on China's central TV in 1998:

There are many things in China that people can do well, but there is a lack of effective organisation and co-operation. In other words, each individual is a pearl, but many pearls cannot be organised into a force. My Japanese friends told me, 'You Chinese people are very intelligent, at least are more intelligent than we Japanese. You are also faster in comprehension and reaction. However, you Chinese are poor in co-operation and organisation.' Japanese often say that they are afraid of one Chinese individual but not two Chinese. As a Chinese person, I feel uncomfortable when I hear such comments. But the Japanese are right. 'A pile of loose sand' is still our nation's biggest weakness.

In everyday life, many Chinese also like to quote the following ancient Chinese anecdote when they suffer from the lack of co-operation among themselves:

When a monk lived alone in a temple, he was able to carry two buckets of water with a bamboo pole on his shoulder from a spring in order to feed himself. One day, another monk joined him, and they worked out that the best way to fetch the water was to carry one bucket of water on the bamboo pole between them. Later on, a third monk arrived. No matter how hard they tried they could not find a way to distribute the water-carrying work evenly among the three of them. So, they had no water to drink since.

Yet when I have heard people quoting it, rarely has anyone gone any further to explore innovative solutions to the underlying problem. For instance, some sort of schedule might be figured out so that each of the three monks participated in fetching the water on alternative days. A brighter solution might be that two monks carried a bucket of water on a bamboo pole while the other monk fetched the wood. More profoundly, few recognise the sense of responsibility involved in the story: no monk was prepared to step forward to take on even a tiny bit more responsibility to ensure collective survival.

So how do we explain the dual individualism–collectivism of Westerners and the inter-relatedness of the Chinese? The answer lies in the fundamental difference between their respective social life orientations in history, which, contrary to what leading culture experts suggest, do not represent two poles of the same continuum.

Group/Individual-Oriented Westerners versus Family-Oriented Chinese

The difference between Westerners and the Chinese with respect to social life is that Westerners emphasise both group and individual, whereas the Chinese emphasise family (see Figure 1.1, where type size indicates the relative importance of a particular social orientation, solid arrow lines clearly defined relationships, and dashed arrow lines vaguely defined relationships).

In the West, although people have families, their intense group life has reduced the importance of their family life. They normally belong to various groups, such as work organisations, sports clubs, hobby societies, political parties, religious groups and so on. They all know that for a group to function effectively and efficiently, which ultimately will be beneficial to all the members, a set of rules has to be established and every member must subscribe to them. As group life is much richer in the West, each individual's personality is also much better developed: in a group, an individual is encouraged to take initiative and play an active, creative role. Freedom of expression, individual accountabil-

FIGURE 1.1

Social Life Orientation Contrast

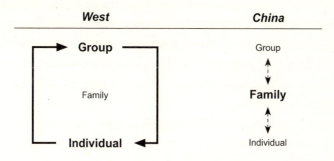

ity and personal rights are valued. Westerners glory in their individual differences, nurture them and value them as the essential features that make them unique and, indeed, make a group viable. Group and individual are therefore the two sides of a coin; one cannot exist without the other.

The group/individual orientation of Westerners stems, to a large extent, from the dominance of religions in the past, and of Christianity in particular, which encouraged group activities beyond the boundary of the family. In modern times, industrialisation further broke the boundary of the family and reinforced the development of group organisation and the role of the individual. Democracy is another factor that has promoted a dynamic group life, although the scope of the group here is the state. In fact, all through medieval, modern and contemporary times, Westerners have been shifting their life orientation between the concept of the individual and that of the group. Choosing what weight to place on each concept has possibly been the single most important issue in their life and ideology.

In China, people regard the family as the most basic social unit and attach much more importance to the relations in the family than to their group/individual life. Moreover, family relations have been extended to the whole of society, so that the sense of mutuality, of being connected through affection, obligation and responsibility to specific people becomes the central theme, seriously overshadowing the functionality of both group and individual. In any social group in China, it is inevitable that informal, personal human relations tend to prevail over group rules. The best teacher–pupil relationship is called a "father–son" relationship, best friends are called "brothers", and the best officials are called "father and mother" officials. The notion of individual "privacy" simply does not exist among Chinese people – people are generally very much aware of the comings and goings of those around them. Even after decades of Western influence, most Chinese people equate individualism to selfishness.

The family orientation of the Chinese originates from the dominance in ancient times of Confucianism, which prescribed five cardinal, interpersonal relations, involving both obedience and accountability, to Chinese society: "ruler and minister, father and son, husband and wife, elder brother and younger brother, and friends". Family-based agriculture had been the emphasis for development throughout Chinese history. After 1949, the central government's measures to bring everything under its control and its use of severe legal tools to prohibit the mass from voluntarily establishing any form of association or society had virtually eliminated the possibility of the rise of any intermediate social groups. Although urban Chinese had a certain industry-based organisational life, the spirit of teamwork was, at times, badly damaged by political upheavals like the Great Leap Forward and the Cultural Revolution.

In a real sense, China's reform since the late 1970s can be seen as the introduction of laws, regulations and rules to reorganise society, i.e. to enhance the group/individual orientation of the Chinese. Although a great deal of new wealth has been created through new forms of organisations, such as private businesses and collective enterprises, most problems, whether political, social or economic, and most obstacles to further development stem from the historical heritage of family orientation. For it is still hugely difficult to draw a clear boundary for any social group by defining a purpose and a set of rules for it, and enabling every group member to adhere to them.

Therefore, compared with rules-based Western society, Chinese society is, in essence, connections-based (see Figure 1.2, where a box represents a group and a line a connection; a bold font and a solid line are more important than a regular font and a dashed line respectively).

FIGURE 1.2

Social Structure Contrast

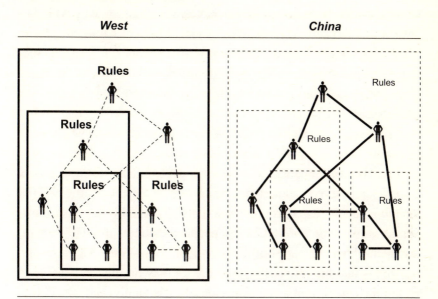

West   China

Characteristics of Connections-Based Chinese Society

Due to the dominance of connections, Chinese society demonstrates
unique personal, organisational, public, political, economic and social
characteristics and, above all, a sense of humour very different from its
Western counterpart, even though there are parallels in the two societies.

Personally: Lack of Independent Personality

"Personality" means the state of existing as a particular person or a
person's whole nature or character. However, the word "personality"
(*renge* in Chinese) does not even exist in *Ciyuan* and *Cihai*, the two
most comprehensive Chinese dictionaries published in 1979 and 1980,
because, once born, a Chinese individual is defined by bilateral rela-

tionships with others. Children develop this sense of being connected through a myriad of daily situations with their parents and others, including shared bedrooms, circular tables, late-night outings with parents, and supervision of homework by elder brothers. Children are told, "Don't question the world around you or try to change it; accept it. Submit willingly and unquestioningly to authority." At school, "a strong character" is normally put as a weakness in the appraisal of a pupil. The Chinese also like to remind each other of the ancient saying that "When one is at home, one should rely upon one's parents; when one goes out, one should rely upon one's friends."

The basic "personality" framework of contemporary Chinese people is made up of three major elements, i.e. "being fearful of officials" (*pa gongpu*), "being dependent on work units" (*kao danwei*), and "following the crowd" (*sui daliu*). Chinese people are utterly afraid of expressing themselves in front of officials or their bosses, especially expressing things that the officials or their bosses may not like to hear. They regard their work unit as an extension of their family, and expect it to look after them by providing welfare services ranging from help at the birth of a baby, help with children's schooling and employment or with reconciliation of family disputes, to assistance at an employee's funeral or even a gift of fuel for cremation. "The tree growing high above the others will be blown down by the wind." "The gun fires at the first bird in the flock." "A fool knows how to celebrate the Chinese New Year by watching his neighbours." These are only a few of the popular Chinese sayings that tell people to "follow the crowd".

Organisationally: Lack of Teamwork Capability

Teamwork capability is the capability to work with others in a team. The key ingredients are the habits of discussing matters and co-operating with each other on an equal basis. Yet the Chinese are not good team players, as some critics of the Chinese say, "the Chinese either give themselves up as hopeless or like practising self-importance; they either do not want the right to speak or want to become an emperor." For example, at Chinese universities, many students devote a lot to the development of the student union, but others have to follow their opinions, otherwise they will become discouraged and distance themselves from the union's activities, and if they feel strongly, they may take action to split it altogether. In local townships or villages, if officials give orders, people are most happy to follow. However, if officials take a democratic step by giving the issue to the public to discuss, endless arguments will occur, making the issue impossible to resolve. And if orders are issued then, people will not follow.

An integral part of teamwork capability is professional ethics and professional capability, i.e. the sense of responsibility and the capability to play one's role. Yet stories of amazingly unethical or unqualified professional practices are abundant in China. There are teachers who arrive at their class with chocolates and snack food to sell and doctors and nurses who directly or indirectly ask patients for "red bags". In Hebei Province, after a deputy head of Xongxian County's Electricity Bureau was refused entry to a dancing hall because it was full, he made an excuse and ordered the operators to switch off half the county's power supply. The poor professional capability of the Chinese is clearly shown in the following statistics. In Asia, China's productivity of labour is only slightly higher than that of Bangladesh and is a lot lower than that of India. China's per capita income is only 2–4% of that in developed countries. The manufacturing productivity of labour in China is about 1/12 of that in the USA or 1/11 of that in Japan.

Publicly: Lack of Discipline Habits

Public discipline refers to the discipline that people are accustomed to in a general public setting without the need to explicitly announce it. What one does is part of a group exercise and should be in rhythm with what others do; only by observing public discipline can things be done in the most efficient manner that benefits everybody. When in a public setting, such as a street, a meeting, a cinema, a toilet, a park, a railway station or an airport, many Chinese seem to think that they are still at home. Their ears, eyes and limbs seem to work only for themselves and rarely sense the group's needs. This is why Bo Yang, a Taiwanese scholar, once famously pointed out that one of the most salient features of the Chinese is their "dirtiness, chaos and noisiness". They also seem not to understand that public assets are there for the benefit of everyone.

Spitting at one's discretion may be regarded as the "habit of the nation". In Beijing, when a tourist was given a fine of RMB5 for spitting inside a railway station, he produced RMB10 and said, "Can I spit once more?" In any public setting, many Chinese also throw rubbish at their discretion. A group of overseas tourists once went into a public toilet in China and immediately came out, commenting, "If the Chinese don't even know how to operate a toilet, how can they modernise a country?" In any service points in China, good, ordered queues are extremely rare. At a bus stop, most people will force their way into a bus before others get off. In Chongqing, some mothers even threw their babies into a bus through windows in order to occupy a seat. When telephone boxes were first installed in Beijing, most suffered from damage within weeks – glass was broken, aluminium doors were removed, handsets stolen, boxes pried open, and coin slots blocked. In Tianjin, of the six hundred copper words on the monument that was built to commemorate the huge civil project to bring in Lianhe River water to Tianjin, two-fifths have been chiselled off and then sold as waste copper.

Politically: Lack of Rule of Law

Rule of law refers to the governing of the behaviour of members of a society by the law, which adjudicates impartially between individual citizens and between individuals and their government, and is supported by the power of government. But in China, instead of subscribing to the principles of rule of law, people have always placed their hope on finding "honest and upright officials" (*qing guan*). One official in the judicial department once vividly described: "Our law and regulations are like a rope. The tall step over it, the short go under it, and only the honest are stopped."

Since the reform, the central government has issued over 80 documents aimed at reducing the use of public funds on eating and drinking, with more specific documents issued by local governments, such as "the prohibition of officials from eating trepan, abalone, prawn, scallop and catfish on official visits". In one document, the central government restricted meals for official meetings to "four dishes and a soup". But suddenly the supply of larger plates on the market fell short of demand because people used larger plates to confine the same dishes to "four dishes and a soup". Some simply learned from the Western style of dish-serving – taking off the old dish when serving a new dish so as to maintain four dishes on the table at any time – and adapted the soup to a chafing dish, which is more tasty (and more expensive) than an ordinary soup.

Because of the lack of rule of law, corruption, i.e. the trading of power for money, becomes inevitable among some officials. From Beijing, the most ordered city, to the poorest province of Guizhou, from politburo and ministries to county and township governments, and from banks and state enterprises to police and judicial bodies, corruption cases have been regularly reported. Yet according to the director of China's anti-corruption bureau, "Chinese media rarely conduct any direct investigations into the corruption of officials, and what is reported in the media are only closed cases."

Economically: Lack of Fair Competition

Due to the lack of rule by economic law and regulation, the principle of fair competition is seriously lacking in the Chinese economy. Many private businesses and township enterprises, which use bribery and kickbacks as business weapons, can beat state-owned enterprises and foreign-invested businesses; underground factories and smugglers, which use illegal methods to become low-cost players in the market, can in turn beat licensed private businesses and township enterprises. As a result, the "Chinese business miracle" has occurred, where "shrimps can eat small fish, and small fish can eat large fish." One Chinese economist summarised: "The market economy is like a basketball game. The current problem is that one side is following basketball rules, the other side football rules. And as the referee disregards what the latter does and takes no measures to stop it, the end result is definitely chaotic fighting,

with the side that used to observe the rules of a basketball game beginning to learn from the other side."

It is widely believed that the average kickback in the sale of all goods
in China is 3–5%, whilst kickbacks for coal mixed with waste rocks,
fake cigarettes and liquor, and fake medicines and publications can be
as high as 8–10%, 20–30%, and 40–50% respectively. According to
various authoritative sources, fake goods occupy 20% of the domestic
market, but fake famous brand liquor or cigarette products occupy over
80% of the respective sectors. A girl tried to commit suicide by taking "deadly" pesticide but failed because the pesticide was a fake. In
Gongxian, Henan, 104 plants were once set up by some several tens of
thousands of peasants to make fake and inferior fertilisers. In 1998, the
State Pharmaceutical Administration found that 112 medicine producers, 39 medicine dealers, 3 wholesale markets, and 40 hospitals and
clinics were involved in the production, distribution or prescription of
fake and inferior medicines. On Chinese national TV, I saw millions of
fake anti-fake hologram labels being found.

Socially: Lack of Healthy Activities

To be sure, given its 2,500 years of interpersonal history, there is no
lack of social activities in China. However, healthy social activities,
i.e. those that promote modern personality (such as competition and
co-operation) and social progress (such as value for innovation and
exploration), are still scarce compared with a Western society. While
people in the West spend a lot of their spare time on activities such
as sports, clubs, camps, concerts, and tours, Chinese social activities
are dominated by eating and drinking, playing *mahjong* and practising
superstition.

Sun Yat-sen (1866–1925), the father of modern China, once wrote,
"China's civilisation in modern times is backward in all but one respect:
its progress in food is unmatchable by other civilised nations." Nearly
a century later, most Chinese still regard eating as their first happiness.
There is a saying, "The Chinese will eat everything in the sky except
planes, everything in the sea except torpedoes, everything on the ground

except tanks, and everything under the ground except land mines." In Guangzhou, a restaurant began offering meals dusted with gold – eating gold is supposed to bring good luck. But does anyone who can afford to eat gold need any more good luck? Some officials complained that the excessive alcohol that they had to drink at banquets had damaged their stomach but still they had to attend with tablets in their pockets.

As a spare-time activity, playing *mahjong* must be the most popular, as a local saying puts it: "Among 1 billion people in China, 900 million play *mahjong* while 100 million dance. Those who neither play mahjong nor dance are idiots." The superstition of the Chinese has made it possible for pseudo-*qigong* masters to swindle money out of a very large number of followers through such "power" as curing diseases remotely. In Hubei, when a lady peasant saw a dragon-shaped pumpkin vine in her garden and claimed that it was "dragon making its presence", tens of thousands of people came to make a sacrifice.

Laughing at Rules – the Chinese Sense of Humour

When Westerners get frustrated with the Chinese, they complain that the Chinese do not have a sense of humour. But I have discovered that the Chinese do laugh a lot among themselves at things that Westerners do not find funny. A sense of humour is a viewpoint, a way of looking at life. Westerners typically laugh at individuals for doing something in a stupid way, i.e. not following the rules. However, the Chinese sense of humour comes from their sometimes over-intelligent attitude towards life. It is characterised by laughing at rules and can be observed more in people's actions than in their conversations. The following two real life stories, which most Westerners will find disgraceful rather than humorous, should give you an appreciation of the Chinese sense of humour:

> Wife: 'What are you doing cutting up the picture album I just bought?'
> Husband: 'Oops! I thought you borrowed it from the library.'

Customer: 'How come the drinks you sell here taste so watered down?'

Waiter (after tasting the wine): 'Sorry, I forgot to mix in the alcohol.'

In general, the Chinese are Taoists in nature and Confucians in culture. When they are winners they are Confucians; when they are losers they are Taoists. Confucians strive and construct, whereas Taoists watch and smile. As a nation, the Chinese can be so great as to establish the most detailed law, but at the same time they can be so great as to resolve most disputes outside the court. They can be so great as to establish the most tedious etiquette, but at the same time they can be so great as to regard this etiquette as part of the joke of life. They can be so great as to condemn evil in the loudest way, but at the same time they can be so great as to take the most tolerant attitude towards evil. Yet, the Chinese sense of humour has a destructive effect when taken to an extreme, because in laughing at the rules they have established in the first place, the Chinese are losing the opportunity to progress collectively.

Finding Your Way Around in China through Networking

Given the network nature of Chinese society, Western executives who are used to working in accordance with rules will inevitably struggle when they want to get things done in China. As they cannot change the network nature of Chinese society, they have to learn the art of networking in order to be effective in China. Yet to ensure long-term success, the adaptation needs to be principle-centred.

The Chinese Concept of *Guanxi* (Connection)

One of the biggest puzzles Western business people have had in China concerns the meaning of "friendship". In the West, a friend is someone with whom you have a close relationship that is based on intangible, shared values and qualities. If someone wants something from you, then their motives for friendship are impure and they are not a true friend of yours. In China, a friend is by definition someone who does extraordinary favours for you, and someone who refuses to do so is by definition not your friend. Among the Chinese themselves, I have noted, friend (*pengyou*) and connection (*guanxi*) are used interchangeably, the only difference being that the former sounds less direct than the latter. We also know that the whole of Chinese society is based on connections. So, to understand Chinese behaviour and to function effectively in Chinese society, we have to understand the Chinese concept of *guanxi*.

From my study of both Western and Chinese civilisations, I have discovered that while the Western worldview has been formed through concepts by *postulation* (with the starting point being the *division* between this world and God), the Chinese worldview has been formed through concepts by *intuition* (with the starting point being how a human being *feels*). As such, while Western society has been founded on religious principles, at the heart of Chinese society have been human feelings (*renqing*). We know that from religious principles have come such necessities as law, regulations, rules, and procedures, which govern everybody in Western society. But how can human feelings be expected to hold society together and make it function harmoniously?

Two and a half centuries ago, Confucius observed that *ren* (the ideograph that is made up of the radical "human" and the word "two") was the most fundamental value for society. *Ren* has been translated as "human-heartedness" or "benevolence", and elaborated as kindness in human relationships. But according to Confucius, "to be able from one's own self to draw a parallel for the treatment of others is the way to practice *ren*," which includes "Do to others what you wish for yourself," and "Do not do to others what you do not wish for yourself." In other words, the "measuring square" for determining conduct is in one's self and not in other things, e.g. "Serve your ruler as you would require your subordinate to serve you;" "Do not use what you dislike in your superior in the employment of your inferior."

In contemporary China, *mianzi* (face) has become the "measuring square" for determining one's conduct. If you want recognition, give recognition to others; if you want attention and appreciation, learn to give attention and appreciation; if you want material affluence, help others to become materially affluent – this is what "giving face" means. And if you do not want to be overlooked, do not overlook others; if you do not want to be insulted, do not insult others; if you do not want to be seen as poor, do not expose the poor state of others – this is what "saving face" means. Thus one's face is a combination of a sense of moral imperatives, social honour and self-respect. This moral aspect of face is particularly important because it demands people to conduct themselves as decent human beings and fulfil their obligations regardless of the pain and cost. Once people gain a bad reputation, it will no longer be possible for them to function effectively in their community because they will lose friends and will be ostracised. As such, for the average person, face is also self-worth.

Thus, when our feelings are used as a standard to regulate our conduct, they do not function as a static code like in Western society but are characterised by a dynamic exchange between two individuals, i.e. the dynamics of give and take. Despite all the effort to give and save face that produces positive feelings, behaviours involving loss of face will cause negative feelings. And while existing positive feelings can offset the negative ones, once the cumulative feelings, i.e. a sense of "trust", become negative, the relationship breaks down.

With this understanding of *renqing* and *mianzi*, we can now define *guanxi* as the emotional bond between two individuals in society, which is founded on the net positive feelings between them that are regulated by reciprocity and manifested as face-work (see Figure 1.3).

FIGURE 1.3

The Chinese Concept of *Guanxi* (Connection)

Getting Things Done in China: The Art of Networking at Work

In the West, the logic of getting things done is largely based on the promise that economic life is predictable and proceeds in a linear fashion – a target is fixed, resources allocated, and implementation monitored. In China, getting things done means building up and maintaining a network of reliable connections, finding the right people to talk to as problems crop up, backtracking or side-stepping when necessary, advancing when possible. Although the resulting path may seem difficult and confusing, applying the art of networking is the most effective way to avoid getting stuck in the complex, dynamic China business environment and, indeed, to accomplish your goals. Specifically, you need to take three critical steps: (1) making first connections; (2) nurturing and enlarging your network; and (3) becoming a master of your network.

Making First Connections

Hank Greenberg, chairman and CEO of American International Group (AIG), has famously summarised, "You can't rush China. You have to take it step by step." Let's begin with that first step.

Finding entry points. Given that the Chinese will rarely initiate an in-depth conversation with someone they do not know, the first step is to cease being a stranger by finding an entry point.

After BC's director of starch development and I were charged with the task of visiting some Chinese starch companies and relevant government bodies in 1995, we did not know anybody in the China starch industry. But I suddenly remembered Mr Wei, a former diplomat at the Chinese embassy in London, with whom I became acquainted when I was the chairman of the Chinese Students and Scholars Association at a British university in the 1980s. He had by then returned to China and became director of the education bureau in the ministry of light industry, which oversaw the starch industry. Although I had not contacted him for years, he immediately offered to "help" me when I telephoned him. He gave me the telephone number of a friend of his in the ministry who was to arrange for us to meet the chairman of the Chinese starch industry association. He also introduced me through telephone calls to Mr Jin, the director of the light industry bureau of Hebei province, and in Beijing he introduced me to Madam Liu, a deputy director in the ministry of agriculture. In the end, it was because of these contacts that we were able to meet many industry experts and factory directors, and develop a comprehensive understanding of the China starch industry.

Apart from employing someone who has connections in China, you can start by making use of intermediaries that have existing connections in China, such as consultants. Attending conferences and seminars, and participating in business missions set up by such organisations as the China–Britain Business Council and the US–China Business Council, can also help you establish bases of familiarity.

Meeting people: saving and giving face. The concept of "face" also exists in the West, but certainly not to the same degree as it does in China. In the West, it basically involves someone becoming embarrassed about something and is regarded merely as a matter of form. In China, however, face is the hallmark of human relationships and expresses a fundamental aspect of life. Therefore you have to adjust your behaviour in your interactions with the Chinese.

Saving face means to head off situations in which you might reduce or are perceived to reduce someone's self-worth. Failing to treat the Chinese with proper respect can have severe consequences: at the very least, co-operation will cease; retaliation may ensue; you may even lose contracts. At its most basic level, saving face means not to insult any Chinese. There are plenty of reasons to lose your temper when dealing with them, but you should try hard not to let any truly felt hostility show through. For example, when things do not go smoothly, instead of criticising the whole Chinese system, you can say, "We do things differently in the West." Saving face also means that you should follow the proper manner when speaking to people at different levels. For example, instead of trying to debate with a Chinese official on any level about anything, you can first agree with whatever he has said, and only then voice the difference by using mild ambiguous language in the hope that he gets the message without appearing to be told to do something.

In China, it is not enough to consciously save face for people, you also need to actively give face to them, i.e. say or do something to enhance their self-worth. Acknowledge someone's presence with a pleasant *ni hao* ("hello"). When attending a meeting or visiting a factory, acknowledge everyone with a handshake; and on departing, give face to them with a wave. Call someone by prefixing their surname with their official title or, for junior people, *lao* ("old") or *xiao* ("young"). Invite someone to dinner or a banquet. Arrange your guest of honour to sit farthest away from the door and, at dinner, invite him to order the dishes. Use both hands to present or receive things like business cards, gifts, or whatever. Escort a departing visitor to the outer door of the office or the elevator, or even the front door of the building if they are a VIP.

Meeting people: giving expressive gifts. When I came to the UK to study in 1985, my luggage was full of Chinese-style gifts because I knew that I would meet a lot of new friends. On arriving at my university, my first task was to choose a supervisor, and therefore I had to see the professors and lecturers. But when I brought a gift to the first professor I saw, he said that he did not deserve it. Seeing me puzzled, he then said that it was not Christmas yet. I subsequently learnt that, even at Christmas, presents are supposedly from Santa Claus.

Knowing the British culture and the fact that I had spent so many years in the UK, Mr Wei specially reminded me, when I asked him for help in 1995, to bring some gifts to his friends when we came to see them in China. I therefore bought mini bottles of liquor for the men and mini bottles of perfume for the women at London Heathrow airport, which all my new China friends loved.

Indeed, in China, gift-giving is a fundamental way for people to express their interest in one another and to establish a basis for continued interaction. In your first encounters with the Chinese, you can bring some company promotional items as business gifts, but as these items are generally too impersonal, whenever possible you should also make an effort to select gifts your new Chinese friends need or would be particularly pleased to have (and, most likely, to show off to others). Knowing that Jiang Zemin, the then president of China, liked to recite the famous Gettysburg address that was originally delivered on 18 November 1863 by President Abraham Lincoln, Gerald M. Levin, chairman of then Time Warner, delighted Jiang by presenting him with a bust of Abraham Lincoln at the 1999 Fortune Global Forum in Shanghai.

Special occasions, such as births, deaths, weddings, New Years and many Chinese festivals, also provide natural opportunities for giving expressive gifts, which are well perceived by the Chinese as important signs of interest and attentiveness.

Nurturing and Enlarging Your Network

After meeting people, you have to know them both in depth and in a large social context so as to nurture and enlarge your network.

Knowing people: interactions and goodwill. Aware of the role of *guanxi* in China, some Western business people expect their newly-made Chinese friends to help them shortly after they have undertaken "throwing banquets and giving gifts" (*qingke songli*), but the Chinese do not seem to hold up their end of the bargain. The misconception here, on the part of Westerners, is to see connection as a "business transaction in one hammer blow" (*yi chuizi mai mai*). Instead, *guanxi* is strongly characterised by your sincere interest in people.

Specifically, you need to take a long-term view – believing that the more you give the more you will receive – as well as show your commitment to an ongoing and deepening relationship. Gestures, such as occasional notes, phone calls and inquiries about their families, will keep the relationship alive. A steady and appropriate exchange of thoughtful gifts and favours will help build up the goodwill, i.e. the positive feelings accumulated over a period of time. Once sufficient goodwill is present, you will find that *guanxi* runs its own course: not only will your friends be willing to meet your request, but they may also help you far beyond what a friend in the West would do for you.

During my market research in 1995, I met a deputy chief engineer of a leading Chinese pharmaceutical design institute in Shanghai. Since then, every time I have flown to China I have tried to meet him. I also tried to arrange for him to meet as many of my BC colleagues as possible when they visited China. Apart from inviting him to share a coffee or dinner with me, I also gave him RMB50 as his taxi fare. Once, when I asked about his family, he proudly talked a lot about his son, who loved collecting stamps. On my next trip, I brought a set of stamps from the UK for him. He was so happy that he brought his son to my hotel to say "thank you" in English. Then in July 1997 when BC was considering participating in the take-over of Zhongyuan Pharmaceutical that CC had been asked to undertake by the government, my friend gave me a copy of an "internal report" on Zhongyuan, from which I could see BC was headed for big trouble. With this unsolicited intelligence, BC cooled down and then gave up the idea.

Enlarging your network. In China, it is a rule that the larger one's network and the more diverse one's connections with people of different positions and abilities, the better one's general manoeuvrability in society. Therefore, you need to extend your first connections into a network of connections with multiple functionalities – some may be able to help you with approvals, some may be able to advise you, and some may be able to provide you with information, for example.

When I met Mr Jin in person in Shijiazhuang of Hebei province, he said: "Old Wei was my teacher when I attended the study sessions in the ministry of light industry, and we have since been close friends. Since it was Old Wei who introduced you to me, it must mean that he trusts you, so I trust you too. Besides, since you are his friend, helping you is helping him too." He therefore arranged for me to have meetings with all the key officials in charge of agriculture, grain and maize in the province, from which I gathered valuable knowledge and data about maize production, distribution and consumption at a provincial level. When I needed to study the maize situation in Shandong, Madam Liu helped me by sending her assistant to accompany me to the province, and I covered his travel expenses. In his presence, I was able to meet not only provincial officials in charge of agriculture and grain distribution but also county officials and local starch factory directors.

Indeed, there is a cumulative effect in extending your network of connections – the more connections you have, the more it is possible to expand your network. For example, merely invoking the name of a mutual friend can provide both parties with a familiarity basis for establishing a connection. In the case of the CC–BC joint venture, my initial contacts have grown into a nationwide network of connections with twice as many people as there are formal employees.

Face-work level 2. As you interact more and more with the Chinese, you will find that face-work can become complicated. At its most subtle, saving face involves "introducing remedies without causing the irritation that attends the exposure of defects". I once assisted a British company in receiving some Chinese visitors. On their first trip, we treated them with upmarket accommodation, but they were unhappy. I then realised that what they really wanted was to take money back home. On their next trip, we booked modest accommodation but we gave them more "pocket money"; and instead of telling them that this was what they wanted, we said this was because of tighter company budgets.

It is advisable that you always work at being aware of when you are given face and when you have an opportunity to give it. At a banquet celebrating the formation of a joint venture I once attended, a junior official gave face to a senior official by saying that the latter had abandoned his birthday party to attend the banquet. At a meeting arranged by Madam Liu, I met three retired agricultural experts in her office. When the meeting was finished, I invited all of them for dinner but none of them reacted. I then realised that the three experts were giving face to Madam Liu because they wanted to be seen as helping me for the purposes of helping Madam Liu. After the three experts left, Madam Liu immediately joined me for dinner.

In its Chinese application, face can seem a formidable challenge to Westerners. But it need not be if you relax, use common sense and keep in mind that everyone's feelings are important. And if you don't like the conventional wisdom that "Flattery will get you anywhere," remember that honest and sincere appreciation will get you anywhere.

Becoming a Master of Your Network

With time and experience, you will realise that the key to mastering your network of connections is to master human nature, which requires intuition, tolerance and human-heartedness on your part.

Intuition: understanding people's emotional world. Mao Zedong was undoubtedly the greatest leader ever in Chinese history, and his secret lay in his mastery of people's emotional world, i.e. what makes them tick. An amusing story has often been quoted to illustrate Mao's intuitive ability. Mao once asked his colleagues President Liu Shaoqi and Premier Zhou Enlai about how they could get a cat to eat chilli powder. Straightforward Liu answered that the only way was to open the cat's mouth by force and pour chilli powder into it. Mao rejected the idea by saying that it was bad to force somebody to do something. Diplomatic Zhou answered that they could hide chilli powder inside a piece of meat and then feed the meat to the cat. Mao rejected the idea too by saying that it was no good to cheat. He then said that they could get the cat to eat chilli powder by applying chilli powder on the cat's bottom because when the cat felt its bottom burn it would happily lick it.

The biggest obstacle to understanding people's emotional world is that we unconsciously use our own mental frame to filter what we see and what we hear. Typically, as soon as we come across something that does not fit into what we believe, we react and when we react we all too often overreact, and that overreaction will stop us from gaining direct intuitive insights into the inner world of another human being. Thus, to understand another person's emotional world, you have to learn to become a great human observer – listen more and talk less; see all but stay obscure. In particular, never dismiss what others say as a nuisance; in fact, if you think about what they say and how they say it, you will be able to discover what is important to them.

Tolerance: weathering the inevitable ups and downs in a relationship. What is it that makes a relationship long-lasting? Many Western business people will say that it is a water-tight contract. As such, as soon as they see that the Chinese are not honouring what they have agreed in a contract, they begin blaming the Chinese or even lose their temper, but the consequence is often the end of the relationship.

To the Chinese, it is tolerance that makes an enduring relationship because ups and downs are inevitable features of a human relationship. Instead of living in *the* world, we all live in our own little world, one constructed by our own mind in order to make sense of what is going on outside it. Thus, we think and act differently, and we want different things from life. If you cannot tolerate the things you dislike in another person, you cannot possibly maintain a relationship with that person.

In particular, people make mistakes, and often agree to do things but then for reasons beyond their control, they are no longer able to do them or may even no longer want to do them. When this happens, it is very tempting to confront the side at fault with "How could you have done that?" "But you said. . ." or "But you promised. . ." Yet, if you can step back, take a moment to listen to the other side's account, and then place it in the perspective of the overall relationship, you may find it in your best interest to let them off the hook. For adversity is the best test of a relationship: the understanding, forgiveness and tolerance you have shown at a time that was difficult for someone else will turn into rewards or opportunities for you at another time.

Human-heartedness: what "old friends" can do to each other. In 1992, among several dozen foreign insurers with a representative office in China, American International Group (AIG) became the first to be granted a licence to operate in Shanghai (and will shortly have no fewer than ten separate licences as well as other approvals).

How did AIG achieve this? Greenberg said: "I worked on it for 17 years." A long time! But the full answer is that AIG has been an "old friend of China", which is not only reflected in *youbang* ("a friend of a country"), the Chinese name of its wholly-owned subsidiary American International Assurance (AIA), but also in the unequivocal trust and goodwill it has expressed toward China ever since it was originally founded by C. V. Starr in Shanghai in 1919. During World War II, AIG shared China's suffering because several of its senior executives in Shanghai were imprisoned by the Japanese occupation army. This pre-1949 reputation and AIG's ongoing post-1949 contact with China enabled Starr's successor, Greenberg, to visit Beijing in 1975 – even before the official Opening Up in 1978. In 1980, AIG was the first foreign financial firm to set up a representative office in Beijing.

In 1990, Greenberg helped Zhu Rongji, then mayor of Shanghai, establish Shanghai's first international business advisory council. In 1992, AIG presented China with windows taken by foreign invaders from the Summer Palace. In return, AIG has held such a sway in China that its executives can meet with the top leaders whenever they visit China.

The Principle-Centred Adaptation

Suzhou Industrial Park was opened in 1994 and has been personally promoted by Lee Kuan Yew, senior minister of Singapore. It was based on the concept that Singapore would provide the development expertise and China the labour, to attract foreign investment. Summing up the lessons learnt, Lee commented to *Forbes Global* in November 1999:

> When dealing at provincial and lower levels, you have to live with their business culture. It requires you to be flexible, to compromise and do things half their way. We thought that they wanted to learn to do it the Singapore way, according to proper rules and strict procedures. That was what the centre wanted. But the reality at the local level could not be overcome.

Indeed, there is no doubt that you will run up against walls in China if you adopt a "no adaptation" approach by trying to do everything on the basis of Western philosophy. For example, if you take the approach of making formal requests to governmental bureaux without the careful work of establishing personal relationships, you can hardly make anything happen in China. On the other hand, if you adopt a "total adaptation" approach by slavishly attempting to do as the Chinese do and forgetting your own cultural values, you will not only be uncomfortable and unsure of yourself but also cede all advantage to the Chinese. And if, in the extreme, you become "more Chinese than the Chinese" in the exchange of favours, you not only contribute to the lack of order and rules but also run the risk of becoming a victim of the bribery game.

The effective approach is therefore the "principle-centred adaptation", which aims for the synergy or, in some cases, a compromise between the Western and Chinese ways of doing things. It is best illustrated as an ancient Chinese coin (see Figure 1.4), in which you take your own principles to heart but adapt your behaviour when dealing with the China reality, i.e. "square inside and round outside".

All too often, "principle" becomes a convenient cover-up word for a bruised ego of some insensitive, insulting Western business people in China. To practise the principle-centred adaptation, you actually need a strong sense of self that gives you the confidence to question your own ways of doing things and consider alternative approaches. If you know who you are, you ultimately feel safe integrating new approaches into your previous ways of doing things. In this sense, doing business in China can truly enrich the potential of Western executives. For example, on top of their analytical skills, Western executives will be able to learn the significance of intuition, sharpen their intuitive edge, and enhance their people skills. Of course, the principle-centred adaptation also enables you to effectively engage the Chinese in the short term and develop them in the long term. And if you accommodate and comfort Chinese sensibilities, while at the same time introducing and enforcing well-defined ethical codes, you will not only profit from your effort but also contribute to the evolution of the China business environment.

The next time you feel puzzled about a situation in China, think about the ancient Chinese coin and what Lao Tzu said in *Tao Te Ching* 2,500 years ago:

> Superior men are square without dividing; honest without offending; straightforward without straining; and bright without dazzling.

FIGURE 1.4

Three Approaches to Doing Business in China

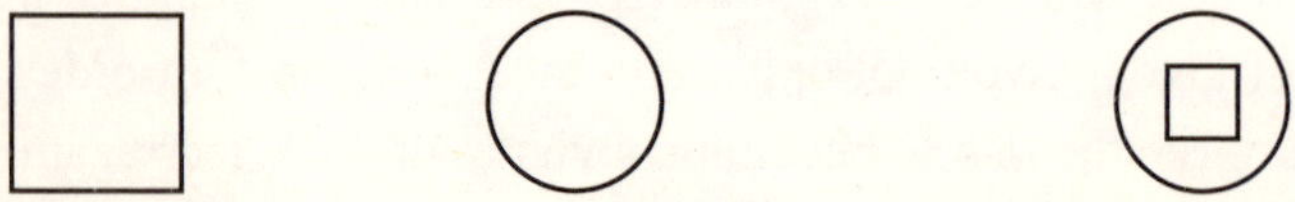

(1) No adaptation   (2) Total adaptation   (3) Principle-centred adaptation

2

READING THE DYNAMICS
OF THE CHINA MARKET

The China market is a difficult market, but at least it is a market.

ANONYMOUS WESTERN BUSINESSMAN

China is the market of tomorrow. But it's what you do today that counts.

DR MARTIN POSTH, CHAIRMAN AND PRESIDENT
OF VOLKSWAGEN ASIA-PACIFIC LTD

WHEN WESTERN EXECUTIVES think about the China market, many think about the population of 1.3 billion and the extremely low per capita consumption rate of almost everything. They then think that if they walk in and supply this population they will certainly make money. Yet, while some companies have produced success stories, many have discovered that China's huge population does not easily translate into a steady stream of customers and, indeed, that correctly reading the China market represents a huge challenge. In this chapter, we examine the major factors that limit the size of the target market and explore the art and science of reading the dynamics of the China market.

Limiting Factors of the China Market

With over one fifth of the world's population and a largely underdeveloped economy, the China market has undoubtedly the highest potential in the world. However, it is essential to note that major factors, such as affordability, regionalism, accessibility, competition and regulation, determine a target market, which can be hugely different from the market potential that is a function of only people's interests.

Affordability

Despite the rapid economic rise over the past two decades, the average purchasing power of the Chinese population has always been very low and severely limited the number of customers who can afford foreign products and services. When McDonald's entered China in 1990, it was perceived as an upmarket restaurant, offering American food to a new class of entrepreneurs and professionals who could afford the experience. As of 1994, a dinner at McDonald's for a family of three cost one-sixth of a worker's monthly salary. Entering the 21st century, eating at McDonald's is still a big treat for most Chinese. In Shanghai, which boasts the highest per capita income of any Chinese province or municipality, getting residents to pay about RMB20 (US$2.41) for a lunch at McDonald's, when they can pick up a Chinese lunchbox for RMB5 (US$0.60), is difficult. "People are rather more inclined to save their money for clothes and housing," says a McDonald's executive.

So far, among foreign-manufactured goods, only lower-priced consumables, such as skincare products, and convenience goods, such as snack foods and soft drinks, can be sold nationwide. One of the most painful lessons learned by multinationals like Pfizer and Hoffmann-La Roche is that China does not have a pharmaceutical market of 1.3 billion people, but at most 10–15% of that figure. The vast majority of the population – 900 million peasants and part of the urban population – find joint venture drugs too expensive an option. For higher-priced products such as cars, the market is similar in size to that of a smaller European country. A poll taken in ten provinces in 1999 showed that 90% of households would not pay more than US$8,500 for a car. This is why, after launching the Buick model targeting chauffeur-driven officials and executives in 1997, Shanghai General Motors soon learnt that luxury and middle-class sedans have a limited market in China and decided in 2000 to launch a small, economically-priced family car.

At the heart of the above market difficulties is the low overall purchasing power of China's 1.3 billion consumers. In 1995, the average Chinese earned just US$530. China's population structure also leads to slow wealth accumulation. At the poor end, about 900 million people are located in rural areas, of which about 100 million still rely on state subsidies to survive. Among members of the 15–45 age group, 7% are illiterate. People aged 60 and above make up 9.7% of the total population. China has about 60 million disabled people, and every year, about one million babies with disabilities are born. The redundancies made in the state sector – 11.5 million, 8.9 million and 11.7 million in 1997, 1998 and 1999 respectively and at least 12 million in 2000 – are creating urban poverty. At the rich end, there are now the nouveau riches and "Chuppies", the Chinese yuppies, but they only represent the tip of a huge iceberg. Thus, in 2004, although China's GDP ranked 7th in the world, its per capita income (at US$1,290) ranked 105th.

Regionalism

Apart from its low overall purchasing power, China must not been seen as a single homogenous market. First and foremost, there are significant regional differences in customers' income and purchasing power. The average income in the poorest Gansu or Guizhou is only less than 1/8 of that in the richest Shanghai or Guangzhou, and the gap is getting larger. While many consumers in developed southeastern coastal areas have become comparatively well off and pursue comfort and brand, most of those in the vast Western region are still struggling to make ends meet and emphasise utility and price. While colour TV sets, video recorders, washing machines and refrigerators have become essentials in major cities like Beijing, Shanghai and Guangzhou, black and white TV sets and classic sewing machines are still at a growth or even introduction stage in rural areas. The market for clothing can be divided into four geographic segments, i.e. coastal areas, large and medium cities, small towns, and rural areas, with each lagging 2–3 years behind the other in that order. This is why McDonald's rightly opened its first restaurant in western China a decade after it started business in eastern China.

Other factors are also at work shaping the behaviour of consumers in different regions. There is the saying: "To eat in Guangdong, to dress in Shanghai, and to play in Beijing." In Xinjiang and Inner Mongolia, local Uighur people and Mongolians have the habit of eating roast whole lambs and they therefore demand that the size of the freezer of a refrigerator must be larger than normal, whereas in Shanghai small and detachable refrigerators are most popular. In mountainous areas, people demand few bicycles; in hilly areas, people demand bicycles that have more gears; in rural flatlands, people demand bicycles that can carry heavy loads; in urban flatlands, people demand bicycles that are light, beautiful and flexible. In northern China, as the air is dry and cold in winter, and extremely hot in summer, the market for personal care products is dominted by skin creams; in southern China, as the weather is milder, more money is spent on hair care products.

Even variations in local family planning policies can produce marked differences in demographics. In Beijing, Shanghai and Tianjin where family planning policies have been more stringently implemented, the population is getting increasingly older, but in Xinjiang, Guizhou and Yunnan where family planning policies were activated later and have been less stringently implemented, the population is still dominated by youngsters. In developed areas, as birth rate is lower and quality of life is higher, demand for products for the elderly and for cultural life is stronger; in poor provinces, as birth rate is higher and quality of life is lower, demand for products for children and material life is stronger.

In short, China, from a market point of view, rather resembles Europe: it is very diverse geographically, linguistically, culturally and economically, and is therefore made up of many different markets, with many different characteristics.

Accessibility

For those Western businesses that have located an affordable market in China for their products with the right regional tastes, the difficulty in getting the products to where customers can buy them is another significant limiting factor to the size of the market they can serve. Because of its history, China has a less developed transportation infrastructure than even smaller, poorer countries like India. China is three times as large as India yet has 20% fewer miles of railways. Almost seven decades have passed since new railway lines were built, and many of those are narrow gauge and single-track, have obsolete switching yards, and still run on steam. China is blessed with excellent natural harbours, but few are developed well enough to handle much traffic let alone containerised cargo. And the few that are suffer from very poor transport links to the interior. While China needs more airports, it already has airports that are grossly under-utilised because they have been built in the wrong places. To make matters worse, the amount of goods that has to be transported around the country has been growing exponentially with the development of the economy.

As a result, Western businesses in China must wrestle with the daily challenge of hopelessly overburdened transport and distribution networks. Rail-freight space needs to be reserved about six weeks in advance, but even then demand often exceeds capacity. Lorries, however, can cost up to ten times as much as the state-subsidised rail system, once pilfering and quasi-legal inter-provincial customs duties are taken into account. One Japanese home appliances company says that up to 25% of its shipments by truck from Guangzhou to Shanghai are damaged en route. According to Cadbury, on a typical long distance lorry route from Beijing to Shanghai, the company can lose as much as 10% of its cargo. On both rail and road, it is also difficult to secure empty containers because so many companies are now shipping their products around China. In Nestle's case, its factories are distributed across seven cities in eastern China. It has a western regional office in Chengdu of Sichuan province, responsible for the distribution of its products from these factories in a vast territory stretching in an arc from Yunnan in the south-west to Xinjiang in the north-west. In reality, Chengdu's operations are limited to only four urban centres: Chengdu, Chongqing, Kunming and Xi'an, and almost all of its "Sichuan" sales are transacted in Chengdu because of the poor transportation infrastructure.

Distribution is not only terribly difficult between provinces or cities but also within cities, such as Shanghai, Guangzhou and Wuhan. In Shanghai, Western ice-cream makers have to use wholesalers who sometimes have to rely on tricycles to peddle their products to retailers, given the complicated and changing traffic rules that inhibit lorry deliveries. In Guangzhou, UPS has to use motorcycles, in lieu of its trademark brown delivery trucks, to navigate the overcrowded streets.

Competition

Apart from the affordability, regionalism and accessibility factors, the competition factor also limits the size of the market that can be served by a multinational. Competition can come from four main sources, i.e. foreign companies, domestic companies, fake products, and smuggled products. In the telecom sector, the existence of a large number of Western giants including Alcatel, AT&T, Ericsson, NEC, Nortel and Siemens has virtually created an oversupply situation. As a result, these companies now have to call for razor-thin or even negative margins to win contracts. At Alcatel's Shanghai Bell joint venture, which was dubbed by *China Daily* in 1995 as the most successful joint venture in China, revenue per switch dropped from US$182 in 1990 to US$95 in 1996.

Competition is emerging not just from other foreign companies but – much more dangerously – from local companies. Chinese home electrical appliance manufacturers, such as Haier, Kelon, Little Swan and Little Duck, have driven America's Whirlpool crazy. The company started off in 1997 by selling refrigerators, air-conditioners and washing machines under its own brand but it is now primarily supplying washing machines that are marketed in China under the brand names of Kelon and Little Swan. In the PC market, foreign investors have seen their hard-won share of the market quickly lost to rising Chinese PC makers. Compaq Computer was the market leader in 1994 with a 21% market share. By 1999, it had 9% while Beijing-based Legend

Computer became the country's largest PC maker, with a 14.5% market share. In early 1999, shortly after Microsoft announced its Venus set-top box Internet-TV product, local TV maker HiSense announced its intention to launch a competing product and "fight Microsoft every inch of the way".

In some industries, fake goods can be a major threat, as illustrated in the case of Longcheng Apparatus Company, which is a Sino-foreign joint venture based in Dongguan of Guangdong. In 1992, Longcheng launched the "KASALA" branded clothes on the market. As the design of the clothes was new and appealing, the quality of the materials was good and the workmanship was first-class, the products became very popular among both domestic and overseas consumers. However, fake "KASALA" clothes, the quality of which was inferior, soon appeared on the market in large volumes and within a few months, the once popular "KASALA" clothes were piling up in stores.

Smuggled goods can be another source of competition in certain industries. In 1990 alone, household electrical appliances worth US$ 1 billion were smuggled into the mainland, according to Hong Kong security authorities. According to local analysts, some 90% of the video recorders on sale in 1992 were smuggled ones. In 1998, smuggled sugar caused the collapse of sugar prices in China, driving several sugar joint ventures and many domestic sugar producers into losses.

Regulation

Given the Chinese government's endeavour to manage the transition of the economy from the formal planning system to a modern market system, new regulations have to be promulgated for new forms of economic activities while existing ones are regularly revised as changes take place. A further aggravation is caused by the fact that the regulations are capable of being variously interpreted by different officials in different provinces and that local governments also promulgate and revise their own regulations. The following two examples illustrate the scale of the impact that changes in governmental regulations can have on the market that a multinational serves in China.

In 1994, Piaggio, the Italian motorcycle maker, established a joint venture with a Chinese motorcycle factory in Foshan of Guangdong Province to ultimately produce 500,000 two-wheelers a year. It poured US$30 million into a moped and motor scooter plant and it appeared that the company had neatly caught the crest of the Chinese two-wheeler wave and would make sure money. By mid-1997, the first phase of the new plant became operational with a capacity of 100,000 vehicles. However, sales had been far below Piaggio's initial expectations. What went wrong? Since 1995, with citizen outcry over mopeds and scooters, which were clogging up bicycle lanes, posing a hazard to slow-moving cyclists, as well as contributing to the city's pollution problem, municipal governments in Shanghai and Guangdong had sharply tightened restrictions on licensing mopeds and scooters. In July 1996, Shanghai announced that moped sales would be banned from January 1997. Similar problems occurred in Guangdong province where the city governments of Guangzhou, Zhuhai and Jiangmen also banned mopeds. These cities were Piaggio's main target markets, which had since vanished. Other cities did not copy the restrictions but were seemingly hesitant to issue formal policy permitting mopeds. In the absence of clear policy, many consumers were reluctant to purchase them.

On 21 April 1998, the Chinese government issued regulations banning homegrown pyramid schemes and direct-marketing systems alike, ordering local and foreign direct-marketers to wind up business by the end of October 1998. With US$100 million investment in China and sales of US$178 million in 1997, Western direct-selling giant Amway had a lot to lose. US trade officials protested against the decision, but the State Administration for Industry and Commerce answered that vague or incomplete legislation was for foreign companies to take into account when they set up business in China. Indeed, for the eight years that direct-sales had been thriving in China, the government had changed its mind four times – each time prohibiting some forms of direct-selling while allowing others. This time round, i.e. three months later, the government lifted its ban, but by then Amway had already opened 40 retail outlets in major cities throughout China.

The Art and Science of Mastering the China Market

Apart from viewing the China market as a demand generated by a population of 1.3 billion, many Western executives often continue their analytical tradition and rely far too much on the "hard data" prepared by their market research teams. Yet, the China market is new and without comparison in the rest of the world, and is still sorting itself out and struggling to define itself. To master it, Western executives must avoid conclusions based on hard data or even symptoms alone, and strive to reach its heart and identify emerging patterns and underlying trends.

Reaching the Heart of the China Market

Given the sophisticated nature of the China market, hard data gathered during market research under time constraints can be very partial and limited, reflecting only the symptoms of the market. To reach the heart of the China market, Western executives need to use a combination of hard data, "soft data", and pilot-operation-based approaches to gathering market intelligence (see Figure 2.1).

Level 1 is characterised by collection of published data, formal visits to potential customers and business partners, analysis of gathered data, and preparation of neat folders presented to management. As the engagement between the research team and the market is limited and insights tend to get lost in the process of converting the raw data into presentations to management, market data gathered at level 1 help man-

FIGURE 2.1

Understanding the China Market at Three Levels

High ▲ **Level 3:** Building and running a pilot operation

Reliability **Level 2:** Establishing and using sources of "soft data"

Low **Level 1:** Collecting and researching hard data

agement paint a picture rather than give precise information.

"Soft data" are intuitive impressions and situational perceptions about the nature and trends of the market, and "inside information" from informal sources. Thus, level 2 is characterised by management setting their own foot physically into the market place and directly establishing and using contacts in the market environment in order to pick up the crucial strategic messages that often get lost at level 1. Because of the direct engagement between management and contacts in the market, market intelligence achieved at level 2 allows management to feel the pulse of the market.

At level 3, market understanding is achieved through building and running a pilot operation in the market. As what you learn about the market is what you actually experience, market intelligence gathered at level 3 is most reliable and allows management to directly touch on the heart of the market. Depending on the nature of the business and the amount of risk you are willing to take, a pilot operation can take the form of an import arrangement, a licensing or technology transfer arrangement, or a pilot venture.

Although the three approaches to understanding the China market are separately defined, they are of course closely related to each other and sometimes overlap. While overly relying on collecting and researching hard data, most executives would establish and use, although inadequate, certain sources of "soft data"; prior to launching a pilot operation, most companies would also conduct some sort of hard-data-based research and "soft-data"-based investigation. And from level 1 to level 3, with the increase in the reliability of gathered market intelligence, there is an increasing cost commitment.

Collecting and Researching Hard Data

Although hard data should not be used to arrive at the decision, they are absolutely essential to supporting and confirming it. To collect and research hard data of reliability, you can consider one or a combination of three options: (1) using published data with care; (2) commissioning a credible agency; and (3) doing your own market research.

Using published data with care. With China's growing importance in the world, there has been a growing list of publications containing data on China. Although their reliability is less than satisfactory for decision-making purposes, picking through reports from multiple sources helps build the real picture.

For data about the Chinese economy or a particular industry, refer to such publications as *China: A Directory and Sourcebook* (Euromonitor, London), *Consumer China* (Euromonitor, London) and *Doing Business with China* (Kogan Page, London). To monitor and keep up with the economic trends and market developments in China, you can subscribe to publications like *Business China* (Economist Intelligence Unit, London) and *China Economic Review* (Alain Charles Publishing, London), and regularly surf websites, such as www.chinaonline.com. The Chinese Ministry of Commerce runs a website at www.fdi.gov.cn, which provides up-to-date information on the Chinese economy and statistics on foreign direct investment. Another official source is *China Statistical Yearbook* (China Statistical Publishing House, Beijing).

Whatever the source, it is important that you should treat published data with care. For a start, the Chinese statistical system is riddled with exaggeration and outright fraud because local officials get bonuses according to the growth rate of their regions and those same officials are in charge of collecting economic statistics. In 1995, China's State Statistical Bureau discovered that previously published output figures in the collective sector were so wildly exaggerated that they needed to be adjusted downward by some 20% for each of the previous four years. Meanwhile, by using the purchasing-power parity (PPP) methodology but secondary price data, the International Monetary Fund (IMF) has published dramatically high figures on Chinese per-capita income, such as US$2,600 for 1990, while exchange rate converted Chinese per-capita income in 1996 was only US$678. Which figure do you believe?

As such, without verification through cross-checking with other sources, published data should not be used as exact.

Commissioning a credible agency. To improve on the quality of the data obtained from published sources, you can commission a market research agency. There are now many market research agencies in China but the key is to find a credible, competent one at a competitive rate.

A large number of Chinese market research firms have been established, particularly in major cities, but most of them are very small and not very trustworthy as they lack professional integrity and standards. For example, one survey done by a local market research firm showed a substantial demand, amongst over 500 million Chinese smokers, for products to help them quit, which turned out to be nonsense because the respondents were simply being "helpful".

A good number of Sino-foreign joint venture market research firms have also been established, which generally charge more but also provide better quality services. For example, Gallup (China) Research Ltd, which opened for business in Beijing on 1 January 1994, is a joint venture between US's The Gallup Organisation and a Chinese trading firm with strong ties to the foreign ministry. To avoid possible interviewer bias, it has rejected direct co-operation with the State Statistical Bureau in favour of working through statistics departments of Chinese universities. With nationwide coverage, China–Britain Business Council has also undertaken many market research assignments.

Many Hong Kong-based market research firms also provide services to multinationals targeting the China market. De Beers, the world's largest diamond producer, for example, laid the groundwork for a diamond market in China by hiring a Hong Kong market research firm to identify jewellery ownership patterns.

Doing your own market research. To collect first-hand data, you can undertake your own market research in China. The key to successful market research in China is a strong team, which has to consist of experienced experts and a reliable, bilingual, knowledgeable and well-connected local guide.

In China, you cannot afford to take anything for granted because it is a different world. Things that work in the West may not exist in China yet; if a narrowly experienced person assumes that they do exist in China, then surprises and holes become inevitable later on. Your team must therefore have a sufficient pool of knowledge and experience to ask the right questions, make the right comments, and cross-check against each other so as to assemble the complete jigsaw of your target market. The jigsaw should not just be about demand and supply, but customers, products, regional differences, distribution and logistical systems, competition and regulations.

Central to your team has to be the local guide, who needs to set up a programme of meetings through mobilising his contacts in China and to provide competent interpretation at meetings. The programme should aim to cover a wide variety of contacts, e.g. customers, distributors, industry associations and government agencies. You can recruit an overseas Chinese professional with Mandarin capability and China experience as your local guide, but sufficient training should also be provided to familiarise him with your business. You can also use a China-based consulting firm to organise an interpreter and a schedule of meetings with their contacts for your team.

Before your team leaves for China, they need to pack introductory literature and small gifts. Presenting introductory literature at the beginning of the meeting and small gifts at the end of the meeting helps achieve both business and relationship objectives.

Establishing and Using Sources of "Soft Data"

Sources of "soft data" or close relationships with contacts in the market environment are important because they enable you to gather unsolicited intelligence and thus improve the quality of your decision-making. To establish and use them, you need to undertake three tasks: (1) setting up a representative office; (2) establishing sources of "soft data"; and (3) using "soft data" in decision-making.

Setting up a representative office. While some connections can be developed in your own market research in China, the lack of a local base neither allows these connections to be strengthened on an on-going basis nor facilitates the development of new connections. To commit yourself to developing sources of "soft data", you can consider setting up a representative office.

The British Oxygen Company (BOC), for instance, established its first footing on Chinese soil in late 1985 by setting up a representative office in Shanghai. It found that the representative office, staffed by an American-educated Chinese national, was invaluable. He was far more than an interpreter, having sufficient stature to open doors at senior level and being there on the ground all the time to keep things moving on while BOC negotiators made frequent trips to China.

Setting up a representative office involves three main steps, i.e. finding a Chinese sponsor, submission of a formal application to the approval authority in charge and registration with the local Administration for Industry and Commerce. The Chinese sponsor will normally be a major Chinese foreign trade corporation, a foreign affairs service unit or other state enterprise with which your company has had prior dealings and which is located within the same region as the proposed representative office. The approval authority is normally the municipal foreign economic relations and trade commission.

A full-scale representative office is expensive and can cost upwards of US$150,000 per year for an expatriate plus one local staff person but some sharing may be possible. For example, the British building materials sector has a joint office representing thirty companies, which was opened in Shanghai on 28 April 1999.

Establishing sources of "soft data". The primary task of your representative at the representative office should be to develop a wide network of connections for the purpose of gathering "soft data" on the market your company is targeting.

There are many contacts that can be targeted. Governmental officials (retired officials can introduce you to existing officials) are in the best position to provide inside information on regulations. Experts in industry associations are generally able to provide an overview on the status and trend of the underlying industry. Contacts with potential competitors are in a position to give you the most real indication of what it is like to be in the business you are targeting. Contacts with potential customers, distributors and suppliers are in a position to give you the most accurate information about customer preferences, and distribution and supply systems. Active researchers can be in a position to provide information about customers, competitors and regulations in the industry.

Once your representative has developed an initial connection with an important target contact, he can introduce the contact to you and other executives from headquarters by inviting him to dinners. Over the dinners, you should make sure that you develop a nice, friendly, personal relationship with him instead of focusing on dry business discussions only. It is also important that you maintain your relationships with local contacts through such gestures as sending a Christmas/New Year card, making occasional phone calls, bringing a small gift and having a chat over lunch/dinner whenever you travel to China.

Using "soft data" in decision-making. With your networking efforts over time, trust and goodwill will emerge between you and your contacts, and then they will be in a position to supply, in an informal way, up-to-date, accurate information that may not be published. Such first-hand information from original sources may prove superior to any formal alternatives in your decision making.

You can talk over breakfast or lunch, and attend social functions to exchange views and ideas – critical market information is often exchanged in social settings. You can travel to local scenes to personally check the reliability of local information, and actively seek out information and search for the critical pieces that will have an impact on your final decisions. You can cultivate intuition and gain instinctive knowledge of the workings of the market through other forms of direct but discreet interactions with your contacts. You can use the odds and ends of the tangible detail, pieced together in your mind, instead of surveys, summaries, conclusions or recommendations, to illuminate the underside of the issues you face and to make fresh connections among variables that appear unrelated at first glance.

Indeed, "soft data" in the form of intuition and gut feeling is essential to recognising market opportunities. Intuition is a combination of natural talent and personal confidence generated from experience. If you wait until everything is perfectly clear, it will probably be too late because opportunities may have gone to your competitors. By using "soft data", you can therefore ensure that you do not waste a lot of time on misplaced hard data collection, and that decisions will not be made without factoring in gut feeling and business acumen.

Building and Running a Pilot Operation

The ultimate way of grasping the nature of the sophisticated China market is to experience its dynamics through building and running a pilot operation. There are three viable options: (1) using an importing arrangement; (2) using a licensing or technology transfer arrangement; (3) building and running a pilot venture.

Using an importing arrangement. To test whether the product would sell well enough in the market to justify any investment in a manufacturing facility in China, you can try to sell it in China through an importing arrangement. An American executive once described the logic behind an importing arrangement: "We invest in China in order to sell our product. If we cannot sell it, then there is no point to invest." Indeed, pharmaceutical companies like Lederle, Glaxo, Upjohn and Hoffmann-La Roche all jumped into their domestic investments off the back of remarkable import sales growth.

In the case of Lederle, it began by selling a range of multi-vitamins and antibiotics to China in the late 1980s, where duties, at 15–20%, were less prohibitive than in many other industries. By the early 1990s, imports of these products had grown enough to sustain 16 sales offices around China. It therefore decided to invest US$12.5 million in a joint venture plant in Suzhou, which came on line in February 1994. With the help of its solid import base, the plant got off to a fast start achieving 70% sales growth during 1995.

To set up an importing arrangement, you need to undertake three major tasks. First, you need to identify who the end users are and gather information on government regulations regarding import of the product. Second, you need to identify those with authorised import and export rights and negotiate import contracts with them. Finally, you need to market the product through, for example, holding seminars and meetings to demonstrate the product, placing advertisement in public media, appointing local agents to generate sales opportunities, and establishing a resident office to monitor the market.

Using a licensing or technology transfer arrangement. A licensing arrangement involves a Western company providing its know-how to a Chinese partner to manufacture and market a product in China for an up-front fee plus royalties for a defined period of time. Similar to a licensing arrangement is technology transfer, which involves a Western company transferring knowledge of its technology and the right to exploit it to a Chinese company for cash payment or other value. Technology transfer can be used in a pilot operation when the technology can be continually upgraded so that the technology transferred, while state-of-the-art at the time, would be quickly rendered obsolete.

Guinness, for example, tested the waters of the Chinese beer market by launching a small-scale licensing operation in China. It learnt through the operation that the market was extremely competitive and Chinese drinkers were not so enthusiastic about a foreign black beer, and as a result, it has recently withdrawn from China. UK-based Courtaulds Coatings, the largest marine paint manufacturer in the world, established a licensing arrangement with Kailin, a Shanghai paint manufacturer, in 1982. Production under this arrangement eventually reached about one million litres a year, and by the late 1980s both companies were ready to convert the licensing arrangement into a joint venture, which sold six million litres of paint in 1995.

Of course, a licensing or technology transfer arrangement also brings risk to the Western investor, and the biggest risk is the potential loss of proprietary rights despite protective terms in the contract because in practice the Chinese tend to share information quite freely. To minimise such risk, you need creativity to structure the right deal.

Building and running a pilot venture. Prior to making a major investment of technology and capital, you can consider building and running a pilot venture so as to acquire real, comprehensive market understanding. Indeed, the success stories of many Western investments in China suggest that the smaller you start in China, the better you do, and that the real profits have gone to companies that invested cautiously and increased capacity in response to, rather than in anticipation of, higher demand. For example, General Electric's Shanghai GE Lighting joint venture costing US$60 million to set up has been the least successful while its Beijing-based GE-Hangwei Medical System joint venture costing US$2 million to set up has been the most successful.

Apart from starting small, you can also choose to build a pilot venture in the form of a co-operative venture or by focusing on low-value-added activities. Unlike a joint venture where investors are restricted from withdrawing registered capital during the life of the contract, in a co-operative venture, the partners remain separate legal entities and bear liability and taxes independently. As such, it can be created without any minimum capital requirement and dissolved with ease – registered capital is recoverable during the life of the contract, say, 5 years.

By initially focusing the operation on low-cost, low-value-added activities that require less capital and less sophisticated technology, you can learn about the market at lower risk and prepare for moving into high-cost, high-value-added activities. Ford, for example, has set up a low-cost parts production joint venture in Shanghai, aiming to get its foot in the door of the Chinese car market and in anticipation of being allowed to develop a full-scale vehicle assembly facility.

Identifying Emerging Patterns and Underlying Trends

Given that everything in China moves fast, Western executives must avoid being confused or carried away by symptoms of the market and aim for the emerging patterns and underlying trends by taking a historical view of the developments in the China market – only history can reveal the nature of things.

"Connection" as a Fundamental Driving Force in Chinese Cosumption

Given the network nature of Chinese society, the Chinese generally spend disproportional amounts of money on their social connections with others. Inside their family, everything is pooled. The elderly save their money to pass along to the young as an inheritance. This is one of the reasons why China has a savings rate of 40%, one of the highest in the world. When they do spend, they first spend on their children or child – for urban families, 50–70% of total monthly expenditure is dedicated to the single child. Grandparents buy what their grandchild wants; middle-aged adults buy health tonics to enhance their parents' lives. Young people between 18 and 28 can afford expensive foreign goods, such as food, drugs and cosmetics, because they live at home and their parents cover their basic living costs.

Outside their family, the Chinese spend heavily on services or gifts for others to enjoy. Families usually save for years or even borrow money for "big occasions" like weddings, funerals, and the birth of new babies, especially if they are boys. The most important way of celebrating Chinese festivals is for one's colleagues, friends, classmates, relatives and other acquaintances to take turns to organise banquets. As an individual, you are expected to treat others when you get a promotion or even when your child enters a university. Gift giving is so rampant that it is not uncommon, for example, for a worker to spend a month's salary to buy a bottle of Martell brandy for somebody with power in order to ask for a favour, such as change of job. Thus, the wealthy and those with higher incomes are not the only purchasers of luxury goods.

In general, because of the role of connection in China, sophisticated statistical analysis centred on either the end user or the purchaser would not be effective for the purposes of identifying the target market and designing a marketing campaign. A more effective approach would be to focus on a specific connection, such as a family, and this is exactly how, having initially failed with its traditional approach, one of the world's top pharmaceutical companies has quadrupled its sales in one year.

"Status" as a Major Driving Force in Chinese Consumption

Of course, the Chinese do spend on themselves, and when they do they first spend on acquiring status because it helps them develop connections. For example, it is not uncommon for people in China to go to extreme lengths, including starving themselves or risking malnutrition by eating only instant noodles, to save enough to buy, say, one of the best colour TV sets on the market. This is another reason why China has a high savings rate. Items that have status value are normally set by a small number of trend setters or opinion leaders with the vast majority of the Chinese being emulators or laggards. The consuming psychology with respect to an item of status value is: "Whether I need or use it does not matter; what matters is that if others have it then I must have it as soon as possible or I will be regarded as lowly in status".

A good indicator of this consuming pattern is the changing concept of the "three big items" (*san dajian*), by which is meant the three luxury items that confer the most status on their owner. During the 1960s and 1970s, the "three big items" were wristwatches, bicycles and sewing machines. In the 1980s, colour TV sets, refrigerators, and washing machines became the new "three big items". By the early 1990s, the "three big items" had become a telephone, an air conditioner, and a VCR. Entering the 21st century, despite the voracious appetite of the Chinese, flat/home improvement, modern IT devices, such as mobile phones and PCs, and a car/two-wheeler have become the new "three big items".

For example, it is common to see migrant construction workers in major cities hold mobile phones in their hands, although their annual wages might not even cover the cost of a phone. This is why Motorola, already the largest foreign investor in China's electronics industry, plans to triple its stake there to more than US$10 billion by 2006. Unsurprisingly, B&Q, Dell and Volkswagen are making similar moves.

"Public Funds" as a Major Source of Purchasing Power in Chinese Consumption

In the West, people's consumption behaviour is largely determined by their income. But in China, the purchasing power of the Chinese is also a function of the public funds they have access to. According to official estimates, the use of public funds on entertainment was US$2.2 billion in 1980, and reached US$8.9 billion and US$15.5 billion in 1990 and 1993 respectively. At the moment, it is estimated that the annual spending of public money on entertainment is around US$24.1 billion, of which US$1.2 billion is spent on saunas. A close investigation of nightclubs in Liaoning Province in 1994 showed that 80% of their income was from the state. Public funds are also commonly used to finance the private purchase and consumption of other goods, such as gifts, tours, mobile phones, luxury cars or even apartments, and some directors of state-owned enterprises are in the most privileged position to do so.

For many of those who do not have administrative power, they can still have access to public funds through using counterfeit receipts, which are widely available on the market. In one audit by the tax authority in Liaoning province, 115,000 counterfeit receipts were discovered, involving illegitimate money of US$26 million. In another audit conducted by the state tax authority, over 400 million counterfeit receipts were discovered. What amount of public funds had been transferred to private pockets through these receipts? And what about the counterfeit receipts that were not covered by the sample audit but were possibly many times more than those discovered?

This perhaps explains why in urban centres, where most state-owned enterprises are located, spending power can be abnormally high among certain consumers, generating demand for high-priced goods like Guangzhou Honda's Accord and Shanghai General Motors' Buick.

"Following the Crowd" among Chinese Businesses

Apart from a few emergent Chinese businesses that have the ability to innovate, the majority of them are driven by the mentality of "following the crowd", which leads to duplicative construction. For example, in home electrical appliance and mechanical engineering sectors, the utilisation of production facilities is less than 50%. While Beijing's consumer purchasing power is only 1/8 of that of Tokyo or New York, its number of large departmental stores is now 8 times that of Tokyo or New York. In some sections of the lower reaches of the Yangtze River, a port has been or is being built every kilometre. Four new airports have been or are being built in the Hong Kong area although the most effective option would have been one airport with high-speed rail connections to the major towns in the area. Between 1995 and 2000, almost every province set automobile industry as its pillar industry.

Underlying the mentality of "following the crowd" has been the poor

R&D capability among most Chinese businesses. For example, the total R&D expenditure of all Chinese-owned pharmaceutical businesses is less than that of even one major pharmaceutical group in the West. According to a Chinese report, 97.4% of 873 medicines produced in China are imitations. Because of the mentality of "following the crowd", the average life of a Chinese business is only 5 years while that of a Western counterpart is 30 years. Thus, for Western companies, the winning business strategy in China may be that based on high-tech and constant innovation through investment in R&D. General Motors, for example, won over Ford in the hotly contested Shanghai investment largely due to its willingness to establish a large R&D centre and transfer up-to-date technology to that centre.

Consumer Goods: From Demand for Quantity to Demand for Quality, Variety and Services

Prior to the economic reform, the Chinese economy was a shortage economy, and if people shopped at all it was for food, clothing or a bicycle. The reform opened the appetite of Chinese consumers who were prepared to buy almost anything they could afford, and created golden opportunities for those who could supply the demand. The story of a retired lady selling boiled eggs who could make three times the salary of a university professor was typical of such demand for quantity. As supplies increased and the novelty of available goods wore off, Chinese consumers began to make choices based on more sophisticated criteria including quality, variety and, increasingly, services.

In 1995, a survey showed that 52% of urban consumers and 42% of rural consumers stated that design was a significant factor in their purchase of underwear products. By 1997, Beijing consumers could choose from more than 100 different brands of foreign and domestic skincare products, and over 70 brands of shampoo; country-wide, there were an astonishing 300 brands of toothpaste, and 400 varieties to choose from. In another survey in 1999, 60.8% of the consumers surveyed rated the assurance of after sales services as the most important criterion in their purchasing decision. French retail giant Carrefour and American fast-food giant Kentucky Fried Chicken (KFC) have been highly successful in China primarily because they sell a unique, valued service, which is also immune to duplication by low-cost local competitors.

Industrial Goods: From Demand for Quantity to Demand for Quality, Variety and Standardisation

Driven largely by developments in the consumer market, the industrial market has been undergoing a transition from demand for quantity to demand for quality, variety and standardisation. The demand for goods meeting international standards has in particular been generated by the presence of a large number of international investors, which have extended their global standards, such as ISO 9000, to China.

Take the steel industry for example. China, with 101.1 million tonnes of steel produced by 1,700 iron and steel works, which represent twice as many as the number of iron and steel works in the rest of the world, became the world's top steel producer in 1996, fulfilling Mao Zedong's economic dream of the planning era. However, fragmented, uncompetitive, unprofitable, heavily in debt and geared to the wrong products, China's steel mills are losing out to imports from South Korea, Japan, Europe and the USA. The range of products now in acutely short supply in China includes galvanised sheets (60% self-sufficiency), tin plate (30% self-sufficiency), cold-rolled sheeting, cold-rolled silicon sheeting and oil pipes, as well as varieties specially for use in the automobile, power, petroleum, container, shipbuilding and chemical industries. Imports of special and value-added rolled steel are also rising. To avoid the seven-week lead-time it has to endure for imports of some of its steel plating requirements, General Motors' Shanghai joint venture has to work actively with local Baoshan Steel Corp.

From Government-controlled to Market-driven

Prior to the economic reform of the late 1970s, the central Chinese government controlled virtually everything, ranging from what crops a farmer should plant in the land through to what goods a state-owned enterprise should produce for allocation. The reform has since seen central government's administrative powers being gradually shifted to the hands of market forces and in particular the government phasing out inferior state-owned enterprises. For example, in the sugar refining industry, the central government decided in December 1999 to shut down 9 out of 14 state-owned sugar mills to reduce annual sugar production capacity from 10.55 million tonnes to 7.5 million tonnes.

Such on-going transition from government-controlled to market-driven economy creates both opportunities and threats. Multinational pharmaceutical companies, such as Xi'an–Janssen, SmithKline Beecham and Bristol–Myers Squibb, had to attribute their success stories in the 1980s to the state-funded health care reimbursement system. As old notions of state welfare are being radically reformed, such golden opportunities have vanished but insurance is set to offer lucrative opportunities for foreign financial firms. While the dismantling of thousands of loss-making state-owned enterprises makes room for more efficient foreign businesses in the long-term, the lay-off of many millions of state employees creates a downward consumption spiral, which can make the life of many existing foreign enterprises difficult. Therefore, the challenge is for foreign investors to be able to grasp the uncertain nature of China's transitional economy and then ride its waves.

From Labour-intensive to High-technology

The first two decades of reform have in essence been catch-up growth, gains that came from disbanding the agricultural communes and from allowing capital and in particular labour to be poured into low-end manufacturing and processing. By the mid-1990s, gone were the days when business success could simply come from the finance of production, and as massive over-capacity had occurred in many manufacturing industries, new business opportunities emerged increasingly in high-tech fields. For example, in the pharmaceutical sector, by late 1994, the heyday of easy money was past, but Western pharmaceutical giants like Pfizer and Upjohn have successfully found lucrative niches in the high-tech end of the market, free from domestic competitors and welcomed by both the pharmaceutical industry and medical profession.

Recognising that more and more domestic enterprises would increase their technical innovation and adopt advanced international technology to boost their technological content and increase their competitiveness, ABB announced in 2000 that it would increase its total investment in China to US$ 1 billion within the next three to four years. Of course, some of the hottest opportunities exist in the booming information industry. For example, the number of fixed-line telephones in China is doubling every three years, the number of mobile subscribers every fourteen months, and the number of internet users every eight months; domestic semiconductor companies and local joint ventures manufacture less than 10% of China's own demand.

From Manufacturing to Services

While competition intensifies in many manufacturing sectors, the most promising market opportunities for Western investors will increasingly be in services, such as education, healthcare, commercial and investment banking, insurance, consulting, and tourism. It is estimated that China currently needs 350,000 business managers but produces a mere 300 MBA graduates a year. This is why Shanghai-based China Europe International Business School has been the fastest growing in the world. And in 2005, with a 37% equity holding, the UK's Nottingham University launched its £20 million campus in Ningbo. Based on regulations effective from 1 July 2000, Sino-foreign joint ventures in healthcare have been allowed. China has a very high savings rate, 43% in 1999, but nowhere to put the money to productive use: its financial institutions are primitive and are only competent at allocating funds to non-performing state enterprises according to government instructions.

In 1999, insurance premium income in China stood at only 1.5% of total GDP, while the equivalent average ratios for developed and developing countries were 8–10% and 3.5% respectively. At a seminar jointly held by the Ministry of Science and Technology and the Asian Development Bank on the Chinese consulting industry in November

2000, it was concluded that the industry is still in its infancy stage. In October 1999, China's first two Sino-foreign tourist joint ventures got underway because, by 2020, China is expected to attract 130 million tourists annually, making it the world's top tourist destination.

From the Coast to the Inland

Over the last two decades, approximately 75% of all foreign investments have been made in coastal areas. But with competition intensifying and costs soaring in these areas and indeed consumer purchasing power growing and governmental incentives being extended in the inland, the latter (in particular its regional centres, such as Wuhan, Chongqing, Chengdu, and Xi'an) can offer increasingly attractive opportunities. Consider Chongqing. Carrefour opened a car park-equipped superstore in Chongqing in 1997, which has since been doing a roaring business. In 2001, Ford invested US$49 to establish a 50:50 joint venture with Chongqing Changan Automotive to make 50,000 family sedans a year, but barely a year into operation, it decided to double its capacity.

Currently, central government is working out the specifics of policies governing foreign investment in infrastructure construction and service sector in central and western regions. It appears that foreign investors will be allowed to hold greater stakes in projects relating to the construction and operation of local railways, bridges, tunnels, ferry facilities and docks, and minority stakes in municipal facilities construction, public services, education and healthcare. China will also adopt additional preferential policies to encourage foreign investment in prospecting and exploring most mineral resources.

In short, central and western regions have their own advantages. For example, Sichuan's fragmented transport system prevents Chengdu from rivalling the eastern powerhouses as a manufacturing centre, but, with 43 universities, and 1.2 million scientists and engineers in the province, the city is regarded by multinationals like Motorola, Siemens and Intel as an ideal R&D base. The UK's University of Liverpool, meanwhile, is planning to set up a university in northwestern China, in partnership with Xi'an Jiaotong University.

3

Approaching and Selecting a Partner

If timing captures the opportunity, geography carries advantages and people are in harmony, then success is bound to come.

ANCIENT CHINESE WISDOM

Do not form alliances with those states whose strategic intentions are unknown to you. It is impossible to conduct the march of an army if one is ignorant of the conditions of mountains, forests, dangerous defiles, swamps and marshes. You cannot gain the advantage of the ground if you fail to make use of native guides. An army does not deserve the title of the invincible Army of the Hegemonic King if its commander is ignorant of any one of the above three principles.

SUN TZU, *THE ART OF WAR*

HAVING RESEARCHED AND IDENTIFIED the market opportunity in China, Western executives can commit themselves to the process of finding a suitable partner. Just like the fact that happy and unhappy marriages are often the result of appropriate and inappropriate partnerships respectively, the process of approaching and selecting a partner often sows the seeds of either smooth or troublesome joint ventures for the future. In this chapter, we first examine the issue of strategic location, which is often overlooked but can make the difference between success and failure. Then, light is shed on the various methods by which partner candidates can be approached and assessed. Finally, we look at the taking of that crucial decision, i.e. the selection of a partner.

Strategic Location Considerations

To a varying degree, opportunity, geography and people all have a great deal to do with the location that is initially chosen for a business. Thus, multinationals must, prior to selecting a partner, take a strategic view as to which part of China the potential business might be located in.

Pitfalls in Choosing an Investment Location

Despite its crucial importance, official development policy and potential partners' rhetoric often lead Western multinationals to choose a location other than that suggested by a purely market-driven calculus.

Official Development Policy

To promote local development, local governments all over China have been trying to woo foreign investors by erecting hoardings declaiming "foreign investment zones" and announcing preferential treatment policies. Yet upon close inspection, most of these zones have had little of substance to offer investors apart from cheap land. China Central Television also reported on 15 October 2000 that 3,081 of the 4,200 development zones in China were unauthorized because they had been set up by sub-provincial government agencies.

Even at authorised zones, caution needs to be exercised. For example, many municipal officials of Wuhan, the provincial capital of Hubei, would quote Wuhan's situation at the heart of China's economic geography and Beijing's drive to promote development of central and western China as reasons why foreign investors should sink millions of dollars into the city. But if we look at Wuhan from the perspective of business operation, we can see that, although Wuhan's geographic centrality makes it look good on a map or corporate strategy slide, what it offers to investors in reality is at most access to a regional market – China is simply too big to think of in terms of one centre. And for retailers especially, but also for manufacturers, central China is simply not yet an attractive enough market. Of course, many multinationals will require a presence in China's seventh largest city, but not necessarily right away and almost certainly for a different set of reasons.

Potential Partners' Rhetoric

Western executives can also be carried away by the impressive introductions of a potential Chinese partner that is actually located in a region unsound for the underlying business proposition. Nowhere can this be more clearly seen than in the case of British brewery Bass, which established a beer joint venture in 1995 with a local partner in Siping, a very remote Jilin town. During the feasibility study, Siping was introduced by the local partner as "a key material distribution centre and a confluence of railroads radiating in all directions in north-eastern China and linking up with the rest of China". And, following the joint venture's establishment, a Bass director proudly commented to *China–Britain Trade Review* that "great care" had been taken to choose the right partner in a geographical area with excellent market potential.

But when the brewery began operating, Bass found that it was in the wrong place, with the wrong people. Distribution difficulties did not help the brewery sell its Tennents lager as far afield as it would have liked, with regular floods blocking road and rail. After being refused licences to sell bottled beer in certain cities, the brewery had to focus on draft beer but, apart from the lack of on-tap facilities, winters at -35°C froze the beer in the draught piping. Coupled with partner relationship problems, the joint venture lost large sums of money during its first years' operation. In April 2000, Bass sold its 55% stake to its local partner, writing off almost all its US$40 million investment.

Understanding the Strategic Consequences of an Investment Location

Depending upon the nature of a business, an investment location brings about five important consequences: (1) proximity to the market; (2) access to supplies; (3) human resource implications; (4) support of local government; and (5) infrastructure facilities and costs.

Proximity to the Market

For service businesses, such as fast-food restaurants and retail stores, proximity to the market is the major factor that determines the location of an investment. While a few years ago only Beijing, Shanghai, Guangzhou and Shenzhen could attract foreign interest, today consumers in a growing number of cities have developed purchasing power. For example, after opening its first restaurant in Shijiazhuang, Hebei province, in 1997, KFC opened the second one in the city in July 2000.

For manufacturers targeting domestic consumers, ventures should be as close to those markets as possible, and probably close to the rail system, which is the best of the poor options available for moving goods nationally. Pfizer, for example, found in 1994 that the location of its pharmaceutical joint venture in north-eastern Dalian created problems with distributing its products to the rest of China. On the other hand, Coca-Cola and Pepsi owe much of their success to their ability to set up nation-wide distribution networks based on building joint venture bottling plants in major cities across China.

For export processors, their facilities would better be near the necessary port infrastructure, such as that found in Tianjin, Shanghai, Xiamen, and Guangdong province. China has also set up over a dozen bonded free trade zones on the coast, in which export processors can freely import materials and equipment, and export finished products.

Access to Supplies

For agribusiness and mining business, access to crops or minerals is the major factor that determines the location of an investment. For instance, ventures for sugar refining have to be located where sugar beet is grown, such as Xinjiang and Helongjiang, or where sugarcane is grown, such as Guangxi and Guangdong. Sino Mining Ltd., an Australian–Chinese joint venture for mining nickel and gold and also currently the only privately owned company with an operating mine in China, is located in Jianchaling of Shaanxi province in the north-west.

For manufacturers relying on local supplies, ventures should be as close to related firms in the industry as possible. In the city of Dongguan in Guangdong province, it is now possible to find 95% of the parts needed for manufacturing computer systems. This is why Dell Computer Corp. made the decision in 1999 to invest in a PC manufacturing facility in Xiamen of neighbouring Fujian province, which can conveniently source parts from Dongguan.

For manufacturers requiring large volumes of imported components, it can be advantageous to locate ventures close to an international port. IBM chose Shenzhen as the location of its desktop PC's manufacturing joint venture in 1994 because its geography and the efficiency of Hong Kong customs allow the venture to source the most expensive components in bulk from Taiwan for significant discounts.

Human Resource Implications

China's best human resources are based in Shanghai, Jiangsu, Beijing, and Tianjin. For example, with the longest history of exposure to Western civilisation, the strongest industrial base and over 50 universities and 700 research institutes, Shanghai hosts China's top talents for Western-style, market-driven business ventures. This is why most top high-tech multinationals have chosen Shanghai as their investment location.

While home to one-quarter of all China's foreign investment, Guangdong lags far behind other high-growth areas in workers with university or graduate degrees – it ranks the 24th out of China's 30 provinces in the proportion of four-year university graduates. So far, it has solved the human resource problem by importing technicians and managers from elsewhere in the country. But these professionals are by nature prone to job-hopping, and this is why Australian conglomerate Pacific Dunlop has scaled back its cable-making operations in Shenzhen and relocated some capacity to Tianjin.

In the vast inland areas, foreign investors generally cannot expect anything but workers of poor quality. However, some urban centres inland do have a good pool of human resources, with Wuhan and Xi'an being the most notable examples, the former having 35 universities and 400 research institutes and the latter 42 universities and 500 research institutes. Chengdu is also strong in this respect.

Support of Local Government

Local government can influence the choice of an investment location in at least two ways. First, local government can grant the status of a "technologically advanced enterprise" to a foreign enterprise to allow it to pay income tax at a 50% reduction for a further three years after the expiry of the standard tax exemption and reduction period. It is also in a position to grant exemption or reduction in local income tax, which is normally levied at 3% of net profit. According to Henry Chow, Chairman of IBM Greater China Group, incentives in the form of tax breaks offered by Shanghai were one of the factors behind IBM's decision to build a US$300 million computer chip packaging plant in Shanghai.

Second, clean and efficient government attracts foreign investors. In 1997, the Shanghai government required all officials to disclose their personal assets. Chongqing's new mayor, Pu Haiqing, has encouraged foreign companies to record and report requests for additional fees. In general, local governments in the underdeveloped interior are conservative in thinking but most can be "friendly" because they want to attract foreign investment, whereas those in the developed coastal areas are open in thinking but some have become "arrogant". In Shenzhen Special Economic Zone (SEZ), for instance, stories abound of the arrogance of officialdom towards less prominent investors.

Infrastructure Facilities and Costs

Investment locations with good infrastructure facilities, such as electricity, gas and water supply, telecommunication and transport links, and residential facilities, are spread along the eastern coast. Xiamen also sells itself as a clean, green place to do business – it treats 40% of its sewage, the top rate in the country and four times the rate of filthy Guangzhou. These zones have successfully attracted a large number of multinationals but they can be expensive. This is why Nestle decided against Pudong as a site for a large foodstuff factory and ended up in Songjiang, a county-level zone an hour's drive outside Shanghai. In Shenzhen, escalating costs have driven some foreign-invested enterprises to depart for less expensive points in Guangdong – Sanyo Electric has moved its television-assembly division to nearby Dongguan.

Although coming cheap compared with the big coastal cities, development zones in large cities like Wuhan and Xi'an in the inland suffer from their lack of appeal as a place to live. As one of the most polluted cities in the world, Xi'an of the north-west, for example, does not yet offer the kind of facilities that might persuade expatriates, especially those with young families, to relocate. In the much less developed rural towns, poor infrastructure and hard living conditions can become the undoing of an investment venture, as the case of Bass has shown.

Approaching and Assessing Potential Partners

Having developed a strategic appreciation of an investment location, potential partners in the appropriate location can be approached and assessed. In practice, these two activities can of course be undertaken in parallel to each other – so long as the former does not give way to the latter. In any case, you need the help of a China guide.

Using a China Guide

A China guide can help you in at least two ways when it comes to approaching and assessing potential partners, i.e. helping you to overcome the language and culture barriers, and giving you inside information, advice and contacts. There are three types of China guides: (1) local guides; (2) professional consultants; and (3) own specialists. They differ in terms of loyalty, experience of China, bilingual capability, industry knowledge and price. If resources allow, you can of course use a combination of these guides. For example, you may combine the loyalty of your own specialist with the wide contacts of a locally based consulting firm. The best China guides are those who are realistic and put your interest first, whereas the worst are those who are mainly interested in luring you into deals for their own benefit.

Using a Local Guide

Local guides range from well-connected individuals, such as retired governmental officials and industry experts, to Chinese banks and Chinese consulting firms, such as CITIC and The Centre for Market and Trade Development (CMTD). They can be found through introductions or in Chinese business directories. Most of them are very small, but they can lead to useful connections. In general, they do not charge much but their services are not very professional either. Their knowledge of a particular industry tends to be limited. The trick for using local guides is to make use of the contacts they can come up with but to severely discount the actual "advice" they will enthusiastically give to you because most of them lack real, strategic business experience and their advice tends to be driven by favouritism.

Hiring a Professional Consultant

Professional consultants differ from the above Chinese guides in that they have a strong Western background and can generally provide services ranging from reliable interpretation, responsible partner introduction and inside intelligence for partner assessment, to sound advice on partner selection. There are three main types of professional consultants. The first are retired diplomats who like to maintain their China contacts in return for comfortable air travel, hotels and a reasonable retainer. Ford, for example, has used James R. Sasser, a former US ambassador to China, as its senior consultant to try to win the right to make cars in Chongqing through a joint venture. The second are the specialist consulting firms focusing exclusively on China business, including Batey Burn, China Concept Consulting and 2W China Investment Consulting. Because of their focus, their services in general are good value for money. The third are global consulting firms, such as PricewaterhouseCoopers and A. T. Kearney, which have the highest professional reputation but their services can be expensive.

Employing Your Own Specialist

You may consider employing a China specialist to facilitate your business development programme. The ideal candidate should be bilingual and have both a Chinese and Western education, and business experience. There is now a well-established pool of overseas Chinese graduates who have received both Chinese and Western education and are working for Western companies. Of course, familiarisation and training programmes are still needed. The beauty of having your own China specialist is the high integration of his activities with those of the rest of the team, and the maximum loyalty, learning and continuity that can be achieved. Employing your own specialist may also cost less eventually than hiring a professional consultant who of course tends to be more experienced and better connected.

Approaching Potential Partners

There are three main types of channels that can be used to find potential partners: (1) existing business relationship; (2) introduction by a third party; and (3) direct contact. Increasingly, there is also the fourth possibility that some Chinese companies may even take the initiative to approach your company directly.

Existing Business Relationship

If your company is already doing other forms of business in China, you may find that your existing Chinese business partner is in a position to become a suitable candidate as a joint venture partner. Texas Instruments (TI), for example, had had a relationship with Baoying Electrical Appliance Factory in Jiangsu province for nearly ten years before their joint venture was set up in 1995. In 1985, Baoying was already one of China's leading manufacturers of thermal protection devices and began purchasing some metal raw materials from TI. In 1992, their relationship developed into a licensing arrangement where Baoying was licensed to produce protection and control devices. As this arrangement went well, TI decided in 1994 to set up a joint venture with Baoying.

Introduction by a Third Party

There are three main types of third parties that you can ask to introduce potential partners to you: (1) existing business partners; (2) government channels; and (3) China consultants.

Existing business partners. If your company has business relationships with equipment manufacturers, component suppliers or financial institutions, which are engaged in business with China, you can ask them to introduce any potential partners they know of. It is even likely that your existing Western customers or suppliers that are already established in China or in the process of doing so may continue to be your customers or suppliers in China if your joint venture eventually takes off.

Government channels. As one of the jobs of embassies abroad is to help their government's nationals make contacts and establish relationships with clients and partners, it is worth making contact with the commercial section of your home embassy in China. Where possible, getting involved with high-level Chinese government delegations or business delegations organised by trade promotion groups, state and local governments and other umbrella organisations on both sides can lead to contacts for potential partners. In particular, the US–China Business Council and China–Britain Business Council regularly organise missions and seminars oriented toward exploring investment opportunities in specific sectors or regions.

China consultants. You can delegate the task of finding potential partners to your China consultants. With the connections they have already established in China, you can expect them to come up with some candidates. CMTD, for example, maintains a databank of 1.5 million industrial and commercial Chinese companies and claims that it can provide a profile of any company in China. Batey Burn has helped an impressive list of foreign investors to find local joint venture partners since it was established in 1989. Although established quite recently, China Concept Consulting has also developed a strong reputation in helping form joint ventures, especially in the Chinese pharmaceutical sector. Big consulting firms, such as McKinsey and PricewaterhouseCoopers, have also established a strong presence in China, but whether their services in introducing potential partners can be justified by the way they charge you is entirely a matter of your own judgement.

Direct Contact

With Western influence, Western-style cold calls are becoming increasingly accepted in China. You can find target companies through combing Chinese company directories like *KAMPASS China* and *China's Top 100,000 Companies* and trade publications like *China Business Review* and *China Britain Business Review* and surfing web sites like www. business-china.com. You are also bound to come across some names of target companies in your market research in China. If a target company passes your basic criteria following checking its business scope, general profile and partnering interest with the help of your China special-ist, comprehensive assessment should then follow.

Assessing a Potential Partner

Too many joint ventures in the past have been established with the wrong partners because, driven by the sentiment of "love at first sight", many Western investors have failed to thoroughly assess their local partners. It is now clear that whatever the pain, it is far better to have it during the assessment stage than after the joint venture is formed. To avoid the fatal mistake of selecting a wrong partner, you need to assess a potential partner from multiple perspectives instead of a single perspective, and at multiple levels instead of a superficial level. In addition, a senior ex-ecutive should be appointed to co-ordinate the exercise and to assemble the whole picture based on discussions and cross checking.

Assessing a Potential Partner from Three Perspectives

While the profile of a potential partner is made up of many parameters, three factors determine its suitability as a joint venture partner: (1) mo-tives; (2) credibility; and (3) capabilities (see Figure 3.1).

Motives are the intentions of the potential partner, i.e. why it wants to form a joint venture with you. The reason for assessing them is to ascertain whether what the potential partner wants from the conceived

FIGURE 3.1

Assessing a Potential Partner from Three Perspectives

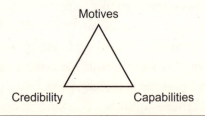

relationship is in conflict with yours. Credibility is concerned with the integrity or trustworthiness of your potential partner. The reason for assessing it is to determine the likelihood of your potential partner's actions being beneficial rather than detrimental to you after the relationship is established. Capabilities are about the strengths and weaknesses of your potential partner. The reason for assessing them is to ascertain whether the two parties have the right complementary skills and resources to make the operation of the conceived joint venture a success.

Assessing a potential partner's motives. Most foreign investors in China form joint ventures with Chinese partners for the purpose of generating returns on their investment. But the motives of a Chinese business for forming a joint venture can be very complicated and are shaped to varying degrees by three factors: (1) government influences; (2) corporate needs; and (3) personal agendas.

(1) Government influences. Many government authorities have a greater or lesser degree of control over state enterprises and an interest in them, often significant enough to make or break a joint venture, although their power and interests may remain hidden from foreign investors without careful research or until it is too late. From local to state level, governments can shape the motives of state enterprises toward "attracting foreign investment" per se, feeding a whole town, developing local economy and/or getting access to export markets. Local government influences can also play a role in shaping the motives of collectively owned enterprises – especially those located inland.

(2) Corporate needs. Most state-owned enterprises lack modern management and advanced technology to compete or even survive in a market economy and such corporate needs may be met by foreign inputs. Most collectively owned enterprises and private businesses also have difficulty in accessing state bank credit and suffer from obsolete technology, although their directors and management are more market-oriented than their state counterparts are. As publicly listed companies are performance-driven, corporate needs, such as making money through pursuing strategic business opportunities or achieving operational ex-

cellence, are their primary motive for seeking a joint venture.

(3) Personal agendas. Many Chinese directors of state-owned enterprises are purely motivated by personal agendas when seeking a partnership with a foreign party, such as higher salaries, overseas trips and other operating privileges including even exploiting the funds to be injected by the foreign partner. As successful entrepreneurs, owners of private businesses can also have strong personal motives for a joint venture. These include capitalising on their business' branding and distribution networks in the China market and enjoying the privileges associated with the foreign connection, which of course are not necessarily in conflict with their corporate needs, such as business growth.

Assessing a potential partner's credibility. In the past, many Western investors have selected wrong partners as a result of their inability to assess their credibility. You can assess the credibility of a potential partner from three perspectives: (1) development path; (2) corporate reputation; and (3) business leader.

(1) Development path. In the past, many Western investors often took a static view by concentrating on examining the existing scope of the potential partner's business. But to develop an understanding of the credibility of your potential partner, you need to assess not only how it is doing currently but also where it has come from and where it is going. Just like the fact that everybody is the product of their past, the character and credibility of your potential partner is much dependent upon its past. Many Chinese companies simply do not have a sensible future direction, and this should tell you that they might be struggling at their existing position.

(2) Corporate reputation. Corporate reputation is concerned with your potential partner's credibility in the eyes of other players in the business environment. For example, its customers should be able to tell you something about the integrity of your potential partner's product and services. Its suppliers should be able to tell you whether it makes payments according to contract terms and whether it has any disputes with

them. Its competitors should be in a position to give you intelligence about its position, strengths and weaknesses in the industry. Its reputation in terms of wage payment and environmental protection in the local community can also be a good indication of its general credibility.

(3) Business leader. The leader of the Chinese enterprise needs to be known by the Western party as a person because their credibility is the focal point for establishing a mutually trusting, long-term relationship between the two parties. Many directors of state-owned enterprises may say that they care about their enterprise, but in practice they are only good at seeking personal gain at the expense of their enterprise and at protecting their position through entertaining their superiors or government officials. On the other hand, some owners of private businesses can be like "cowboy entrepreneurs", who practice a brand of business that no multinationals would feel comfortable with.

Assessing a potential partner's capabilities. All too often, many Western investors concentrate on analysing a potential partner's technical capability. But such analysis lacks a feel of the whole, which can be achieved by assessing three critical areas: (1) managerial competencies; (2) functional assets; and (3) human resources.

(1) Managerial competencies. Although this is one of the key areas in which Chinese companies are supposed to learn from the West, a thorough examination of your potential partner's current managerial competencies and of its potential for managerial development is important. You need to examine its management profile, such as the number of management levels and the ratio of the number of managers over the number of other employees. Generally speaking, the older and the less educated, the more difficult for them to learn and, because of their market-driven culture, collective and private businesses tend to be more receptive to Western business management concepts.

(2) Functional assets. You need to get your company's relevant specialists to China to thoroughly assess your potential partner's functional assets. Your marketing people need to develop a feel for its customer

base and distribution channels. Your production and technical special-ists need to have an in-depth knowledge of its technology, facilities and production and quality control systems. Your supply managers need to develop an understanding of its raw material or components supply situ-ation and of how the local supply network works. Your financial experts need to thoroughly assess its financial health from such perspectives as solvency and liquidity.

(3) Human resources. In the past, Western investors rarely sent their human resource specialists to assess their potential partner's human re-sources. But experience shows that human resource problems account for many of the difficulties suffered by Western investors because eve-rything is carried out through people. Therefore, your human resource specialists need to develop an in-depth knowledge of your potential partner's existing practices in the areas of recruitment, training, per-formance appraisal, promotion, and financial rewards. They also need to establish its personnel profile, concerning the age, education, and skills of the workforce so as to determine its desirability.

Assessing a Potential Partner at Three Levels

In assessing a potential joint venture partner, some Western investors in the past relied on their traditional wisdom of "seeing is believing" or even "hearing is believing" to form their judgement. Yet, due to cultural differences and the lack of business credibility among some Chinese, what they heard could be fabricated stories and what they saw could be decorations for visitors, leading to the selection of the wrong partner. To form an accurate judgement on your potential partner, you need to learn to practice the art of "listening, plus seeing, plus checking, plus testing, is believing", i.e. assessing it at multiple levels (see Figure 3.2).

Assessment at level 1 consists of the introductory activities formally prepared by your potential partner. At level 2, assessment is concerned with the investigating activities informally conducted by you or your China guide. Assessment at level 3 is done through any pilot operation designed to test your potential partner. It is worth noting that from level

FIGURE 3.2
_____

Assessing a Potential Partner at Three Levels

High	▲	**Level 3:** Real "engagement"
Reliability	│	**Level 2:** Informal investigation
Low	│	**Level 1:** Formal introduction

_____

1 to level 3, the emphasis is shifted from analysis to intuition; and with insight of increasing reliability being generated, increasing commitment is needed. And because of the limitations of level 1, you should, as a minimum requirement, assess your potential partner at both level 1 and level 2, and where possible, you should go through all three levels.

Formal introduction. Most Western investors rely on formal introduction, which is done in three main ways: (1) presenting formal documents, (2) holding formal meetings, and (3) arranging formal visits.

(1) Presenting formal documents. If you ask, your potential partner will give you a company brochure, product specification sheets and other formally prepared publicity materials. To develop a feel of its managerial capability, you may ask for its management structure and any operating procedures. To understand its financial position, you should insist that they give you some financial data even if they are reluctant.

(2) Holding formal meetings. Many introductions to a potential partner take place at formal meetings. At these meetings, you should seek first to understand by listening carefully, inquiring with questions, testing your assumptions, and taking detailed notes. You may also request to have an in-depth meeting with a particular manager to establish detailed knowledge about a particular area.

(3) Arranging formal visits. Although site visits arranged by your potential partner could be a show in some cases, you can still take the opportunity to develop a view of your potential partner at its best. If the

best form cannot even convince you, then you may forget it completely. Of course, such visits are essential to your development of a feel of your potential partner's physical location and facilities.

Informal investigation. With the help of your China guide, you can investigate into your potential partner in three informal ways: (1) collecting intelligence from the public, (2) getting inside stories from internal sources, and (3) making informal visits to the site.

(1) Collecting intelligence from the public. If your China guide has contacts in the local Administration for Industry and Commerce or the local tax authority, he may over a dinner get intelligence on your potential partner's financial health. He can also gather intelligence on your potential partner's strengths and weaknesses from officials and experts in the relevant industry association and from those who are with your potential partner's customers, suppliers and competitors. If he spends some time reading local papers or chatting with people at restaurants close to your potential partner in a small town, he may well read or hear gossip, rumours or speculations about it.

(2) Getting inside stories from internal sources. If your China guide has contacts in your potential partner, you may well get some inside stories. One British animal feed company once approached a Chinese producer in Sichuan province and subsequently became convinced that it was a suitable partner. But the China guide had developed such a good personal relationship with one Chinese employee that the young graduate employee, who spoke some English, privately told the British side that the Chinese side was lying at formal meetings. Alerted by the warning, the British side probed more thoroughly into the Chinese company and eventually concluded that it was not a suitable partner.

(3) Making informal visits to the site. Given that formal visits may contain water, your China guide can try to make visits to the site without formally notifying your potential partner. A working environment full of rubbish and chaos is the result of poor management while a clean and ordered working environment is the result of good management. If

the guide observes that some employees are reading newspapers while cracking melon seeds in the offices or simply sleeping at desks during office hours, then it is not a properly managed company. If he observes that everyone is preoccupied with doing their job, then the management of the company is in a different league.

Real "engagement". The most reliable method is to enter into a real "engagement" with your potential partner, which can take one of three main forms involving varying degrees of commitment and risk: (1) low-risk alliance; (2) co-operative venture; and (3) pilot joint venture.

(1) Low-risk alliance. There are three main types of low-risk alliances that are suitable for the purpose of assessing a potential joint venture partner, i.e. licensing, technology transfer, and compensation trade. In the mid-1980s, Polaroid set up a compensation trade arrangement with a factory of Shanghai Motion Picture. Polaroid provided capital equipment, trained the work force, and upgraded the Chinese factory. In return, the Chinese side assembled and supplied printed circuit boards to Polaroid manufacturing plants around the world. Polaroid in the meantime had the chance to evaluate operating conditions in China, cement ties with its partner, build up the Chinese side's production skills, and assess the feasibility of a larger commitment. In the mid-1990s, the two parties signed an agreement to set up a joint venture, and because of the evolutionary nature of its relationship, the transition from assembly to a fully fledged joint venture had gone practically without a hitch.

(2) Co-operative venture. To test the water, you can also consider proceeding first through a co-operative venture, which can be dissolved with minimum legal restrictions. Oregon-based Tektronix Inc set up a five-year co-operative venture in 1991 with Yangzhong Electronic Instrument Factory. As the contract approached expiry in 1996, Tektronix was encouraged by the local government to convert its stake into an equity arrangement. But Tektronix was acutely aware of the financial difficulties that the local industry was in throughout China. One symptom of the Chinese partner's financial difficulties was the way it was trying to renegotiate clauses in the co-operative venture contract that

stipulated that 100% of the venture's profits must be reinvested. In addition, the Chinese partner was arguing that it should receive a greater share of the profits. After careful assessment, Tektronix only agreed to extend the co-operative venture agreement for a further six years.

(3) Pilot joint venture. In high-tech industries where protection of proprietary property is vitally important, it is worth considering setting up a small, pilot joint venture to assess the local partner before expanding it into an integrated, full-scale operation or developing with the same partner into other products or geographic markets. In 1994, IBM established International Information Products (Shenzhen), its first joint venture with Great Wall Computer, which was a leading computer manufacturer in China backed by the People's Liberation Army. Following the initial success, IBM established four more joint ventures with the same partner: the Shenzhen GKI Electronics Co. in 1995, the Shenzhen Hailiang Storage Products Co. in 1997, the Shanghai IBM Leasing Co. in 1999, and the Beijing Xing Chang Ke International Electronics Co. in August 2000. In addition, the first joint venture was expanded to include a new branch in Futian duty-free zone in October 2000.

Selecting a Partner

Having fully assessed the potential partner, it is now possible to bring all the issues together to establish the business proposition and to decide on whether to pursue it jointly with the potential partner.

Structuring the Business Proposition

When structuring a joint venture business proposition, you need to pay attention to three critical areas: (1) business philosophy; (2) complementary skills and resources; and (3) supporting business relationship(s).

Business Philosophy

The business philosophy of a joint venture is concerned with three sets of assumptions that must fit reality and each other, and be known and understood by both partners. The first are their assumptions about the joint venture's environment concerning the society, the market, customers and competitors, and technology. The second are their assumptions about the meaningful results of the venture, i.e. the product and services valued by the customer. The third are their assumptions about the core competencies, i.e. bundles of skills and technical methods needed to deliver the product and services. In the past, some joint ventures have failed simply because the partners have failed to define a consistent and shared business philosophy. For example, in establishing Beijing Jeep in 1983, the Chinese intended to persuade the Americans to design and produce a four-door jeep with a soft-top that could be used by the People's Liberation Army. Meanwhile, the Americans hoped to persuade the Chinese to accept one based largely or, better yet, entirely on the Cherokee Jeep they were selling in the USA. Although the Americans later managed to string the Chinese along to assemble its Cherokee, the reliance on knockdown kits imported from the USA and the resultant high sales price at US$19,000 (with Chinese customers' lack of foreign exchange) made it almost impossible for the venture to survive.

Complementary Skills and Resources

Liu Chuanzhi, president of then Legend, the leading Chinese computer manufacturer that formed a 51:49 joint venture involving US$200 million with AOL Time Warner in June 2001, once vividly described a joint venture as "a blind carrying a lame":

> Since the blind can carry the lame to walk while the lame gives the direction to the blind, the joint venture for walking becomes meaningful. If one can see and walk on his own, then there is no need to collaborate with somebody else. It is not dangerous to be a blind or a lame, but it is dangerous for a blind person to ride a blind horse in

an environment full of obstacles and pitfalls.

Indeed, complementary skills and resources represent the marriage of strengths and are at the heart of a successful joint venture business because they settle to a large extent the issue of who does what. Yet, many Sino-Western joint ventures have failed in the past because Western investors looked for similarity rather than complementarity when selecting a partner. The problem with partners of great similarity but little complementarity is that, although similarity leads to easy understanding at the discussion stage, each party may seek to challenge the other at the operational stage because they both think they know what they are doing. This is why AOL had looked at and passed over dominant Chinese Internet portals, such as Sina.com and NetEase.com, and chosen Legend as the partner. The AOL-Legend joint venture would see the Chinese company's computers making use of AOL software.

Of course, there are many successful joint ventures with partners in the same industry, but their operational success has followed because the partners have looked beyond similarity and based the joint venture on complementary skills and resources. Texas Instruments and Jiangsu Baoying Electrical Appliance Factory, for example, saw their joint venture combining the application experience and technology of the former with the manufacturing and local market experience of the latter.

Finally, a joint venture must be based on complementary skills and resources that are sufficient to make up its core competencies. Peugeot formed a joint venture with the Guangzhou government in 1985, which was then found to be unable to develop adequate marketing and sales for the cars. The Chinese partner, meanwhile, maintained that the French carmaker had failed to provide up-to-date equipment and models. The result had been a long-running and bitter stand-off between the "partners", and by 1996 the venture ran up losses of US$600 million and forced Peugeot to pull out of China in 1997.

Supporting Business Relationship(s)

In many joint ventures, the business proposition can be further complicated by one or more side business relationships, where, for example, one partner is also in a technology license arrangement with the joint venture or is also a supplier or customer of the joint venture. Without a side business relationship, the partners' respective stakes in the venture make them consider the maximisation of economic returns from the operation of the venture as their top priority. However, with a side business relationship, the partners' priorities or motivations in the venture may get entangled. For example, when a partner is also in a technology licensing arrangement with the joint venture, it may receive a return primarily through sales royalties, levied as a fee for its closely guarded proprietary technology, rather than from the operating profits of the joint venture. In the early days of Beijing Jeep, while seeking a return from the capital invested, the American side was actually reaping much richer rewards from selling knockdown kits, spare parts and equipment to China for payment in hard currency. Thus, in structuring the joint venture business proposition involving one or more side business relationships, it is important to make the latter supportive to the former.

The Final Decision

The decision on the selection of a partner is the source of many benefits or problems for establishing a joint venture business in China. In making the final decision, senior executives need to consider three further criteria: (1) quantitative evaluation – the role of financial modelling; (2) qualitative factors; and (3) consequences of failure.

Quantitative Evaluation – The Role of Financial Modelling

It has been a Western corporate tradition to use financial models to evaluate a proposed investment. While "correct" in theory, discounting methods like net present value (NPV) and internal rate of return (IRR) are, arguably, too technically sophisticated to evaluate a joint venture business whose cash flows are subject to great uncertainty. In practice, non-discounting methods, such as yearly return on investment (ROI) and payback, give decision-makers a more real picture.

To calculate ROI and payback, a projected five-year profit and loss statement, which shows in hard numbers what the operation of the proposed business will look like if it is established, needs to be constructed. The construction of the model is an exercise that seeks to challenge everybody involved to express their part of the business in the best possible clear-cut numbers. A good financial model is the result of good teamwork requiring input from all related functions, and is assembled by an experienced accountant. Help also needs to be sought from the local partner regarding local data. ROI can be computed by dividing the prospective investment's annual net profit by the total investment, and ROI in the fifth year may give an indication of the acceptability of the investment in financial terms to the decision-makers. The payback method involves estimating the number of years, over which the cost of the investment is "paid back". As such, it is a good rough screening device – a short payback period may provide some assurance that acceptance of the project is unlikely to have serious consequences.

Yet, despite the role of financial modelling, it is crucial to note that it is human beings rather than the financial model that have the ability to make the decision. It is wrong not to build a financial model to support your decision-making, but it is equally wrong to let the financial model make the decision for you. A financial model is only a simulation of the future in numerical terms, and the future is full of uncertainties, especially in the China business environment. You should therefore use the model to get a feel of the certain or quantitative side of the future, and use human judgemental capability to bring into consideration the uncertain or qualitative side of the future.

Qualitative Factors

Although fundamental, the structure of the business proposition and the implication of the financial model are by no means the only factors determining the suitability of the potential partner, two other important qualitative ones being: (1) partner credibility, and (2) partner motives.

Partner credibility. How much can you trust your potential partner? The answer to this question clearly has a significant impact on whether to select it as your partner. At one extreme, you may find that you cannot trust your potential partner at all because, for example, it has years of loss-making history, a poor reputation for product quality, and a leader who is known to have created the phenomenon where "the temple is bankrupt, but the priest prospers". Then, no matter how much your potential partner promises, what assurances local government officials give you or how attractive the financial prospect of the business proposition may seem, you should not select it as your partner. At the other extreme, having known your potential partner through previous engagements, you may be completely impressed by its credibility, as reflected in its successful track record, its good reputation in the industry or even the country, and the integrity and resourcefulness of its leaders. In this case, it is possible for the decision to be based on the rapport between the leaders of the two partners. Between these two extremes, partner credibility must be carefully balanced against other factors, such as complementary skills and resources, and results of financial modelling. If you are unsure about your potential partner's credibility, it is much better to allow time to assess it than to rush the selection decision.

Partner motives. What are your potential partner's real motives? The answer to this question has an equally significant impact on whether to select it as your partner. Ideally, you would like to select a partner whose primary motive is identical to yours, i.e. to maximise the long-term economic returns of the joint investment so as to maximise the returns of each partner's stake. In reality, however, this is an unlikely scenario because the partners are also determined to retain their separate identities, to the extreme where the two partners may, as the Chinese proverb vividly puts it, "share the same bed but have different dreams" (*tongchaung yimeng*). For example, if a local partner's motives for forming the joint venture are primarily to "milk" the Western investor's technology and special skills, then the long-term survival of the venture is unlikely to figure highly among its goals. On the other hand, partner motives are more likely to be moving targets than set objectives because mutual benefit is not a static element but rather flows positively or negatively from one partner to the other throughout the life cycle of the relationship. At times, a benefit that was there at the beginning of the relationship may, as a result of market, industry or partner changes, no longer be present; of course, new benefits can also emerge. Thus, keeping an eye on the evolution of partner motives is essential.

Consequences of Failure

It is also important to bear in mind that once the decision is made your life will be associated with that of your partner regardless of whether you like your partner or not. The idea of a "divorce" in a joint venture can be extremely complex and costly, given the underdeveloped legal systems in China and the tendency for them to be prone to political influence and regional protectionism. Case in point: US-based battery maker Revpower. When its partner relationship soured, Revpower elected to pull out of its Shanghai joint venture established in 1989. A Stockholm arbitration panel subsequently awarded Revpower some US$5 million in damages, but it got nowhere when it sought to enforce this.

Thus, if you cannot find a suitable partner for the time being, you are well advised to conduct further research instead of forming a joint venture with an unsuitable partner. Or if you are really convinced of the market opportunity, then a wholly foreign-owned business can be the right option subject to government regulations. The biggest advantage with this option is that you have full management control and are insulated from partner problems commonly existent in joint ventures. The biggest disadvantage is that you have to rely on yourself to get everything done. Companies like 3M and DEC have shown that this type of venture can be operated successfully.

Overall, since its accession to the WTO, China's regulatory environment has rapidly been evolving toward one that is fairer and more flexible as far as equity share holding is concerned. This is why, knowing that China was to allow wholly foreign-owned retailing ventures from December 2004, Tesco, the UK's largest and the world's third largest retailer, still invested US$260 million cash to establish a 50:50 joint venture with Shanghai Ting Hsin in July 2004.

4

NEGOTIATING WITH THE POTENTIAL PARTNER

If you have trouble in waiting for the change of traffic light, then you are not for China.

AN ANONYMOUS WESTERN BUSINESSMAN

If you know only how to move forward and not backward, you will reach a dead end.

ANCIENT CHINESE WISDOM FROM *I CHING*

TO MANY WESTERN BUSINESS PEOPLE, negotiating with the Chinese is one of the most challenging business tasks in the world. Some have been so overwhelmed by the frustrations and pains involved in Sino-Western negotiations that they begin to believe that the Chinese have a negotiating "advantage" as a result of their use of deliberately designed, deception-based negotiating tactics. In my years of experience at the core of many Sino-Western negotiations, I have discovered that these claims are largely speculative. In this chapter, I seek to uncover the myth of the Chinese negotiating advantage and explore the art of effectively negotiating with the Chinese. Consideration is also given to negotiating finance and management control, the two most important issues in setting up a Sino-Western joint venture.

The Myth of the Chinese Negotiating Advantage

Much is made of the difficulties of negotiations in China, but these difficulties can only thoroughly be understood when examined from both a Western and a Chinese point of view.

Western Speculation upon Chinese Negotiating Tactics

Trying to interpret things within a Western frame of reference, some Western "China hands" in their published works attribute negotiation difficulties in China to the use, by Chinese negotiators, of deliberately designed, deception-based negotiating tactics. They claim that before foreigners arrive in China, the Chinese will have decided to use the strategy of "keeping the foreigner off guard", including the tactics of "controlling the location and schedule", "playing off competitors", "changing negotiators", "exploiting 'friendship'", and "driving a hard bargain". During the negotiations, the Chinese will deploy the strategy of "establishing principles first, worrying about details later" while "getting to know the foreign side thoroughly and exploiting contradictions" and also "exploiting the Chairman's visit". They will try to get their way by "exerting psychological pressure" and "using guilt". They will "push to find the bottom line" by "using time pressure", "feigning ignorance" and "feigning anger". If everything else has failed, the Chinese will adopt the strategies of "using intermediaries", "re-opening closed issues", and finally "considering a signed contract as a draft". These "China hands" further claim that these Chinese "strategies" have given the Chinese an "advantage" and, as a result, that Western business people have paid a "comparable premium".

Influenced by these types of warnings, many more Western business people get spooked as soon as they come across seemingly puzzling circumstances. For example, some consider that the reason that the Chinese arrange visits to tourist sights or banquets is that they want to fill time with irrelevant activities so as to "use stalling" to exploit foreign impatience. Others suspect that the true motive behind the Chinese side's sudden cancellation of a pre-planned banquet on the grounds that a senior official cannot attend it is to "wear them down". And when the Chinese negotiators indicate that they need to consult a higher authority, many immediately hear the alarm ringing that the Chinese are deploying the strategy of "using false authority".

Yet, upon closer examination from both Western and Chinese perspectives, we can see that such claims are largely speculative. For a start, instead of being in an advantageous position in joint venture negotiations, the Chinese have often been in a disadvantageous position because of their lack of knowledge of Western technology and equipment and of experience in international business negotiations. This is why many Chinese believe that they have paid "tuition fees" in joint venture negotiations, as indicated by one official report that among the sampled 8,550 state-owned enterprises that entered into joint venture with foreign companies in 1992, about 5,000 did not even conduct their own asset valuation. One Western businessman also observed that "while it is a common complaint by foreign investors that Chinese parties overvalue their assets, it is equally fair to mention that Chinese complaints about the overvaluation of know-how and technology are as common." In my years of experience at the core of Sino-Western negotiations, I have also frequently heard the Chinese side expressing worries that they have possibly been ripped off in deals with Westerners.

But how do we explain negotiation difficulties in China? The answer lies in the natural differences between Western and Chinese negotiating philosophies, beyond which negotiations mostly run into trouble in China for the same reason that they run into trouble elsewhere – the parties involved cannot agree on what is best for both.

Five Differences between Western and Chinese Negotiating Philosophies

If we take an orbital view of the world of both Western and Chinese negotiators, we can see that there are five natural differences between Western and Chinese negotiating philosophies (see Figure 4.1).

FIGURE 4.1

Negotiating Philosophy Contrast

	West	China
Negotiating Goal:	Contract	Relationship
Constraints:	Company	Country
Way of Thinking:	Logic	Intuition
Communication Style:	Frankness	Face
Language Used:	Western	Chinese

Difference 1: Western Contract versus Chinese Relationship

In the rules-based West, business is generally conducted in a public-ly verifiable manner, i.e. using contracts, under laws that are widely known and consistently enforced. Thus, Westerners are looking for an airtight contract, and focus on discussing business issues and reaching agreement with the Chinese on the terms of the contract through formal negotiation sessions. In connections-based China, however, business is traditionally done on the basis of mutual trust rather than written contracts because laws have provided the Chinese with relatively little protection. Thus, the Chinese are looking for a relationship that will provide some assurance that an agreement can come to fruition, and have to "get to know the foreign side thoroughly" in order to assess its trustworthiness. They also see the negotiating process as part and parcel of the relationship between the two parties, which begins prior to any face-to-face meeting and continues into the implementation of the con-tract. This is why they seem to "consider a signed contract as a draft".

Difference 2: Western Company versus Chinese Country

When negotiating in China, the majority of Western executives repre-sent private business and therefore they work in the context of a busi-ness organisation, where there is a fairly direct relationship between action and profit but little or no need for them to consult government agencies. Even those who represent non-profit-making organisations are generally used to a decision-making system that links actions with efficiency. However, the majority of the Chinese negotiate on behalf of state-owned enterprises. Thus, instead of "using false authority", they often have to cope with the huge constraints of Chinese bureaucratic life, negotiating with many different constituencies and seeking official ratification before concluding an agreement with the Western side. In some cases, they may have to bring officials to the negotiating table – thus "changing negotiators" frequently. Even when Chinese negotiators represent private or collective business, they cannot escape from having to meet government demands.

Difference 3: Western Logic versus Chinese Intuition

The Western way of thinking is based on logic, biased toward an analytical and linear view. Westerners are used to breaking apart a complex issue so as to analyse each piece, and when they try to see the whole, they simply reassemble all the pieces in their mind. They tend to think that the way from A to Z is a straight line, i.e. right through the alphabet. However, the Chinese way of thinking is based on intuition, biased toward a synthetic and spiral view. The Chinese emphasise gaining overall intuitive impressions rather than analysing the way all the details actually fit together to form a whole. This is why they like to "establish principles first and worry about details later", and instead of "exploiting the Chairman's visit", they regard his words as principles. They tend to think that the way from A to Z is like a spiral – going through A, B, C, D and E, with an excursion back to C and D, then on to E, F and so on, until reaching Z. This is why they may "re-open closed issues". And don't forget that their Z is not exactly the same as yours.

Difference 4: Western Frankness versus Chinese Face

Western communication style has traditionally been characterised by straight talk, open debate, friendly disagreement and loyal opposition. From childhood Westerners are taught to say their piece and not to worry what others think because their legal systems protect their right to express their ideas. In Chinese communication, however, great attention has to be paid to face, i.e. the light in which they appear, because of the respect that people traditionally have for the feelings of others. They are taught not to dispute the instructions of their superiors or in any way offend those with power. They are therefore particularly sensitive to what is said in public, valuing comments that bolster others' reputation, prestige and status, and are used to exercising caution in expressing opinions that are critical of others. This is why they sometimes use vague phrases, such as "in principle it is OK" and "I will do my best", to avoid that too confronting word "no", and also why they prefer to "use intermediaries" to pass on messages.

Difference 5: Western Language versus Chinese Language

A Western language, say English, is completely different from Chinese, and interpreting between them is one of the hardest of all arts because of the extraordinary differences between the two cultures. When a negotiation involves large negotiating teams on both sides, it takes approximately three times longer than is required if only one language is used. Yet, too many people regard interpreting as a mechanical function – input English and out comes Chinese and then the other way round. Many Western negotiators make the fatal mistake of assuming that they do not have to have their own interpreter because the Chinese side will prepare one or that they can use any local who speaks English as their interpreter. But the interpreter prepared by the Chinese side is unlikely to be familiar with you and your business, and is unlikely to work hard for you – he may lean heavily to the Chinese side and fail to pass on vital information to you. And an interpreter who has studied only language may have problems with technical interpretations.

The Art of Effectively Negotiating with the Chinese

In essence, joint venture negotiation is the process of seeking to establish a business relationship between two parties, which is legally specified by a written contract but also contains an intangible element of mutual trust. This element of mutual trust is especially important in the highly uncertain China business environment. Thus, the shared goal of any joint venture negotiation must be to efficiently reach a win-win position represented both by a mutually beneficial contract with minimum scope for problems to occur in the contract's execution, and by sufficient mutual trust formed on the basis of adequate knowledge of each other. To achieve this goal, we need the art of effectively negotiating with the Chinese that reconciles the differences between Western and Chinese negotiating philosophies (see Figure 4.2).

It is important to note that successfully performing a lower-level activity is a prerequisite to successfully performing a higher-level activity. Also, as negotiation is a dynamic process, you should consider undertaking all five levels of activities for each negotiating session.

Preparing the Team

In *The Art of War*, Sun Tzu said:

FIGURE 4.2

Negotiating with the Chinese: Five Levels of Activities

Level 5	Employing A Combination of Western and Chinese Behaviours
Level 4	Thinking From both Western and Chinese Perspectives
Level 3	Keeping A Balanced Emotion throughout
Level 2	Preparing For the Negotiation
Level 1	Preparing the Team

The skilful generals in ancient times first made them invulnerable before seeking the chance to defeat the enemy. To be invulnerable depends on yourself, but whether you can defeat the enemy depends on whether it makes mistakes.

Western negotiators often complain about the large number of people in the Chinese negotiating team without questioning themselves whether their own team is of sufficient capability. Too often, the answer is "no", which means vulnerability. To be invulnerable in negotiations with the Chinese, you need to prepare a strong team at three levels: (1) personal qualities; (2) team structure; and (3) phased encounters.

Personal Qualities

Whether you are sent to China to negotiate on your own or as a member of a team, you need to work at preparing yourself in the areas of emotional fortitude, intellectual skills, and China knowledge. As differences and surprises are the name of the game in China, patience becomes of paramount importance. You should not be characterised by restlessness, aggressiveness, speed and extreme competitiveness but be good at controlling your temper and naturally predisposed towards conciliation over confrontation. You should also have as much experience and knowledge about the substantive area to be discussed as possible so as to ask the right questions and give the right explanations. Finally, you need to learn about China, about how to relate to the Chinese, about the differences between Western and Chinese negotiating philosophies and the methods for handling them by reading books like this one and by talking to those who have had experience of negotiations in China.

Team Structure

In most cases, you need to send a team to China to undertake complicated negotiations. A team of sufficient capability needs to consist of a leader of sufficient stature, an adequate number of team members, and a competent interpreter. Given the toughness and complexity of the job, the team leader should be someone who is strong yet caring, firm yet flexible, experienced yet inquisitive, and is in a position to co-ordinate internal resources and has sufficient authority to make certain decisions so as to maintain his credibility. It is also essential to have individuals of the necessary expertise to cover all the areas to be discussed, a knowledgeable outside consultant who knows how to get things done in China, and a lawyer experienced in the legal aspects of setting up China ventures. Finally, you should spare no expense in finding and using your own competent interpreter. Even when the Chinese side provides an interpreter, having your own interpreter improves your reading of Chinese signals, reduces the chances of misunderstandings, and enhances your information gathering. The best candidates are those who, apart from speaking fluent English and Mandarin, have been educated and have worked in both China and the West. Internal training should also be provided to allow them to familiarise themselves with the substantive areas to be discussed.

Phased Encounters

Negotiations with the Chinese for the purpose of forming a joint venture generally go through the stages of initial discussions, substantive negotiations and the end game, each of which requires people of different stature. Initial discussions should be made at a level that is neither too low nor too high. If a low-ranking representative is sent to China to do initial reconnaissance, the Chinese side may not arrange representatives of sufficient stature to meet him. On the other hand, there is a strong argument that the chairman or CEO should not lead the pioneering trip because what he or she says during such a trip may undermine the negotiating position of the team that must follow. At the substantive negotiations stage, your company needs to send a complete negotiating team headed by a competent leader. This stage normally takes months or years, and generally involves a lot of twists and turns. To maintain continuity, it is important to use the same team members throughout the talks if at all possible. Constant rotation of personnel makes it possible for the Chinese side to cite ostensible "understandings" reached during earlier talks. At the end game stage, senior executives of your company can be very useful in getting stalled negotiations back on track, and your company's chairman and CEO are the right people to come to China for signing ceremonies.

Preparing for the Negotiation

In *The Art of War*, Sun Tzu said:

> Knowing yourself and knowing the enemy, in any battle you will not be in peril.

> A triumphant army will not fight until victory is assured, whereas a defeated army hastily challenges to fight first and thereafter strives for victory.

There is no doubt that the more you are prepared for the negotiation, the more effectively you will be able to influence the Chinese. Yet, one of the most common mistakes Western negotiators make in China is insufficient preparation. There are three critical areas of preparation you need to consider prior to the negotiation: (1) intelligence on your counterpart; (2) your own negotiating stance; and (3) supporting materials.

Intelligence on Your Counterpart

You can gather intelligence on your counterpart by collecting published reports, approaching relevant contacts and using pre-negotiation occasions. With the help of your own interpreter, you can study your potential partner on the basis of the information contained in its brochure, Chinese company directories, industry yearbooks, trade publications, and any reports in the local press. With the help of a professional consultant, you may be able to gather intelligence, in an informal way, from your potential partner's customers and suppliers and even the local people. You can seek knowledge on industry policies from the relevant Chinese ministry and gather industry intelligence from foreign competitors. You can also use pre-negotiation occasions, such as banquets and visits, to probe the attitude of the Chinese side to the negotiation and find out how familiar it is with the substantive areas to be discussed.

Your Own Negotiating Stance

Successful negotiation with the Chinese requires clarity about your own negotiating stance concerning your goals and objectives, negotiating limits, and concessions to be made. When it comes to figuring out what to achieve in China, some Western negotiators confuse wishes with objectives because of their poor knowledge of the China business reality and their lack of understanding of the key issues involved in joint venture negotiations. "They form partnerships but then cannot figure out why they did it," as one expatriate observed. You should drop the idea of a vision, and concentrate on what will work and what will be achievable. Objectives should therefore be clearly defined, prioritised and realistic. You also need to work out your negotiating limits, such as your bottom line, beyond which the potential deal may become unacceptable to you, as well as "crunch points", which cannot be compromised. Having some non-negotiable items will give you a number of focal points on which to stand against Chinese pressure. Without a clear idea about your negotiating limits, you will run the risk of being carried away by your counterpart. Finally, you should prepare some items, which can be given to the Chinese when they insist on a concession, because making the gesture is often more important than the substance of the item.

Supporting Materials

There are three main types of supporting materials, i.e. business cards and company brochures, evidence for supporting your negotiating stance, and gifts for relationship building. Having a Chinese name given and printed on one side of your business card not only helps the Chinese to memorise your name but also projects a gesture that you respect the Chinese tradition. You should also prepare a company brochure introducing your company's track record and its product or service, in Chinese. As Western technologies and many modern business concepts are new to Chinese negotiators, any documentary, audio and visual materials illustrating these concepts will support your negotiating stance. Chinese negotiators can also take such materials to their superiors behind the scenes, thus facilitating their decision-making. As a small token gift given to someone you first meet means that you respect them as an individual and that you are willing to develop a friendly relationship with them, you should prepare some gifts, which are not expensive but have a unique Western cultural value.

Keeping a Balanced Emotion throughout

According to Confucius in *The Analects*:

> Don't hope for quick results; don't see just petty gains. If you want quick results, you can never complete your tasks. And if you only see petty gains, you can never achieve great things.

There are generally plenty of reasons to lose your temper when negotiating with the Chinese. However, blowing up tends to make matters worse because it puts you at risk of losing the respect of the Chinese and may even lead to disastrous consequences. To keep a balanced emotion throughout the negotiation, you can take three steps: (1) anticipate frustrations; (2) allow time; and (3) think positively.

Anticipating Frustrations

You should anticipate that frustrations are the name of the game. Without due mental preparation for what you will face, it is likely that these pressures will defeat you. Indeed, the greater the gap between expectations and reality, the greater the disillusionment. Frustrations can come from three main sources, i.e. strains from being in China, challenges from Chinese negotiators, and twists and turns in the negotiation. First, if you have visions of China as an exotic, storybook land before you come to China, you can be fazed by what you experience because jet lag, Chinese food, pollution, solitude and the isolation of being unable to speak the Chinese language can all become strains on you. Second, if you set off for China with only feelings of kindness, you will be frustrated when you come face to face with Chinese negotiators and find them unsympathetic. During the encounter, you may find your cherished values challenged – for example, the Chinese may question not only your products or services but also the rationale behind them. Third, the negotiation process will not be smooth, and if you do not anticipate such twists and turns, you will feel frustrated. You should therefore accept as normal prolonged periods of no movement or progress, and be prepared to walk out of some negotiating sessions empty-handed.

Allowing Time

If you go to China and expect to negotiate a mutually satisfactory contract within a short period of time, you will inevitably be under pressure. To be removed from time pressure, you need to take three critical steps, i.e. controlling head-office expectations, giving the Chinese side time, and giving yourself time. First, there are always expectations from headquarters for you to produce results in a short time no matter what it takes. But such expectations unwittingly put you in a vulnerable position negotiating with the Chinese. You should therefore educate senior people at home about the reality of China – for example, what takes half a day to be resolved in the West takes at least three days in China. Second, given the constraints imposed on Chinese negotiators by such factors as unfamiliarity with Western legal concepts, the complication of the Chinese bureaucratic system and lack of experience in modern business, you should give the Chinese side time to digest new ideas, go through their consultation process and solve their internal problems. Third, you should negotiate as it goes, never push yourself into tight schedules. You should give yourself plenty of time to learn about the China reality, to really understand Chinese perspective, to assess a deadlock situation and find alternative solutions, and to think about the issues and prepare for further negotiating sessions.

Thinking Strategically

As there are so many distractions placed in your way, it is essential to think strategically by keeping an emotional distance, avoiding obsession with details, and thinking positively about the big picture. First, whatever happens, you should never give full rein to your natural responses because emotions can be your undoing. The most effective response is to be sympathetic, fair and controlled. When things are difficult, instead of getting emotionally involved in the drama, you should step back and watch; and when a contentious issue comes up, instead of trying to get it resolved there and then, you should leave it and try again after a cooling-off period. Second, as it is ineffective to give equal attention to or try to win on every issue, you should identify a number of major issues that are important to you and keep them as mental signposts through the negotiating process. Third, research in psychology indicates that it is entirely their subjective view of the situation that makes one person feel stressed and leaves another unperturbed. When things are difficult today, you need to remember that they will be easier tomorrow. When you cannot walk away with a signed contract, you need to remember that you have gained vital learning for further negotiations.

Thinking from both Western and Chinese Perspectives

According to Confucius in *The Analects*:

> There are four things that mark a man of superior mind. He takes
> nothing for granted; he is never over-positive; he is never inflexible;
> and he is never egotistical.

Western negotiators who do not take account of Chinese concerns, needs and constraints can easily find themselves in situations where the relationship between the two sides breaks down. As such, you must think from both Western and Chinese perspectives and this can be achieved by taking three critical steps: (1) dropping false assumptions; (2) understanding the Chinese perspective; and (3) searching for creative solutions.

Dropping False Assumptions

There are three main false assumptions that act as barriers to effective thinking from both Western and Chinese perspectives, i.e. the assumption that the Chinese think the same way, the assumption that the Chinese should think the same way, and the assumption that Chinese interests do not matter. For example, you may assume that the Chinese are also logic-driven and that you can convince them through the use of logical arguments. Yet the truth is that logic will not fully persuade the Chinese because their history has provided them with a frame of reference that emphasises intuition and relationship. And when you fail, you may blame the Chinese on the grounds that they should think the way you do, but while you adopt such a superior attitude, the Chinese may be proud of their own way of thinking. Finally, you want to make a profit in China and bring that profit home, but when the Chinese have a different aim, to benefit themselves, and pursue it with vigour, you may feel that the Chinese have no right to do so. But such a false assumption will bring you nothing but a broken-down relationship.

Understanding the Chinese Perspective

To think from both Western and Chinese perspectives, you need to really, deeply understand the Chinese perspective by understanding before judging, listening actively, and discovering hidden needs. First, you may be very good at speaking your mind, but this strength can become a weakness in negotiations with the Chinese because it may lead you to judging before understanding. By judging first, you never fully understand – for example, in trying to quickly reach agreement on something, hoping it will work out well, you may fail to understand the Chinese frame of reference. Second, active listening enables you to hear what they are trying to say, understand their perceptions, and feel their emotions. It requires you not to phrase a response while listening, to pay close attention to what is said, and to enquire with specific questions. Third, to avoid loss of face, the Chinese may sometimes choose not to speak openly about a sensitive issue but to deflect it onto something else, such as standing on a fixed position while signalling that they are open to finding a solution. With experience or with the help of an experienced China consultant, you can be alert to such signalling. You can discover these hidden needs through discreet discussion of the problem, asking for evidence, going behind the scenes and using an intermediary – to "poke around with a stick to find what is under the stone".

Searching for Creative Solutions

Ultimately, thinking from both Western and Chinese perspectives is about being flexible and creative so as to find solutions that are of mutual benefit and acceptable to both sides, three skills being critical: thinking win-win, focusing on interests rather than positions, and inventing options for mutual gain. First, given the frustrations involved, it is tempting for you to think of ways to "beat them", but such win-lose tactics may damage people's feelings and lead to lose-lose in the long term. Win-win is a frame of mind and heart that constantly seeks mutual benefits, even in hard situations. It is a belief in the third, better, higher alternative. Second, a negotiating position is a concrete, explicitly expressed want, but it often obscures what people really want. As focusing on stated positions is not likely to produce a solution that will effectively take care of the human needs that led people to adopt those positions, you should look behind them to the underlying interests. Third, a creative solution that satisfies the interests of each side can be constructed by identifying shared or compatible interests and by dovetailing differing but complementary interests. You can also develop a creative solution by moving between issues or parts of a negotiation and by working together with the Chinese to look for a way that appears to conform to Chinese "regulations" while actually getting around them.

Employing a Combination of Western and Chinese Behaviours

According to Lao Tzu in *Tao Te Ching*:

> A man living is yielding and receptive. Dying, he is rigid and inflexible. All things, the grass and trees: living, they are yielding and fragile; dying, they are dry and withered.

Western negotiating style is characterised by initiative, straightforwardness, confrontation, and progressiveness. But to be effective in negotiations with the Chinese, you need to adapt your behaviour to Chinese behaviour in three main ways: (1) combining contract negotiation with relationship building; (2) combining frank communication with face saving; and (3) learning to apply ancient Chinese wisdom.

Combining Contract Negotiation with Relationship Building

Contrary to the conventional wisdom held by many Western negotiators that relationship building has nothing to do with contract negotiation, the two are closely related. While any progress in contract negotiation strengthens the relationship between the two parties, informal relationship building behaviours can act as buffer and lubricant for any problems and knocks in formal contract negotiation. As such, instead of rushing straight into the formal negotiation, you should allow time to get to know each other well by giving priority to informal socialising activities. You can present token gifts to key Chinese negotiators at the end of the first negotiating session. You can invite some Chinese negotiators to your hotel for a dinner and a *karaoke* session. If possible, you may even invite some senior Chinese people to visit your company.

With goodwill established, you can take better control of the negotiation by occasionally raising your voice to express your serious concerns or by spelling out the ultimate consequences if the Chinese do not do as you ask – without causing resentment. You can also insist on having some safeguards in the contract by pointing out that this is your company legal requirement, and negotiate the negotiating procedure.

Combining Frank Communication with Face Saving

When Western negotiators communicate in a frank style and Chinese negotiators a face-saving style, tensions can run high. For example, if in expressing your frank view on a business matter you make a Chinese person look like a failure in public or represent them as disobeying the instructions of their superiors, they will cease to co-operate and may well take revenge sooner or later. Sometimes, such tensions can lead to severe or even disastrous consequences. Face-saving is thus important to securing the co-operation of others because it aims to show consideration for their feelings and convictions. Yet, negotiations cannot be conducted purely on a face-saving basis – frankness and face must be discreetly balanced. You need to be polite and firm, nice and tough: what matters is the form, i.e. the way you do it. You need to put your concern in a way that sends your message to the Chinese but does not insult them, and instead of rejecting Chinese demands outright, you can negotiate around face by acknowledging the Chinese demands but also getting something back. Although you may argue back and forth in formal negotiations, many deadlocks can be resolved much more easily through operating in the private arena, such as having a one-to-one conversation or using an intermediary.

Learning to Apply Ancient Chinese Wisdom

You can immensely broaden your negotiating behaviour by learning to apply four pieces of ancient Chinese wisdom, i.e. using the yielding to overcome the rigid (*yirou kegan*), using inaction to control action (*yijin zhidong*), using retreat as advance (*yitui weijin*), and using defence as attack (*yishou weigong*). With *yirou kegan*, you can counter a preposterous proposition by drawing your counterpart into a discussion of the issue and then steer the discussion into a more constructive vein, instead of rejecting it outright. Inaction does not mean doing nothing. For instance, when the Chinese side brings up individual problems, instead of immediately reacting as they are brought up, you can listen to all of the problem areas first and only then decide what to do – this is what *yijin zhidong* means. With *yitui weijin*, you can retreat from a sticky position first and then seek to advance through a completely different route, such as using a third party to mediate or influencing officials who have authority over the Chinese party. When the Chinese side seems to have a stronger bargaining position, instead of turning the negotiation into a gun fight, you can greatly strengthen your hand by exploring what you will do if you do not reach an agreement, i.e. *yishou weigong*.

Negotiating Finance and Management Control

Although problems will inevitably come up during the operation of a joint venture, its proper setting up, as represented by the *Joint Venture Contract* and the *Articles of the Association* fully covering all the critical issues, is absolutely essential to its operational success. These critical issues can be grouped into finance- and management control-related areas – these two areas being also closely related.

Negotiating Finance

Chinese legislation provides two fundamental concepts for the financing of a joint venture, i.e. registered capital and total investment. Registered capital refers to the total of the capital contributions of the Chinese and foreign parties, and total investment is the sum of the registered capital and loans borrowed by the joint venture. A joint venture must also meet the mandatory requirement of a minimum ratio between its registered capital and total investment. As such, capital contributions serve as the financial foundation of the joint venture, with negotiations centring on three main issues: (1) equity share holding; (2) valuation of capital contributions; and (3) capital contribution schedule.

Equity Share Holding

Under Chinese law, the foreign party is required to invest a minimum of 25% of the total registered capital. Chinese government regulations, which also change from time to time, specify certain sectors, such as car manufacturing and telecommunication, in which foreign investors are not permitted to be the majority shareholder. In general, however, the legislation does not impose a legal maximum ceiling on the foreign investor's proportion of the registered capital.

Although there are Chinese partners, such as certain government authorities, which may choose to take minority stakes and have little direct involvement in the day-to-day management of the joint venture, many would press for a 51:49 or 50:50 equity split. In fact, given that corporate control or representation on the joint venture's board of directors, not to mention dollars and cents, hinges to some extent on the respective capital contribution or equity of the parties, there can be tough negotiations between the Chinese and foreign parties over equity sharing. To secure a majority equity share, some Western investors choose to offer technology and export concessions to their Chinese partners. Bausch & Lomb, a US-based optical product manufacturer, went as far as opting for a co-operative venture agreement limited to three years with its Chinese partner in 1987 when it believed that it would not be able to achieve an equity share greater than 50%. In 1989, the co-operative venture began to make a profit, and this solid achievement, far ahead of the initial targets, formed the basis of the next move, the conversion of the business into a joint venture in 1991, in which Bausch & Lomb was then able to hold a 60% stake.

However, it is easy to exaggerate the role of majority equity share in corporate control. In the past, there were foreign investors with as little as 5% stake (e.g. Nissan-Zhengzhou) securing effective management control of a joint venture, while others with a majority share (e.g. Xerox Shanghai) faced problematic vetoes at their board of directors' meetings because they had not negotiated effective board control. To gain real control over the venture, you therefore need to consider equity share in conjunction with other factors, such as the structure of the business proposition and management control, and bear in mind that associated with majority equity share is also majority business risk.

Valuation of Capital Contributions

Chinese law allows both Chinese and foreign parties to contribute cash, machinery, equipment, buildings, intellectual property, know-how and other types of assets or transferable proprietary interests. Apart from cash, Western investors often choose to contribute technology as part of their equity. Under Chinese law, the value of any contributed technology cannot exceed 50% of a party's contribution or 20% of the registered capital unless the joint venture qualifies as a "technologically advanced" foreign investment enterprise.

The toughest negotiations tend to occur in the valuation of Chinese assets because cash-starved potential Chinese partners normally put forward their state-owned assets, such as land, buildings, plant and equipment, as equity. During preliminary negotiations, only book values are available for reference. With progress comes an official valuation, the size of which can sometimes surprise Western investors and cause them to doubt their prospective partner's good faith. Bausch & Lomb, for example, found that the Chinese party seemed to be looking at every single aspect of the site that could be ascribed a value. This ranged from broad issues, such as land rights (but the Chinese partner could not make it clear whether they were full land rights or merely "allocated" land rights), right down to the value of the pipes in the building and the frontage of the building.

In the absence of a non-administered market for land, it can be difficult for both sides to agree a "fair" price. The Chinese party may seek to have its land classified by the local government as "zoned for commercial use", in which case its value is raised. The other problem is the gap between the Western engineers' complaint that the equipment the prospective Chinese partner is keen to contribute would, in more competitive economies, be sold for scrap, and the Chinese view that the equipment at least has a value as recorded in the book.

To successfully settle the above differences through negotiations, you should remember first that the assets being valued do not belong to Chinese directors but the state that is represented by the local branch of the State Land Administration or the State Asset Administration. Chinese directors often have no way either of understanding how the land price is worked out and how formal valuation procedures will inflate the book value of the fixed assets. Therefore, your doubt should be directed at the quality and the experience of the licensed Chinese valuation firm. To establish the bottom line for further negotiations, you can commission a professional Hong Kong-based valuation company to conduct a separate valuation. To avoid the awkwardness associated with the valuation of ageing equipment, you may try to make a hard and fast rule of accepting only land and buildings from the Chinese side. As local valuation companies are often unfamiliar with, and fail to properly value, intangibles, such as branding and distribution networks, you can use intangibles to resolve any disagreements on the valuations.

In the end, it is important to recognise that the valuation of partner contributions is a very uncertain art rather than a precise science, and depends very much on corporate politics and the respective attitude of each partner toward the future partnership.

Capital Contribution Schedule

Chinese government regulations require joint venture partners to stipulate in their joint venture contract a specific capital contribution schedule. The regulations further provide that if the parties decide to make contributions in one lump sum, such contributions must be made within six months from the date of issuance of the business license. If the contributions by both parties will be made in instalments, the first instalment must be no less than 15% of the total amount of contributions by each party, and be made within three months of the date of issuance of the joint venture's business license. Given the potential risk involved in a one-lump-sum contribution, it is prudent to negotiate a schedule where contributions are made in instalments as determined, except the first instalment, by the board of directors according to, for example, the progress of construction and actual cash requirements of the joint venture. It is also important that both parties must inject their proportional cash into the joint venture's account at the same time. In the past, a few foreign investors allowed their Chinese partner to make its contribution in the form of a letter of credit (LOC) opened for paying imported equipment and then got themselves into trouble because the Chinese partner was short of funds.

Negotiating Management Control

Due to lack of understanding of the potential partner's management capability and thus the failure to think through at the earliest stage the human resource needs of the joint venture, some Western companies in the past have suffered serious difficulties in management control. Too often, they have equated the right for the nomination of the general manager to the control of the joint venture's operation, but, in reality, a lot more needs to be done in order for the nomination to be effective. To secure real management control, you need to take an integrated view towards all three levels of the joint venture organisation: (1) board structure, (2) management structure, and (3) labour structure.

Board Structure

The board of directors is the highest authority of the joint venture, the structure of which is determined largely by two variables, i.e. the total number of directors together with the number of directors appointed by each party, and the appointment of the chairman.

Given the bureaucratic web most Chinese enterprises have, it is no surprise that the Chinese party normally likes to have a large board so that more can be appointed from their side, while efficiency-focused

Western investors tend to favour a smaller board. With negotiations, the parties should be able to agree on a board consisting of five or seven directors. Normally, the respective equity shares of the parties determine their representation on the board. However, the role of board control as represented by a majority of directors at a Sino-foreign joint venture should not be overstated for two reasons. First, under Chinese legislation, any resolution on critical issues like change to the total investment or registered capital, termination of the joint venture, and amendment to the articles of the association, requires the unanimous vote of all directors. Second, to avoid developing an "us-versus-them" attitude among the partners, control over the operation of the joint venture cannot be sought from frequently exercising majority-voting power.

While concentrating on securing board control as represented by a majority number of directors, some multinationals carelessly let the Chinese side nominate the chairman. The potential problem is that in the China business context, people inside and outside the joint venture tend to see the chairman as the boss of the business and expect him to intervene in its day-to-day operation. In the contract of the joint venture between Orsan, the French subsidiary of Belgian starch manufacturer Amylum, and the Guangzhou Monosodium Glutamate Factory, Orsan had 51% equity stake and four out of seven members of the board of directors, but it allowed the Chinese side to pick the board chairman. This enabled the Chinese side to block almost any major capital spending proposals because it wanted to boost profits as quickly as possible. The lesson here is that the Western side should try to secure the right to appoint the chairman and that if it cannot, then it is essential to have the term in the contract that the chairman does not have the casting vote.

Management Structure

Management structure is concerned with the appointment of senior managers, such as the general manager, deputy general manager(s), financial controller, and human resource manager, who will be in charge of the day-to-day operation of the joint venture business.

To secure management control, Western investors typically like to have the right to nominate a general manager from their own side and let the Chinese side nominate the deputy general manager. They envisage the role of the general manager as analogous to that of chief executive officer of a company in the West and that the role of the deputy general manager is to assist the general manager in his work. In reality, the Chinese side sees the role of the deputy general manager as a check upon the powers of the general manager. The situation gets worse in reality when the chairman is from the Chinese side because having been cultivated under the planning economy, the Chinese deputy general manager is often more interested in seeking power than in assisting the Western general manager, leaving the latter in a lose-lose position.

One way to reduce the above problem is to set up functional deputy general managers, such as a deputy general manager for production and a deputy general manager for marketing. This would help your general manager manage his deputies through keeping them balanced in political powers as well as focused on business tasks. Of course, the nomination of a Western general manager is not always the most appropriate, because despite his enormous experience gained in the Western corporate world, he will inevitably struggle on language and culture. As such, creative alternatives must be considered. You can differentiate between short-term and long-term management control by nominating key managers from your own side only for a fixed term, such as four or five years, during which they will not only fulfil managerial responsibilities but also train up Chinese candidates to replace them eventually. You can also nominate Chinese people working in the West or experienced bilingual professionals in Taiwan, Singapore, Malaysia and Hong Kong. Ecolab, for example, found a Chinese-born, Western-educated manager with the right combination of attributes for the general manager position. Finally, if the Chinese boss is trustworthy and capable, then it can be appropriate to let the Chinese side nominate the general manager. This is especially so if the joint venture is based on taking over a Chinese factory including existing employees. Of course, it is important that you secure the right to appoint the chairman, and the deputy general manager(s) who may well be from the Chinese side but having the right helps balance the power of the Chinese general manager.

Equally important but sometimes ignored are the positions of financial controller and human resource manager. Texas Instruments, for example, let its Chinese partner nominate a local finance director in 1995 and then found that he was not at all used to international accounting. And without a professional human resource manager setting up the proper labour structure, your nominated general manager will lack the human resource foundation necessary to run an efficient business.

Labour Structure

To secure management control, it is also important to think through and negotiate a sound labour structure covering employee recruitment, training, performance and remuneration for the joint venture. Otherwise, the old Chinese-style employee policies will be inherited and easily destroy any hope of Western companies to build an efficient business.

First and foremost, you should insist on the right to hire and fire free of interference or consultation because pruning staff after establishment is generally difficult. Ecolab, for example, attributes part of its success to its joint venture contract, which allowed it to hire managers and staff independently, in particular, Chinese nationals who spoke English, making it easier both to implement Western-style management systems and to communicate with foreign managers of client hotels. If the joint venture is based on developing an existing Chinese business, you should, as Avon did for its joint venture with a Guangzhou partner, negotiate for the power to decide which staff to hire from the old Chinese factory and for the training of all candidates. Sometimes, the parties can be so substantially at odds in relation to the number of employees to be hired by the joint venture that you may have to accept a compromise. In either case, it is important to state in the contract that the recruitment process is to be operated by the general manager of the joint venture with supervision from a Western human resource specialist.

Another management control pitfall is the inability of foreign managers to set salary incentives because they have overlooked this point at the negotiation stage. Thus, you should negotiate for the power to establish performance-based employee remuneration schemes, abandoning, at least to some extent, old "big wok"-style schemes.

PART II

MASTERING THE "FAMILY" LIFE

Yang corresponds to what is masculine, active, creative, hard and bright. Yin is the feminine, the passive, the receptive, the soft and the dark. The interaction of Yin and Yang gives rise to all changes.

CHINESE WISDOM FROM THE YIN YANG SCHOOL

5

BRIDGING
COMMUNICATION GAPS

Nothing could be more fallacious than to judge of China by any European standard.

LORD MACARTNEY, 1794

The significant problems we face cannot be solved at the same level of thinking we were at when we created them.

ALBERT EINSTEIN (1879–1955)

AS THE TWO PARTNERS ARE FROM "DIFFERENT PLANETS", the central challenge in effectively running a Sino-Western joint venture is to bridge the communication gaps between them arising from the differences in their assumptions, expectations, use of languages, and communication styles. In addition, there is the communication gap between expatriates and their headquarters caused by the difference between reality on the China ground and head-office expectations in the West. In this chapter, the nature of these communication gaps is examined and the methods for bridging them developed.

The Post-Contract Negotiation
as a Communicating Challenge

Because of the contrast between Western contract and Chinese relation-ship orientations, post-contract negotiations have to be seen as an inte-gral part of the on-going communication between the two partners.

The Clash between Western Contract
and Chinese Relationship Orientations

Having signed the joint venture contract and other associated agree-ments, many Western executives have in the past expected that the deal with the Chinese partner was now closed and that the contract was fixed and would be implemented in line with the printed documents. In real-ity, they have learned to their surprise that "The establishment of and the operation of a Sino-foreign joint venture are one and the same thing. You start off negotiating, and end up doing the same thing."

For example, the Chinese might fail to stick to the capital contribu-tion schedule. They might begin seeking new concessions by hiking their prices or asking for additional overseas trips. They might press to get their relatives and friends to work in the joint venture despite the contractual term that the employees will be recruited publicly. They might resent having to pay for technology in perpetuity once it was as-similated into the joint venture.

There are generally two types of reasons, one concerning the con-tract itself and the other uncontrollable factors, why the Chinese would act irrespective of the terms in the contract. First, there can be mis-understandings and ambiguities at the formal negotiation stage. Many Western business people, especially newcomers to China, tend to be efficiency-driven and seek to close a deal quickly. Yet, if not given de-tailed and sufficient explanations, the Chinese can easily be mistaken as having understood something that they actually did not because they are still learners regarding many aspects of a market-driven modern business. In the case of the CC–BC joint venture, because of the time pressure, Tony once asked Mr Zhang, who could not read any English, to read and accept the 200-page supply contract that BC had negotiated with ES on behalf of the future joint venture within a week. After the joint venture was formed, Mr Zhang began arguing that "after-sales services", as it was printed in the contract, included some trips, paid by ES, for the joint venture's technical staff to visit ES in Europe, but ES (and Tony) maintained that that was not what BC had agreed with ES.

Sometimes, if only general principles regarding a particular issue are agreed in the contract, their interpretation from a Chinese perspective can also be in conflict with the Western interpretation at the implementation stage. For exmaple, by the time Beijing Jeep opened for business in 1984, American Motors and its Chinese partner had not even decided what sort of jeep the new joint venture was going to produce. Under the 1983 contract, there was general agreement that American Motors was to help China to design and manufacture a completely new Chinese jeep, using some of the basic technology of its American Jeeps. It soon emerged that the sort of vehicles Chinese officials wanted could not be made from any of American Motors' existing Jeeps. But in signing the contract, the two sides had glossed over this point.

Second, a change of circumstances can also make it impossible for the Chinese side to implement certain terms of the contract. For example, when there are a number of parties on the Chinese side and each party has temporarily agreed to things as they stood just to get the contract signed, disputes between them thereafter may result in breaches of the contract. I was once involved in establishing an agribusiness joint venture. The representative of the Chinese partner, the director of a local state-owned enterprise, signed a memorandum with the Western side concerning the price of the raw materials supplied by local farmers who were under the administration of the local government. At the negotiation stage, the county governor, who was the superior of the Chinese director, agreed to what the Chinese director had signed. But shortly after the joint venture was established, a new county governor was appointed. He had a different view on agricultural policies and demanded that a new price formula be negotiated. This was of course entirely beyond the control of the representative of the Chinese partner, who was now a director and general manager of the joint venture.

Of course, at the core of the post-contract disputes is the clash between Western contract and Chinese relationship orientations. While the Westerners see a signed contract as the final word in defining a relationship, with the future behaviours of the parties governed by the neatly defined terms in the contract, the Chinese see trust, i.e. the positive emotional bond between the parties, as being at the heart of the relationship, with the future behaviours of the parties characterised by the continued, dynamic exchanges between them. As such, post-contract negotiations are an essential feature of a Sino-Western joint venture.

Undertaking Effective Post-Contract Negotiations

To be effective in post-contract negotiations, you need to take three critical steps: (1) have your people on the ground; (2) assess the case for re-negotiation; and (3) walk the line between sticking to the contract and keeping the relationship.

Having Your People on the Ground

If you or your negotiators go home and leave the implementation of the contract to the Chinese, you should not be amazed or outraged when things on the ground do not turn out as you expect. To make sure that the contract is implemented according to the agreed terms, you must have your people on the ground to influence the implementation immediately after the contract is signed. It is only through people that enforcing actions like face-to-face discussions, and checks on quality standards and financial arrangements can take place.

When an important post-contract problem comes up, it is better to send in the business development people who negotiated the deal to re-negotiate than to leave the task to the expatriates assigned to make the joint venture work. The original negotiators can better remember the views expressed and the verbal promises made, and command a better degree of trust and confidence among the Chinese given the great value they place on personal relationships built up during the course of the negotiations. Conversely, asking expatriates who are sent to China to run the joint ventures to re-negotiate can negatively affect the effectiveness of their operational job because of the perceived conflict of interests. Of course, asking them to deliver the concessions on behalf of headquarters actually helps them build goodwill.

Assessing the Case for Re-negotiation

When a post-contract problem comes up, the worst possible thing you can do is immediately confront the Chinese and accuse them publicly of dishonourable behaviour. It is important that you should try first to develop a deep understanding of their case for re-negotiation before deciding on the course of action. Typically, the Chinese side might seem to have come up with all sorts of stories or even excuses, but you should neither be carried away by what they say nor draw your own conclusions too quickly. Instead, you should probe with questions, demand specific evidence, conduct informal investigations, and finally ascertain whether the cause of their request is ambiguity and misunderstanding during the formal negotiation or a change of circumstances.

In the case of the above agribusiness joint venture, the first thing we did was to develop an understanding of the local government politics with the help of reliable contacts in the region. We learnt that in rural areas in particular, as it is individuals rather than impersonal entities that shape relationships, it is quite normal for any personnel change in local governments to produce post-contract problems. We also reached the conclusion that it would be very damaging to the joint venture's relationship with the county government, and ultimately to the joint venture, if we completely ignored the new governor's point of view and kept on pressing the Chinese director to stick to the original term.

Walking the Line between Sticking to the Contract and Keeping the Relationship

In addition to assessing the case for re-negotiation, you should be clear about your bottom line, and express your principles. If you do not express your principles, the Chinese side may view you as somebody stupid, weak and easy to cheat. It can also suggest that you have money to throw away and may give them another opening. On the other hand, so long as the issue does not cut into your bottom line, it is important that you demonstrate consideration and flexibility by discreetly asking for something else to compensate as well as stressing your commitment to the relationship. Never give in without getting something in return. In the case of the above agribusiness joint venture, we eventually entered into negotiation with the Chinese side. We accepted the new price formula proposed by the new country governor but we were compensated by a new tax rebate rate. This eventually led us to a position where not only the joint venture's total economics had remained almost intact but an important relationship had also been nicely strengthened.

In the case of the CC–BC joint venture, after placing Mr Zhang's request in a bigger context, BC realised that it needed to consider the dispute as an opportunity to develop both the competencies of the joint venture staff and the partner relationship. Therefore, instead of arguing in a "chicken and egg" way, BC accepted its responsibility in not giving enough time for CC to digest the supply contract and sponsored Mr Zhang (plus a local official and Mr Chen's daughter) to visit ES.

Even when operating difficulties have reached such an extent that you wish to dissolve the joint venture, it is often better to preserve the joint venture as a going concern with new partners than to play the game of zero-sum division of assets. This is because under Chinese legislation, the foreign party cannot dissolve the joint venture without the co-operation of the Chinese party and related authorities.

Cultural Barriers to Communication between Westerners and Local Staff

Apart from the post-contract negotiation, there are other profound cultural barriers to communication between Westerners and local staff.

While most of these barriers can only be overcome by using a combination of approaches varying in temporal and spatial dimensions, the barriers created by the use of different languages and of different communication styles need to be overcome at the earliest possible time.

Riding the Waves of Cultural Diversity

Because of almost oppositely developed Western and Chinese histories, Western and Chinese cultures are in sharp contrast, creating a huge expectation gap in communication between Westerners and local staff. To be effective in running a Sino-Western joint venture, you need to learn to harmonise the cultural differences.

The Cultural Divide between Westerners and Local Staff

In describing the cultural divide at the American joint venture Beijing Jeep in the 1980s, Jim Mann said in *Beijing Jeep* (1989):

> For any Western reaction there was an equal, and often opposite, Chinese reaction. At Beijing Jeep Americans and Chinese frequently gave different meanings to the same events. They had different attitudes toward work, toward management, toward money, toward the importance of foreign advisers, toward nearly everything. Amid the large business disputes over the future of Beijing Jeep were smaller daily conflicts inside the factory. The Chinese and Americans had been trying to coexist and adapt to one another, but it wasn't easy. Both sides found that the cultural differences were even greater than either had expected before the joint venture opened its doors.

To be sure, two decades of Western business interactions with China have greatly helped bridge the cultural gap. In particular, in places such as Beijing, Shanghai, Jiangsu and Guangdong, which have attracted much Western investment, Western cultural influence upon the younger

Chinese generation has become highly visible, with more and more young graduates with English communication capabilities looking to Western values and beliefs. But inside joint ventures, the cultural divide still exists, as Jim Mann reported in 1997 on Beijing Jeep: "Chinese workers still believe the foreign executives are overpaid; while Western managers complain that the Chinese leaders have to spend too much time on social problems, such as housing, that have little to do with production." And in places that have attracted little foreign investment, Chinese culture still dominates almost every corner of society.

A summary of the major differences that make up the cultural divide is given in Table 5.1, where they are best understood from the outer layer, the middle layer, to the core (see Figure 5.1):

TABLE 5.1

Cultural Differences between Westerners and Local Staff

	Westerners	Local Staff
Cultural Symbols	• Use literal and precise Western languages. • Eat individualised Western food with cutlery. • Dress either formally or casually. • Used to advanced infrastructure, e.g. car. • Observe public code, e.g. queuing. • Distinguish between private and public life. • Leisure activities are rich, well organised. • Celebrate religious festivals.	• Use figurative and ambiguous Chinese. • Eat shared Chinese food with chopsticks. • May wear formal and casual clothes together. • Used to poor infrastructure, e.g. bicycle. • Disregard public code, e.g. pushing. • Like personalised greetings and talks. • Leisure is largely limited to eating and *mahjong*. • Celebrate seasonal festivals.
Business Practices	• Follow work rules. • Job has priority over position. • Plan activities ahead of time. • Give priority to business issues. • Use people who have the required skills. • Realise sales through product integrity. • In purchase, technical merits have priority. • Make decisions based on data.	• Follow authoritative orders. • Position has priority over job. • Deal with problems as and when they arise. • Give priority to personal issues. • Use people who have personal loyalty. • Realise sales through personal connections. • In purchase, price is almost everything. • Make decisions based on intuition.
Personal Values	• Value organisational/personal achievement. • Emphasise equality of individuals. • Work and money reign supreme in life. • See time as sequential; emphasise efficiency. • Aim for objectivity and progress. • Regard responsibility as personal. • Self-motivated to take initiative. • Value freedom of expression.	• Value feelings and relationships. • Admire status and authority. • Consider work and money as part of life. • See time as synchronous; just flow with it. • Pursue reasonableness and satisfaction. • See responsibility flow in two directions. • Happy to go with the flow. • Value harmony and orderly society.

FIGURE 5.1

Culture as a Three-layer Onion

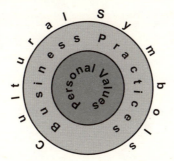

- **The outer layer – cultural symbols:** Cultural symbols are the first things people encounter in another culture. They are the observable reality of the language, food, dress code, buildings, signs, rituals, and other explicit objects and social behaviours.
- **The middle layer – business practices:** Business practices are the way business activities, such as negotiation, production, sales, purchase and decision-making, are undertaken in another culture.
- **The core – personal values:** Personal values are rooted in survival needs, and express what people really believe in, such as their part in society, and their attitudes towards the most important topics in life, such as relationships, time and nature.

Harmonising Cultural Differences at Three Levels

Given the above cultural divide, you can easily hit the mental wall or experience "culture shock" if you take on all differences. Culture shock, the experience of foreignness, occurs when so many expectations do not coincide with reality that you feel disoriented and anxious, and do not perform well. To minimise culture shock, you need to distinguish between cultural differences from both temporal and spatial perspectives and adopt the appropriate coping methods (see Figure 5.2).

In any given situation, there are only a limited number of cultural

FIGURE 5.2

Harmonising Cultural Differences at Three Levels

Cultural Differences		Coping Methods
Level 3: Related practices and values	▲	Training and learning
Level 2: Immediately relevant practices	|	Communicating and balancing
Level 1: Symbols and irrelevant practices	|	Ignoring and tolerating

differences that are directly relevant, while the vast majority of them are not. It is therefore important that you focus on bridging only the most immediate, relevant cultural gaps. It is easy to link many of them together, but if you do so you can easily get yourself into a non-resolvable situation for the simple reason that cultural gaps formed, in a sense, over a period of 2,500 years cannot be bridged instantly. As for the irrelevant cultural gaps for the given situation, they should, depending upon the degree of their relevancy to the attainment of long-term business goals, either be tolerated and ignored or be bridged, over time, through training on the part of local staff and learning on the part of Westerners. Indeed, while some gaps in business practices may be relatively quickly bridged through intensive training, it can take years to bridge gaps in personal values. This is why the running of a joint venture should be seen as both an operation and an evolution.

Level 1: Differences in symbols and irrelevant practices. All too often, Westerners feel culture shock because they overreact emotionally to differences in cultural symbols and irrelevant business practices, i.e. things that are not worth drawing too much of their attention to, for a given situation. You can take two key steps when facing such differences: (1) ignoring differences in symbols and irrelevant practices; and (2) tolerating differences in symbols and irrelevant practices.

(1) Ignoring differences in symbols and irrelevant practices. You should be sensitive not to intentionally expose irrelevant cultural differences to

the locals because they do not know what to do with them either. There are also gaps that may not be able to be bridged in the foreseeable future or even during the life of the joint venture, and it is best for these not to be exposed for the time being. In the West, people like to be perceived as young, but in China older people deserve to be better respected. You will only get yourself into an increasingly awkward position if you keep on discussing this difference with the locals. At a joint venture in rural China, my Western colleagues used to be fussed by the fact that many local staff ate raw garlic at the canteen. But they soon learnt that they could not win the argument because while they were concerned with the smell inflicted upon others, the locals regarded raw garlic as a food that, according to Chinese traditional medicine, "can cure one hundred diseases" (*nengzhi baibing*) . This is why one European expatriate executive reflected: "My approach is never to compare – better, worse – but to recognize the differences and leave it at that."

The worst possible thing you can do is joke about cultural differences in front of local staff because a joke in Western culture can easily be misunderstood as an insult in Chinese culture. Imagine you joke about the lack of religious meaning of the Chinese New Year, the seemingly unhygienic chopsticks or the fact that many Chinese like to wear Western-style suits but without a tie, even on formal occasions! I once chatted with a Chinese driver on my way to a joint venture in the rural area. He boasted that he could drink a bottle of Chinese liquor (which has an alcohol content of over 50%) and still maintain the capability to drive. With his Chinese boss also sitting in the car, I did not laugh at his stupidity as I would in the West, because many locals regard the driver as a hero. In general, you have to wait until you have achieved a certain familiarity with the locals before employing humour. If in doubt, don't joke; when you do, avoid the petty cut-them-down language!

(2) Tolerating differences in symbols and irrelevant practices. If ignoring differences in symbols and irrelevant practices is to bury your head in the sand, tolerating them is to put yourself in the shoes of the locals. It requires you to try to understand why the locals think and act as they do. By asking "How would I feel and react if I were in their shoes?" you will save yourself time and irritation because by becoming interested in

the cause, you are less likely to dislike the effect. Indeed, without the awareness that you and the Chinese are supposed to be different, you and local staff will be at odds with each other. Both sides can become demanding, resentful, judgemental, and intolerant – you expect the Chinese to think and react like you while the Chinese expect you to think and react like them. Therefore, with time you have to learn to transcend the limits of your own conditioning so as to become sympathetic with, and tolerate, at least to some extent, the Chinese way of work and life.

For example, it is tempting to want instant progress, instant change, instant everything, but if you try to achieve that in China, you simply will not succeed. At an agribusiness joint venture, for quite some time we expatriates had to travel three hours each way by car between the hotel in a small city and the joint venture site on a daily basis. Aware of the lack of a sufficient number of vehicles and the uncertainties associated with road conditions, some of my expatriate colleagues got so nervous that as soon as they saw a vehicle had disappeared from the site they started worrying that they might not be able to get back to the hotel that day. They then began questioning the local administrator and digging into who was actually using the vehicle and on what mission and so on. They eventually became so preoccupied with the administrator's job that they not only had little time left to do their real job but also seriously demoralised the administrator.

Level 2: Differences in immediately relevant practices. To bridge immediately relevant business practices, you need to enhance the effectiveness of your communication with local staff through overcoming the language hurdle and adopting an effective communication style. This is dealt with in more detail in the next section of this chapter. In a broader sense, you need to learn to balance managing and leading in a dynamic way so as to achieve both successful business results and harmonious partner relationships. Chapter 8 is devoted to this topic.

Level 3: Differences in related practices and values. By nature, the Chinese do not like being managed. In other words, they do not like complying with rules or standards. As a result, their sense of management must be developed over time through comprehensively organised training programmes. Chapter 6 is devoted to this topic. On the other hand, as the Chinese are inherently different from Westerners, you have to learn skills for leading the local staff so as to improve your chances of getting them on your side. Chapter 7 is devoted to this topic.

Achieving Effective Communication with Local Staff

Sino-Western communication involves three essential issues, i.e. the content of the message, the language that is used to express the message and the style or method in which the message is got across. The content of the message is largely dependent upon the expectation gap between you and local staff, which in turn is dependent upon the balance that you decide to achieve between managing and leading (this is addressed in Chapter 8). Below, the issues of overcoming the language barrier due to the use of different languages and of adapting your communicating style due to the tension between frankness and face are addressed.

Overcoming the Language Barrier to Communication

Even people who speak the same language can have misunderstandings. When communication takes place in two completely different languages, the risk is very much greater. According to some research, less than 5% of Western business people working in China speak any Chinese at all; and to make matters worse, of the remaining more than 95%, few know how to use an interpreter properly. To minimise the chances of misunderstandings in Sino-Western communication, which can lead to mistrust and even conflicts, every effort needs to be made to break through the language barrier.

The language barrier. One of the most amusing stories about the language barrier was told by Carolyn Blackman in *Negotiating China* (1997). When the Western team arrived in China, the interpreter provided by the Chinese side showed them around the hotel garden. Pointing to an exotic flower, he said, "They taste very nice." When a Western engineer went to put it in his mouth, the interpreter rushed to stop him. He had meant, "They smell very nice," but the Chinese expression for the two English expressions is the same (*weidao bucuo*). Meanwhile, as the Westerners did not have their own interpreter, it took them two years to realise that the hotel they were staying in had a menu – before, they just accepted whatever Chinese food was put in front of them even though much of it was not to their liking.

In another case, an American was assigned to a caviar factory in northern Heilongjiang as a quality-control engineer. She had to struggle hard in the factory to improve, among other things, sanitary conditions there. By doing so, she upset the factory manager who did not think sanitary issues were important. She therefore dreamt about her American boss suddenly arriving on the premises to arbitrate some of the disputes that had arisen. But when he did show up midway through the caviar season, he created more problems than he solved because the interpreter provided by the Chinese was so incompetent that his interpretations were often either meaningless or offensive to the Chinese, making her assignment more difficult for the rest of her time there.

Indeed, the Chinese language is completely different from the English language. There are no common or similarly written words. In Chinese, the message contained in a statement is determined not only by the words themselves but by the context in which they are used. For example, in English "yes" simply means "I agree with you", but in Chinese "yes" could mean, "I have understood what you have said," or "I have not understood what you have said," or "I have heard what you have said," or "I agree with you." The last of these Chinese interpretations is very unlikely unless the speaker has made it quite clear to what he is agreeing. Most nods or affirmative noises used by the Chinese during conversation mean "I have heard you" or "I have understood what you are saying" instead of "I agree with you."

To avoid any damage that a categorical "no" can do to a relationship, the common ways of saying "no" in Chinese are "Let's talk about it again next time", "In principle, it's OK" and "I'll do my best". Also, if you ask a question a second time about something you wish to pursue and they again say, "It's under study," or "It is not a convenient time," you can conclude that the subject is closed, or very nearly so. If interpreted literally, *meiyou wenti* means "no problem" but this is rare in China because the Chinese expression is more an indication of intention than of accountability. Often when the Chinese say *meiyou wenti*, they do not even know what the problem is let alone how to solve it. The only time when *meiyou wenti* can truly be understood as "no problem" is when you have developed a deeply trusting relationship with your Chinese counterpart because then your concern becomes theirs.

As such, interpreting to and from Chinese is one of the most difficult of all arts. Yet, all too often, people use unknown or incompetent interpreters without realising how damning misinterpretations can be to their case. If the interpreter does not know you well, he may not do justice to the complexity of your message, report back to you on what is really being meant by the Chinese, or give the wrong feeling or tone to your words making you sound aggressive and arrogant. If the interpreter has a background in electrical engineering but the discussion involves chemical engineering, he may not understand the importance of certain issues or why particular points are stressed. Also, few realise that as the amount of talking the interpreter has to do is the sum of what all the others do, he can easily get exhausted and start missing the meaning or detail of what is being said if others drive him hard.

Breaking through the language barrier. Obviously, employing bilingual employees wherever and whenever possible and arranging English language training for local staff help break through the language barrier. There are three further steps that you can take: (1) building an adequate interpreting capacity; (2) mastering the art of speaking through an interpreter; and (3) making an effort to learn the Chinese language.

(1) Building an adequate interpreting capacity. Compared with the serious aftermath of misinterpretations, it is worth spending resources on building an adequate interpreting capacity made up of experienced, competent interpreters. Competent interpreters must be both bilingual and bicultural to a very high degree. They must be extraordinarily sensitive to myriad nuances of the languages they are using, as well as to the relationship between the speakers, the political climate, and the personalities and even the moods of the speakers. They must be actors

in the strongest sense of the word – self-confident and aggressive when the occasion demands. As competent interpreters are scarce, you can build a team of interpreters, each specialising in a particular area, such as engineering or finance or, at the very least, recruit both language graduates and graduates specialising in other subject areas so that they can complement each other. You need to have somebody with solid interpreting experience to head the interpreting team, giving him an attention-catching title like "assistant project manager". It is also imperative to pay and treat your interpreters well and arrange training programmes for them so that they can familiarise themselves with your business before being asked to play that pivotal role.

(2) Mastering the art of speaking through an interpreter. For a start, advance preparation greatly improves the quality of interpretation. Whenever possible, you should use your own interpreter or have him available to assist with the communication. As your interpreter knows you well, he may save the day by taking account of Chinese sensitivities when you inadvertently say something inappropriate; you can also have some feedback afterwards on the nuances behind what was said. You should provide your interpreter with adequate briefing on the subject matter, make sure he understands what you are aiming to achieve, and give him as much background material as possible. You can prepare translated written materials and visual information, such as photographs and a video, for use during the presentation or meeting. If a presentation or meeting is to last all day and, especially if it is to go on for several days, more than one interpreter should be prepared. In situations where a great deal of sensitive matter has to be transmitted, it is wise to prepare a backup interpreter as a monitor.

During the presentation or meeting, you should take extra care to speak in short, straightforward sentences, with regular pauses between them. Rambling on for paragraph after paragraph before pausing or speaking in short phrases and unfinished sentences makes the interpreting job impossible to do. When large numbers are involved, you should give plenty of time to the interpreter to help him get around them because they are particularly tricky and can easily be interpreted wrongly, sometimes leading to a mistake between millions and billions.

You need to make a deliberate effort to avoid slang, jargon and figures of speech like "what's the bottom line" and "it's all above board" unless you know your interpreter is familiar with the terminology. Finally, you should avoid jokes and witty asides because they may well fall flat in interpretation and your Chinese counterpart may just laugh politely without understanding the punch line.

(3) Making an effort to learn the Chinese language. According to an American expatriate who has been involved with China for over 30 years and is now fluent in Mandarin: "You can get by using English, but you may be missing 60 percent of what's going on. And that can't help but have an impact on productivity and the bottom line." Indeed, coming to grips with the basics of the Chinese language will help you get around when your interpreter is not with you and get a feel of what is happening around you. While a thorough knowledge of the written language takes years to acquire, getting by in basic *putonghua* is not that difficult at all. The vocabulary required for activities, such as ordering meals, buying food and getting through to the person you want on the telephone, is minimal and can be picked up by anyone within a fairly short time. But the impact on communication of learning Chinese goes beyond the language itself. If you make an effort to learn a little Chinese, communication will improve almost magically, and soon people around you will be much friendlier, with many Chinese who previously stared at you in silence going out of their way to be helpful.

Getting Your Message to the Heart of the Chinese, Not Just their Face

Western and Chinese communicating styles are characterised by the emphasis on frankness and the preservation of face respectively. To be effective in your communication with the Chinese, you need to master the art of getting your message to the heart of the Chinese, not just their face. There are three critical steps: (1) understanding the tension between frankness and face; (2) learning to balance frankness and face; and (3) learning to get your message to the heart of the Chinese.

The tension between frankness and face. One of the most frequently voiced complaints of local staff about their Western colleagues is what they see as the latter's unacceptable behaviour, including arrogance, an unwillingness to listen, and the lack of consultation. The larger than average size and louder speech of many Western people also appear threatening to the Chinese. On the other hand, Westerners find that the Chinese consider matters that apparently relate merely to form as being of substantial importance, and that they will typically not admit an error or ignorance, often compounding what would otherwise be a fairly minor problem. They also find that the locals are easily offended and that they are most unlikely to give any outward indication of genuine hurt or offence, "with a broken arm kept inside the sleeve".

Indeed, playing around face alone can cause the locals to lose the courage and ability to stay honest, face truth, and pursue quality and efficiency in what they do. When people concentrate only on gaining face for themselves or giving face to others, the truth of the matter can easily get lost in the process. Many locals like to tell their boss what they think their boss wants to hear rather than what they actually think to be true; over time, they develop a habit of not being concerned at all with right or wrong. When there is a serious quality or efficiency problem, local staff are also likely to avoid mentioning it because they want to save face for the fellow worker, and when many locals hold such an attitude towards work, many quality or efficiency problems will get hidden beneath human face and never get resolved until it is too late.

Balancing frankness and face. Given the tension between frankness and face, effective Sino-Western communication must be that which involves balancing frankness and face. Specifically, you can consider the following three principles:

(1) Frankness first and then face. When a local employee makes a mistake, it is essential that you let him know it by pointing it out in a frank and polite way. If you do not do this, he will not learn a lesson from it because he is likely to think that you do not care about it. However, the communication between you and the local regarding the situation

should not stop there – you should also pave the way out for him, i.e. giving face to him or making space for him to learn from it. One Western expatriate described a situation where a Chinese receptionist noticed the fax machine was out of paper but did not put any more paper in until four hours later. The "frankness first and then face" approach to handling the situation is to politely instruct the receptionist to add the paper immediately, and then make comments like: "What would have happened if someone was trying to fax us something very important and urgent? Maybe we should write a note and stick it to the fax machine so that everyone will know to put more paper in even when you are away. Here, help me write a Chinese translation to my note. Thank you!"

(2) Face first and then frankness. Sometimes, you can come across locals whose face is so thin that you need to help them build up their face in the first place so that they can stand your frankness. For instance, it is common that when Western managers in China tell their Chinese staff what to do, the latter's fear of losing face can once again cause serious miscommunication. The manager explains what is to be done, and the locals assure him they have understood. But the task is done wrongly or not done at all. The reason is that the Chinese were too embarrassed or afraid to admit that in fact they did not fully understand the manager's instructions in the first place. A more effective approach is first to praise them and help them build the confidence, and then to move onto the frank part of the communication. As another example, when dismissing an employee, it is far better to begin the conversation by saying something like "It may be possible to find a better place for your talents than here", than just telling him that his performance is not acceptable or that he is no longer wanted.

(3) Adopting a moderate style. In general, speaking in soft tones gets you a great deal further with the Chinese than shrill complaining. Often, a few kind words, softly spoken, can take the edge off potentially tricky situations; and the softer your tone of voice, the louder your message to the Chinese. A moderate style is also characterised by adjusting your verbal content to the feelings of the Chinese individuals, i.e. to avoid the loss of face by allowing them maximum freedom of manoeuvre if

they cannot accept your true position. It is therefore a good idea to speak less directly than you might otherwise prefer, and to imply things rather than state them outright. For example, when criticising someone, you can put the emphasis on the fact that you simply want it done differently instead of causing him to think he has been doing something wrong. Other features of the indirect verbal style include referral to previous discussions, repeating of the stated Chinese position before presenting your own, questions and suggestions instead of statements and orders, and use of adverbial modifiers like "fairly" and "somewhat".

Getting your message to the heart of the Chinese. Ancient Chinese wisdom says that in communication, "the supreme policy is to influence the person's heart." To get your message to the heart of the Chinese, you can consider the following non-confrontational methods:

(1) Having a private conversation. This is the most common Chinese way of communication that leads to both learning and face-saving. By making an appointment to see the individual, you have showed your respect for him. In addition, when you communicate your frank messages to him in this way, his attention will be focused on digesting what you say rather than worrying about what others around may think of him.

(2) Writing a letter. A letter can be drafted in the most effective style. Of course, you need to make sure that you have someone trustworthy as well as bilingual to translate it accurately. This way, the individual concerned may learn from it by appreciating that you have respected him by writing a special letter to him. In addition, you will have avoided the possible adoption of overreacted behaviours when you face him.

(3) Sending out a story. Sending the message indirectly to the individual by telling a packaged story to others and letting others spread it around. This way, the individual may learn from it by assuming that apart from him, others may have made the same mistake. In so doing, you obviously need to be very careful in packaging your story so that everybody gets the correct message but nobody loses the face.

(4) Using a third party. Sometimes, the best way to get the message across to the individual concerned is to find a third party whom the individual trusts and let him pass the message on. Facing someone he can trust, the individual can relax, hear the message and digest it instead of being overwhelmed by tension. Obviously, it is important that you make sure the third party you choose is trustworthy to you too.

(5) Putting up a poster. Due to tradition, the Chinese like to see messages – usually two lines of characters – on a wall. You can arrange for someone with a fine hand to put key company messages into couplets and write them out, and then hang them on the wall. This way, you can maintain a very smooth interface with the workforce because you cause nobody to lose face while getting your message to everybody's heart.

The Communication Gap between Expatriates and their Headquarters

Sun Tzu states in *The Art of War*:

> There are three ways in which the ruler can bring misfortune to his army. First, when ignorant that the army should not advance, to order an advance, and when ignorant that the army should not retreat, to insist on a retreat and this is interference with military command. Second, when ignorant of the internal affairs of the military, to participate and interfere with its administration and this causes officers and soldiers to be perplexed. Third, when ignorant of matters relating to the exercise of military authority, to interfere in the execution of responsibilities and command and this creates doubts in the minds of officers and soldiers. If the army is confused and suspicious, the neighbouring states will surely create trouble. This is like the saying: A confused army provides victory for the enemy.

Indeed, the difference between the "banner" held by headquarters and the "reality" experienced by expatriates in China can mean the difference between success and failure, and every effort needs to be made to bridge the communication gap between them.

The "Banner" and the "Reality"

All too often, senior executives who visit China return home, believing that they understand China well and that they get along splendidly with Chinese business leaders. If a company has difficulty after the contract is signed, then they feel it is the fault of their soldiers on the ground: they must be seeing the wrong people or approaching the Chinese in the wrong way. They also tend to wonder why their people out in China are always so negative and cynical about the place and the Chinese.

But expatriates commonly complain that their superiors and colleagues back at headquarters do not understand their circumstances. When they report their problems and frustrations to their superiors at headquarters, the latter tend to think that it must be the former who do not handle the situation properly because on their visits to China things do not seem so bad. At best, they think that you are too tedious, reporting to them a lot of details that they do not expect to hear from you, or that these are your problems and you are paid to sort them out yourself. When some of the expatriates want to take a strong public stand against exorbitant costs, unpredictable fees, protracted delays and other problems in China, the chances are that head office does not support them to do so because they do not want to rock the boat. As the board chairmen and chief executives, who live in the West, do not confront the daily frustrations of life in China, they see that the joint venture project is much more important than the daily problems reported by their expatriates. According to the expatriate general manager at a US electrical appliance joint venture in Shanghai:

> One of the biggest problems confronting foreign companies in China is that senior management at head office in the West have no idea about China. They did no homework, have over-invested, and

now they expect you to make them a fast return. They then suffer
a big turnover in their management team, because they just cannot
achieve the results the bosses want. The objectives they set are impossible, but they won't listen to their people on the ground.

While head office executives have problems with their expectations
from their China operation, expatriates are not all up to the necessary
standard of operating in a remote country. According to some independent consultants, many foreign executives often "do nothing but fool
around". A lot of them are on a very nice expatriate package and although they have objectives to meet, if they fail, they just pass the buck,
blaming it on the difficulties of doing business in China.

Interestingly, when commentators and consultants talk about foreign
expatriates in China, they like to categorise them into "three types".
According to Jim Mann in *Beijing Jeep* (1997), the first were the China
hands, those who had studied Chinese history and language and then
gravitated to jobs in business that would take them to China. The second
were the overseas Chinese, Hong Kong Chinese or Chinese-Americans
who were employed by Western companies to help make contact in
China. The third were the careerists who had no particular background
in China but had gone for money or career advancement. Kent Watson,
chairman of PricewaterhouseCoopers China, also has his "three types".
The first comes for a fixed term as part of a career plan. Ensuring the
long-term success of the venture cannot be high on their agenda. The
second comes sometimes for longer and does an outstanding job for
his company, but lives essentially within the expatriate community and
often expects China to be much like the home country. The third tries to
be more involved in the Chinese environment.

According to China business consultant Laurence Brahm, the first
type is the "lazy, disinterested, self-entertaining, and self-gratifying executive", who comes to China without any interest whatsoever in developing his company's business. But as he is full of information about the
best entertaining places in China, he will be considered a real "China
expert" when head-office bosses visit China and promoted to the highest level within his company. The second is the "non-risk-taking, obedi-
ent, and somewhat paranoid executive", who is so afraid of taking risks

that he will do nothing without consulting the headquarters. The result is that he will not be able to do anything in China at all, but as he makes no mistakes he is likely to advance himself within his company structure. The third type is the "aggressive, ambitious, and self-disciplined executive", who comes to China to achieve business targets. However, as he needs to take calculated risks and often acts independently of the views of, and the constraints imposed by, the headquarters, the latter will invariably be afraid of the risk he is taking and will find fault with his practical adaptation to China's reality. He will probably be fired.

Which type(s) are you or your company's China executives?

Bridging the Communication Gap between Expatriates and their Headquarters

To bridge the communication gap between expatriates and their headquarters, some form of education for bosses and colleagues at headquarters needs to take place regarding the China business reality and the kind of support expatriates need. Yet, it can only be effectively accomplished when both headquarters and expatriates take responsibility.

Responsibility of Headquarters

Most of those who never come out of headquarters or have only had a touch of the China ground naturally assume that expatriates should deliver the same professional performance in China as they would in the West. And when the latter come under great pressure in achieving targets and need understanding and support, further pressure can come swiftly from the former. To show their understanding and support, staff at headquarters have a responsibility to build their China knowledge. Specifically, they need to take three critical steps: (1) taking on the self-educational job; (2) engaging all their senses when visiting China; and (3) creating a China knowledge pool.

Taking on the self-educational job. In general, head office staff need to get rid of the usual assumption that they know best and that they need never change their beliefs. And instead of regarding any China-related issues as irrelevant to their job, they should actively seek out knowledge on the business reality in China by reading publications that reveal the fabric and texture of doing business there. In addition, they should read books on Chinese history and culture, watch Chinese films, pay attention to stories in the press on China's current affairs, and make friends with those of Chinese origin.

Engaging all senses when visiting China. For those who have the opportunity to travel to China, instead of insulating yourself behind the typical perks of limousines, Western-style luxury hotel and dutiful staff, you should try to put yourself in the middle of China – its economy, political system, market, and culture. And instead of being only interested in learning something about the Great Wall, you should look for opportunities to dive deep into the waters of the society and develop an understanding of what shopping, education, homes, work, and life at large are really like for the local people.

Creating a China knowledge pool. Corporate executives should formalise a process for disseminating the lessons gained from travels to China. For instance, after a trip to China, the traveller may be asked to present what he or she has learnt about China. Knowing that one must make a presentation enhances the motivation to extract lessons worthy of being presented to peers back home, and as a consequence, enhances the level of learning during the trips. Of course, the presentations also facilitate learning at headquarters and enable others to build from a higher base of knowledge when going to China.

Responsibility of Expatriates

In educating people at headquarters, it is no good pathetically exclaiming, "But you don't understand China!" This will serve to make your bosses at head office feel more and more insecure and anxious about this expensive, volatile, unpredictable operation they have in the world's largest market. Life for you would be much easier if your bosses recognise the difficulties you face and consequently the kind of understanding you need and the results you can be expected to achieve in China. Specifically, you can take three critical steps: (1) take on the educational job; (2) stay connected with headquarters; and (3) welcome head office bosses to visit the site.

Taking on the educational job. "It's your job to educate your boss," says one American expatriate. You should start from scratch, make no assumptions and, like any other kind of education, keep up the process of reinforcement and review. You need to help your bosses understand the differences between operating in China and operating in the West, and the need to blend cultures. You need to help them appreciate the fact that infrastructure problems, difficulties in getting around, limitations surrounding shopping and entertainment, and inexperienced staff can all take their toll on you.

Staying connected with headquarters. Even though you may be tempted to take "home leave" and go off with your family to new and exciting countries for a holiday, make sure that you have time periodically to remain connected to people at headquarters. Typically, chief executive officers and other big bosses hate being taken by surprise, especially if it is bad news – they do not even like good news sometimes, unless they know it is coming. You must keep in touch with head office, delivering both good and bad news, if only to give them some comfort that they know what is going on.

Welcoming head office bosses to visit the site. Another effective form of educating your bosses at headquarters is to encourage and welcome them to visit the site of your business in China so that they can develop a feel for the reality. During their visit, you should neither complain constantly nor play down your problems, but show factual evidence so as to put them clearly in the picture. "They come here and look and listen, they can see my way of thinking, and they can follow my line of reasoning afterwards when they have left," commented one expatriate for a trade publishing operation in Shanghai.

6

TRAINING THE CHINESE TO MEET MANAGEMENT NEEDS

By nature men are pretty much alike. It is their learning and practices that distinguish them.

CONFUCIUS, 550 BC

China is the great story of the next century, and we have the chance
to contribute a part of the DNA to a future business culture.

LEO BURKE OF MOTOROLA UNIVERSITY, 1997

TO PRODUCE DESIRED BUSINESS RESULTS, people of the necessary
quality and with the necessary skills are essential. Yet, there is an
acute shortage of qualified human resources in China because genes of
2,500 years of Chinese agricultural civilisation, thirty years of command economy and a backward education system have not cultivated
human resources suitable for businesses operating in a modern market
economy. To effectively cope with this challenge, Western companies
must take a long-term view by initially bringing in and relying more on
expatriates and then gradually evolving towards localisation through
comprehensively organised training programmes for local staff.

The Human Resource Challenge in China

In many ways, the greatest challenge to investment ventures in China is the human resource challenge because no nation has ever undertaken so vast an economic and industrial revolution on so weak a human resource foundation.

The Shortage of Qualified Labour

China has been renowned for its "cheap labour" since its door was reopened to foreign investors at the end of 1970s. Yet, in reality, "cheap labour" has also been synonymous with "unqualified labour". In the 1980s, most foreign investors had no choice but to take on existing employees of their Chinese partners – almost invariably state-owned enterprises. Public recruitment was next to impossible because a residence registration system (*hukou*) controlled the movement of all Chinese citizens. Although many state employees did have some skills, foreign executives found it difficult to convince Chinese workers of the importance of showing personal initiative and going beyond the usual "do as little as possible" attitude. "Local employees find being given responsibility for a task or being asked to develop their own initiative very daunting, too big a commitment, too dangerous and with only negative connotations," reflected an expatriate. Another at a computer manufacturer concluded: "The idea of being part of a team that is doing something important is something we have to teach here."

Entering the 1990s, the torrent of foreign direct investment, which has increased from just over US$4 billion in 1990 to over US$40 billion since 1996, has led firms to scramble for a limited pool of qualified labour in the frontline commercial centres like Shanghai and Beijing. Many foreign-funded businesses have reported staff turnover at about 20% and a common 30% or more yearly pay rise since foreign investment began flooding in in 1992. The government decided to loosen its control over the population moving from region to region. This has created a sea of 100 million migrant workers. Some are highly skilled professionals in search of greater opportunities, many more are un-skilled and anxious to find a foothold in China's new economy. The World Bank estimates, "One quarter of all investment in rail systems, power plants and other infrastructure is wasted through technical inef-ficiencies largely due to poorly trained operators." In 1997, China was ranked the last, among the world's forty-six major countries assessed, in the availability of competent senior executives and in the mobility and competitiveness of human resources in the Global Competitiveness assessment by the World Economic Forum. According to a survey by *Business China* and consulting firm A. T. Kearney in 1997, "lack of quality local managers" was ranked the top constraint for doing busi-ness in China. Executive search firm Korn & Ferry forecast in 1997 that the demand for executives among large corporations in China would increase by at least 400% over the next decade, with general manager, human resource manager and financial controller being the most fre-quently requested search assignments.

Entering the 21st century, skills deficits are so critical in China's banks that the mainland government has looked to Hong Kong and is bringing in overseas talent to accelerate needed financial reforms in such institutions as the People's Bank of China. In insurance, China's regulations specify a firm must have a certain number of qualified insur-ance professionals to operate a licensed business, and this has prompted many Chinese insurance firms to woo Chinese people working in over-seas insurance companies back to China because of the lack of quali-fied local staff. At a seminar jointly held by the Ministry of Science and Technology and the Asian Development Bank in November 2000, Vice-minister Xu Guanhua said that China is in great need of profes-sional consultants capable of producing detailed market and industry analysis reports. While reforms that will eventually bring compliance with International Accounting Standards (IAS) have been in the pipe-line for years, including a World Bank-funded programme that aims to provide IAS training to 25,000 Chinese accountants per year, real reform is not coming any time soon. The number of MBA graduates currently needed in Shanghai alone is about 9,000 whereas China has produced only 5,000 in the past decade.

Why then is the shortage of qualified labour so acute in China? The

answer lies in the fact that genes of 2,500 years of agricultural civilisation, thirty years of command economy and a backward education
system do not readily support the massive industrial development that
has taken place since 1978.

The Quality of the Chinese: From Genes of Agricultural Civilisation to Modernisation

At a press conference during his visit to the USA in April 1999, Premier Zhu Rongji said: "China has a history of several thousand years
of a feudal system, feudal society. So people have very deep-rooted
concepts influenced by this historical background. It's quite difficult
to change such a mentality or concept overnight." Indeed, much of the
Chinese character as it is known today, including the failure to exhibit
individuality and accept personal responsibility, the tendency to blindly
obey those in authority, the reliance on connections, and the inability to
put any invention into wide-spread, large-scale applications, has been
shaped by genes of 2,500 years of agricultural civilisation.

After Qin Shihuang united China and established the Qin Dynasty
(221–207 BC), he ordered that all books except those in his own library
and a few on medicine and agriculture be burned so as to eliminate
possible criticism of his reign. The founder of the Han Dynasty (206
BC–220 AD) ordered that all schools of thought except that of Confucianism be banned. This "unification of Chinese thought" generated an
all-encompassing pressure for obedience to any authority figure without question. Private enterprise was also made taboo, stifling innovation. Another critical development was the establishment of the "impe-
rial examination system" during the Sui Dynasty (581–618), which was
to last until the last dynasty fell in 1911. Those who passed the exams
became scholar-officials even though none of them had any hands-on
work experience. Being an official brought power, and power brought
money. There had never been a proper legal system, an official with
power being the law. Not being able to read, receiving no instruction
in anything beyond household and farm work and proper behaviour
toward superiors, over 90% of the Chinese population were simple-

minded peasants, subject to flourishing superstitions and taboos. In this atmosphere, money and connections with those with power were the most important things in life, without which no Chinese could feel safe from the depredations of officialdom or random violence.

Within the confines of this highly structured, emotionally, intellectually, and spiritually limiting system, the lives of the mass of Chinese remained virtually the same for century after century, but their brilliance in intellect or imagination, at least on the part of the intelligentsia, had never failed. Their technological inventions (blast furnaces and piston bellows, gunpowder and cannon, compass and rudder, paper and printing press, suspension bridges, porcelain, wheeled metal plough and horse collar, and the decimal system, for instance) pre-dated similar developments in the West by at least eight hundred years. In the fifteenth century, China would have been the candidate who was about to conquer and colonise the rest of the world militarily and to pull ahead of it economically by converting an agricultural base to an industrial one. But it did not happen, because the feudal system not only did not reward innovation or invention but also, for the most part, opposed such changes. So the Chinese rejected, did not use, and forgot the very technologies that would have given them world dominance.

The assault on China by Western powers since 1840, as a result of industrialisation and modernisation in the West, was a wake-up call to many Chinese. Revolutionist Sun Yat-sen wrote: "Since the birth of the ancestor, China's four hundred million people have been used to being slaves of autocratic monarchs. There have been so many people who do not know that they should be a master, do not have the courage to become a master, or do not have the capability to become a master." In 1905, Sun Yat-sen and educationalist Yan Fu had a debate on whether revolution or education should come first. Yan advocated the theory of using education to save the country. He considered that military and economic reforms were all "symptoms" whereas the quality of the people was the "root cause". He further believed that without the end to improve the quality of the people through education, not only could democracy be started from nowhere, but also economic reform would ultimately become empty talk. In the end, Sun Yat-sen overthrew the Qing Dynasty through the 1911 revolution because he saw that the type of education Yan was proposing could not be carried out in a feudal kingdom. But Sun's revolution and indeed the first republic he established provided no basis of agreement for further progress because of the quality of the people at all levels. Warlords were only interested in taking a grip of affairs in their own regions; many educated and patriotic Chinese were sincerely attached to the traditional culture; the mass of Chinese could hardly be touched by ideas from the West. This is why writer Lu Xun said: "What I want is a transformation of the Chinese character. Otherwise, whether the state is despotic or republic, the substance will remain hopelessly the same." But the question was how to transform the character of the Chinese, given the continuing grip of foreign powers on China's life. Sun Yat-sen's conclusion was collectivist: "On no account must we give more liberty to the individual;" he wrote, "let us secure liberty instead for the nation."

Ultimately, it was the ideological genes of Mao Zedong – wealth redistribution and human equality – that proved to fit in best with Chinese conditions at the time. Mao was born in 1893 in Hunan Province where geographic conditions had shaped people to be both straightforward and flexible. He was always in rebellion with his wealthy father who tried to force him to accept his authority, while collaborating with his Buddhist mother to help the poor by giving them food. But the very ideological genes that allowed Mao to secure liberty for China in 1949 were to mould the Chinese in ways he had sought to eradicate. The residence registration system (*hukou*) restrained people from free movement between geographical regions. In 1955, he collectivised agriculture by reorganising peasants into "communes", and nationalised all industry and commerce. The consequences were that rural cadres and enterprise officials were only concerned with window-dressing to show central targets had been achieved while peasants and workers had no incentive or responsibility to work. In the "Great Leap Forward" of 1958, as Mao believed local officials' claim that they were producing more than six million pounds of potatoes per acre, words became divorced from reality, responsibility and people's real thoughts. In 1966, Mao turned the country over to radicalised students to "purify" China. All schools were closed. The millions of students were urged to attack party officials, prominent intellectuals and even parents, and destroy old buildings, temples and art objects. In 1969, Mao took another turn by sending some fifteen million young people to the country for "re-education" by peasants because he maintained that people with some education were inferior to illiterate peasants. By the time Mao died in 1976, the ten-year Cultural Revolution had created a moral void: there were no principles governing the behaviour of the people because moral principles of the agricultural civilisation, such as respect for parents and sincerity to friends, had been destroyed. Many had been reduced to a state where they did not dare even to think, or if they did think, they only thought of Mao's quotations.

Given the cult of Mao, it took two years for the country to begin to think that it was wrong to follow Mao's every word to the letter and for pragmatic Deng Xiaoping to emerge as the new leader. While Mao almost always relied on China's past experience, Deng developed perceptual knowledge of Western capitalism when he studied in France in his early twenties. From 1949, whenever he got the chance, he would try to advance China's course of economic development. His pragmatism was vividly shown in his remark in the 1960s: "It doesn't matter whether the cat is white or black, as long as it catches mice." But his endeavour never lasted because it was not his era. As such, the ideological genes Deng had sought to propagate in China since 1978 were essentially the opposite of Mao's, i.e. wealth creation and human diversity; as he said, "we have to allow some people to become rich first." Since then, Deng had been called the "general designer" of the reform. But the title completely missed his greatness because he was only liberalising the country by allowing the people to do what they wanted to. In a sense, he led by walking behind the people: the household responsibility system was originated by a few peasants in Anhui Province well before the central government decided to allow it; the idea of Special Economic Zone was initially proposed by the Guangdong government.

Of course, the government did have its influence at every juncture of the economic reform. But the process was essentially one of "crossing the river by feeling the stones" instead of one based on neatly defined and strictly enforced rules. It became an age when order and disorder, good and bad, beautiful and ugly, rich and poor, civilised and uncivilised were born side by side. While some officials could not resist the opportunity of easily using their power for personal gains, some have stood the test of time and developed a true sense of political responsibility. While some peasants engage in the production of fake and inferior goods, some have built enterprises of international competitiveness. While some youngsters promote the culture of patriarchal clans and have become gangsters and charlatans, some have become professionals of modern quality and skills. Overall, money worship seems to have gripped a large part of the population and there is a spiritual crisis among many Chinese. This is why when an eminent Chinese scholar asked his students at a university, "Tell me what our society lacks most today," they replied with one accord, "Morality!" This is also why the new state leadership under Jiang Zemin has keenly recognised that ultimately China has to prosper on the basis of science and education.

Could China's reform have started with the political system? In as early as 1980, Deng thoroughly brought to light the limitations of the Chinese political system and their root causes, and pointed out the importance and necessity of reforming the political system. He said, "A good system can make it impossible for bad people to prevail, while a poor system can disable good people or even change them from good to bad." However, by 1986 when he met a Japanese visitor, he commented: "The reform in the political system is too difficult and too complex. We still haven't decided where to start." Indeed, how could China reverse its 2,500 years of connections-based political history to a rules-based system overnight? China's democratic process is not dependent upon poems or slogans but rather its economic foundation, cultural tradition and people's quality. As many Westerners observed during Tiananmen Square in 1989, "democracy" was more a slogan than a deep belief among most demonstrators, with most Chinese being either unaware of these Chinese demands for democracy, uninterested in them, ambivalent about them, or critical of them as impractical and irresponsible.

Could China's reform then have started with education? One of the first things Deng did was to raise the social status of intellectuals but it was unthinkable for him to decide to raise the education level of China's 1.2-billion predominantly agricultural population before finding ways to feed them. He also sent selected students and scholars to the West but only one in three returned, and this showed the serious limitations of using education as a breakthrough point in China. Of course, the backwardness of the Chinese education system has been well known. There are still 145 million illiterate people in China; the way of teaching at Chinese education institutions has led to a further weakness in most Chinese, that of passivity and a lack of active criticism. Yang Chen Ning, American Chinese scientist and Nobel Laureate, pointed out that from elementary, secondary, higher, to post-graduate education in China, students had been driven to an increasingly narrow valley and had become pedants who were used to accepting but not thinking let alone questioning and investigating. He concluded that Chinese education is unsuccessful in cultivating talents of creativity, independent view, and explorative capability. Of course, the problem often starts with Chinese family education, where parents tend to educate their children by switching between the two extremes of "pampering" and "autocracy".

All this has left foreign investors with one option: they have to develop the human resources they need by themselves. Indeed, to educate the Chinese in modern quality, the teachers themselves have to be of modern quality, supported by a suitable environment. In a very real sense, the best teachers in such education are Western expatriates and the best environment is a Sino-Western joint venture.

Evolving from Expatriate Support to Localisation

According to a Chinese proverb, "It takes ten years to grow a new generation of trees, and one hundred years to grow a new generation of people" (*shinian yushu, bainian yuren*). There is therefore no quick fix to the human resource challenge in China. To be effective in dealing with the challenge, multinationals must take a long-term approach, consisting of the following two elements:

- **Bringing in effective expatriate support to achieve control in the short term.** Given the poor quality of the Chinese in general regarding modern market-driven business management, failure to bring in adequate expatriate support at the initial stage of the joint venture is equal to asking for loss of control. Indeed, once bad norms are formed or managerial control falls into the hands of irresponsible locals as a result of inadequate expatriate influence, it will be much more difficult to re-establish good norms or win back control.

- **Systematically training local staff to achieve localisation in the long-term.** Through comprehensively organised training programmes for local staff, management structures consisting increasingly of local talents should be developed over time. This is essential to ensuring the long-term competitiveness of the China business in terms of both its cost base and its sensitivity to the changing local market. Those multinationals that do not pay any attention to localisation will inevitably find it harder and harder to compete.

The above long-term approach to coping with the human resource challenge in China can also be graphically represented (see Figure 6.1). In general, it takes several years before locally trained executives can replace expatriates on a wide scale. In the case of J. Walter Thompson Advertising, one of the most prominent advertising agencies in China, it was only after more than six years of training local staff that the Western firm could begin to utilise local talents to train new employees and to fill middle management positions. Of course, each company's situation is unique. To find the right balance between the use of expatriates in the short term and the use of local staff in the long term, you need two distinct abilities: (1) to bring in effective expatriate support; and (2) to understand the consequences of localisation.

FIGURE 6.1

Coping with the Human Resource Challenge in China

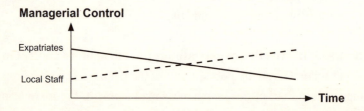

Bringing in Effective Expatriate Support

Latest numbers show that a China assignment can be very tough. According to some studies, the failure rate of expatriate senior executives in China is as high as 30%, which is twice the world average. One human resource specialist says in *Management Review* magazine that 75–80% of China expatriates become burnt out after a two or three-year stint. A high divorce rate also exists among expatriates. The mother of one China-based executive even wrote to her daughter: "Can't you get another job in another country where the people are more like us?" To enhance the effectiveness of your working life in China, you need to undertake three essential tasks: (1) preparing for posting in China; (2) coping with stress in China; and (3) taking on the training role.

Preparing for Posting in China

Before embarking on a career, or at least part of your career, in China, you need to assess the consequences of doing so and make sure that you are absolutely clear about the reason you are going there in the first place. Is it for career advancement, to make money, to learn, or to make a contribution? You also need to be aware of the downside, including missing your friends, your home and your culture – your total way of life in your homeland. To help make up your mind and prepare for your posting in China, you need to undertake three critical activities: (1) learning about China and its business reality; (2) gathering information on expatriate life in China; and (3) preparing for the challenge.

Learning about China and its business reality. If this is the first time you have contemplated the problems of entering China, you will need to develop a basic knowledge of Chinese history and culture, current facts, and how business is done there. You can find what you want to know about China by browsing and searching such websites as www. china-window.com and www.chinatoday.com. Even www.bbc.co.uk maintains a good body of information on China. If, however, you want to read a single, coherent volume, then Tim Ambler and Morgen Witzel's *Doing Business in China* (2000, Routledge, London) is probably the best. If, having gone through all the above, you would like to have a grasp of only the most important issues, then read John Stuttard's *The New Silk Road* (2000, John Wiley and Sons, New York).

Gathering information on expatriate life in China. Websites like www.shanghai-ed.com and www.expatsinchina.com feature a wealth of information on topics from community groups to schools. You can talk to those who have gone before you, but it is important to remember that every person's emotional responses to living in another country are very nearly unique. If you want to have a feel of the worst possible scenario, read Tim Clissold's *Mr. China* (2004, Robinson, London). You should also seek support from your company to make "look-see" visits to China. With your own perception and others' opinions, you can then develop a realistic expectation about your expatriate life in China.

Preparing for the challenge. If, after reading *Mr. China* or hearing others' worn-out prejudices, you still have a basically healthy and positive attitude toward China and its people, then China is for you. Indeed, once you realise that no matter how different, strange or even bizarre the Chinese may seem, you have no option but to see them for what they are, you will be mentally prepared to rise to the challenge. Of course, pre-departure cross-cultural training for you, lasting at least two days and focusing mainly on basic, day-to-day, survival-level concerns, including general cross-cultural and China-specific issues as well as language needs, will equip you with the basic, tactical tools necessary to deal with the daily challenge once you arrive in China.

Coping with Stress in China

Several surveys of expatriates indicate that of the skills needed to work effectively in China, the most important is the ability to cope with stress, which can come from both living- and work-related sources. To conquer what is often termed as the "China syndrome", you need to have a strong internal motivation to adapt to a new environment and to accept the inevitable setbacks as a necessary part of the process. In addition, you need to understand the four phases of adaptation: (1) honeymoon; (2) crisis; (3) recovery; and (4) adjustment.

The honeymoon phase. As a newly relocated expatriate, you will find that everything is interesting, quaint and exciting. You are willing to suppress minor irritations in favour of concentrating on the nice things about the new surroundings. In fact, for the most part, it is the *similarities* that stand out at this point, and you may feel ready to accept whatever comes. As there is a lot of euphoria and optimism, it is easy for you to rush things and develop an erratic work pattern, such as undertaking teleconferencing calls with head office in the evenings. Yet, you should avoid the temptation to promise to make money fast, and take things slowly. You should also remind yourself that what you initially experience is fairly superficial and that you need more time to know things, and in particular the local people, in a deep way. If you try too hard and rush too much at this stage, you will soon hit the crisis stage.

The crisis phase. The honeymoon phase normally lasts around a month because, gradually, your focus turns from the similarities to the *differences* that suddenly seem to be everywhere and are troubling. Your initial excitement wears off and what was quaint only last week, such as the traffic jam, is now seen as bad. Things start going wrong, with workload, pollution and local food making you feel generally run down. You begin to blame all your frustration and anger on the local culture. Some Western expatriates never go beyond this stage, while others leave China all together. Yet, if you want to succeed in China, you should use the symptoms as a clear indicator that it is time to change your approach, and try to enter the recovery phase by engaging in some form of self-development. The worst you can do is ignore the symptoms or adopt a rigid stance of believing that it is all the locals' fault.

The recovery phase. There are five positive steps you can take to recover. First, realise that the crisis you are experiencing is natural and not a sign that you are deficient or strange because virtually every Western expatriate experiences it to some degree, and keep in mind all the positive things about your present situation including the fact that your experience of the Chinese culture, as painful as it may be, will broaden your cultural horizon. Second, maintain good health by watching personal hygiene, bringing vitamins and food supplements with you, joining health clubs or gyms, and flying to Hong Kong or your home country to relax and stock up on vitamins and health foods. Third, cultivate an interest in a Chinese national sport and/or a Chinese cultural heritage, such as calligraphy or furniture, and use every opportunity to investigate it while fulfilling your work responsibility. Fourth, make friends with those expatriates who have been in China longer, gone through the crisis, and have a positive attitude toward the Chinese (but avoid those who spend their days seeking company to commiserate with), and try to develop a deeper, more intimate relationship with one or two locals who can speak some English. Finally, attend relevant training programmes, such as the one-week orientation programme at Shanghai-based China Europe International Business School.

The adjustment phase. After a period of recovery, you begin forming a realistic picture of the local culture, your sense of humour returns, and you realise that the situation is not hopeless after all. You not only start to feel at home in your new surroundings and comfortable getting around but also know the limitations of your skills, are willing to be flexible and can begin to integrate your new experiences into your "old self". You may even begin to find things that you enjoy and that you will definitely miss if you pack up and return to your homeland.

Taking on the Training Role

It goes without saying that multinationals send their expensive expatriates to China to achieve business results. Yet, from a long-term perspective, training is an even more fundamental role for expatriates, as Stephanie Jones quotes one expatriate in *Managing in China* (1997):

The reason why we as expatriates are in China is to train our staff.

> We are too expensive to be here just to do a job. Our task is to rep-
> licate ourselves, 10 times, 20 times, 30 times over. And we have
> to make clones who are better than we are, who will inevitably be
> more culturally sensitive and who will be more committed to China
> in the long term. We are just here to find successors, many of them.

Indeed, expatriates serve as the conduit for transferring to local staff
the most vital information about running a company, including technical know-how, managerial skills, business knowledge, corporate culture, and familiarity with people back at headquarters. As an on-the-job
training approach, training by expatriates has the key advantage of being highly practical. For example, to train teamwork attitude, expatriates
can organise task meetings, in which all the relevant people take part,
involving discussions, joint decision-making and responsibility sharing. And if such activities are encouraged throughout the business and
undertaken frequently, people will gradually develop a habit of opinion
exchange and information sharing, and a sense of joint mission.

Yet, the multitude of tasks that an expatriate is asked to perform in
China rarely includes training their replacement. Companies that want
to make the most effective use of their expensive expatriates thus need
to redefine each expatriate's job priorities. Specifying that the expatriate is responsible for training a local manager is an important starting
point. As requiring an employee to train himself or herself out of the job
is hardly natural in the corporate world, companies should reward expatriates who achieve this goal in the same manner that attaining other
business goals would be rewarded.

Understanding the Consequences of Localisation

Localisation, i.e. the use of locals to replace expatriates, is fundamentally important. Yet, it is equally important to put it in perspective.
Depending upon the joint venture contract and the initial managerial
quality of the local partner, localisation should be seen as an effort-con-
suming *process* rather than a quick fix. And the challenge of localisa-

tion clearly lies in training and developing the local staff rather than immediately giving up important positions to them. Specifically, you need to understand both the benefits of localisation and the dangers of localising too fast.

Benefits of Localisation

The long-term logic of localisation is indisputable because it offers three key benefits: (1) huge immediate cost savings; (2) lifting the morale of local staff; and (3) creating long-term business advantage.

Huge immediate cost savings. Localisation is good for the bottom line since the savings from sending an expatriate home can be substantial. A typical expatriate package for a middle manager with a family tends to be about US$200,000 to US$300,000 a year. It includes base salary, foreign service premium, hardship allowances, tax equalisation, company-rented Western-style house/apartment, children's education allowances, regional rest and recreation, home leave (once or twice a year), and all moving and relocation expenses. A high-calibre local manager is likely to command a salary of roughly US$36,000, plus pension, housing, education and insurance, which add US$23,000 to the costs.

Lifting the morale of local staff. Localisation is good for the Chinese staff whose morale is lifted by promotion. For example, at the end of 1998, the general manager job of Wall's ice cream in Shanghai was transferred to local management, and the joint venture viewed this transition as "a matter of pride". Multinationals that drag their feet on localisation – especially those that send more and more expatriates to China – risk seeing their brightest local managers leave because of the perception that promotion opportunities for local staff are limited.

Creating long-term business advantage. Localisation is good for the joint venture that benefits from a management in touch with the needs and culture of the local market. With language and cultural barriers, expatriates can be limited in their interaction with the locals and consequently in their effectiveness in the local business environment. Even those who do speak some Chinese can be ignorant of the best ways to get things done in China, with their local staff running rings around them. For example, it is difficult to imagine that a marketing or brand manager can be truly effective if he does not have a full, deep understanding of the cultural details of the target market.

Dangers of Localising Too Fast

The promise of saving on expatriate expenses can also propel companies into a rushed programme of localisation that may prove more trouble than it is worth. Specifically, localising too fast can bring about three dangers: (1) resurgence of Chinese practices; (2) difficulty in reversing the process; and (3) threat to the future of the joint venture.

Resurgence of Chinese practices. It is only natural for local staff to revert to old-style behaviours and practices if they are left alone before their mindset has been adequately re-framed through training. At Shenyang Tambrands, as the US side did not give sufficient attention to the training of local staff before it pulled out the expatriate managers in order to cut costs and overhead, the joint venture was forced to practise Chinese-style management. For example, the budget and daily allowance for sales people on business trips had been reduced to conform to Chinese standards, and this seriously damaged the morale of the sales force and led to the resignation of several key local managers.

Difficulty in reversing the process. Localisation is a process that also touches on some of the most sensitive areas between people working in a joint venture, including trust, transparency, racial discrimination and the huge differences in management experience, education, pay, opportunity and local market understanding. In addition, it takes a long time for a new expatriate executive to get up to speed because of the need to build relationships with the locals. As such, once Chinese staff have been promoted to senior management positions, it will be difficult to reverse the process. One manager of an international consulting firm warned: "There are companies that have localised and made mistakes. And if you do not do it right, it will come back and bite you. It is very difficult to recover from that because then you have race issues."

Threat to the future of the joint venture. Without a trustworthy, competent local management team, multinationals that shed expatriate staff too fast will inevitably place their businesses in China at peril as a result of the loss of financial discipline, quality control and corporate identity. One expatriate manager of a Sino-Western joint venture pointed out: "Doing business the Chinese way is much less well-documented and can be dangerous. There is a serious risk when you give up financial control." At Shenyang Tambrands, following the departure of the expatriate general manager and marketing manager, the vice president of Tambrands (Far East) took over the general manager position. But because of his commitment to other businesses, he had no choice but to leave the venture's day-to-day operation in the hands of the local deputy general manager, whose incompetence demoralised other local staff.

Training Local Staff

Given the scale of the human resource challenge, the job of training is too mammoth and too sensitive (due to the Chinese face issue) to be accomplished by expatriates using on-the-job training alone. For on-the-job training to be effective, off-the-job training programmes have to be conducted to prepare the right orientation and mentality. In 1997, when Motorola China expected to triple its Chinese national workforce from 3,500 to 10,000 by the year 2000, its vice president of human resources Leo Burke and his team at Motorola University came up with CAMP, the China Accelerated Management Programme. CAMP consisted of six weeks of classroom work, spliced into 14 months of on-the-job training, including action learning, project management, expatriate coaching, and rotation through Motorola's worldwide facilities.

Training is also costly, and therefore it needs to be employed in conjunction with other human resource policies in order to bring maximum benefits to the business. Specifically, you need to undertake three critical tasks: (1) understanding the ingredients for effective training; (2) generously committing training resources; and (3) creatively using training to find and retain local talents.

Ingredients for Effective Training

Training in China is different from training in your homeland. In the latter, cultural factors, such as mentality and language, can be taken for granted, whereas in the former, such cultural factors often play an important role. Effective training in China involves three key ingredients: (1) having an executive in charge of training; (2) combining training in professional skills with training in professional personality; and (3) taking account of "Chinese characteristics".

Having an Executive in Charge of Training

In the past, many foreign companies tended to focus on rapid expansion in China and did not think about training until the operation of their established ventures was badly hurt by human resource problems. To make human resources an integral part of a firm's growth strategy, it is necessary to have an executive directly in charge of training. Employing an expatriate human resource executive appears to be the preferred option among multinationals looking to establish China-wide human resource policies for their operations. Companies like Siemens, Motorola, Ford and Nokia have all brought in expatriate vice presidents for human resources to spearhead the development of human resources. In addition to having an intimate knowledge of Western training practices, these expatriate managers boast the corporate familiarity and clout necessary to jump-start the process of formulating and implementing an effective human resource policy.

As expatriates do have problems in overcoming the language barriers and understanding local staff, it is therefore necessary to appoint a local, in-house training manager. The training manager can assist the

senior human resource executive by undertaking such tasks as identi-
fication of training needs, accurate translations, follow-up evaluations,
repetition of basic tenets, and maintenance of training records.

Combining Training in Professional Skills with Training in Professional Personality

To ensure that the right job is done the right way, multinationals rightly
organise programmes to train local managers and employees in professional skills, ranging from production planning and control, accounting
and decision making, sales and marketing, recruitment and performance appraisal, to business planning and operating procedures.

However, an employee with the necessary skills can still fail to accomplish their job because of wrong attitudes toward the job or toward
the necessary co-operation with others. For example, the mastery of
sales skills cannot stop a sales person from doing personal deals with
customers if he lacks ethical standards in external relationships. At
BOC's joint venture in Shanghai, it was found that both the attitudes
and practices of the local partner's employees had been inherited from
its state-owned parent company.

Therefore, it is equally important to train local staff in professional
personality, including independent thinking, initiative taking, sense of
responsibility, teamwork attitude and business ethics. In general, the
minds of the locals need to be opened and their horizons widened so
that they can see their work in a wider context, view external relationships from an organisational perspective, and share the responsibility
for the overall results. This can be achieved through basic training and
staff orientation, emphasising the nature of a modern business and the
fundamental importance of the "I need you and you need me" mentality when working in an organisation. To be effective, these sessions are
best illustrated with practical examples and participating role-plays that
are real and where the consequences of not working as a team are all too
obvious. In addition, training in this area should be conducted in short
but frequent sessions to reinforce habit building. At Du Pont in China,
all employees have to go through regular ethics training, and the top

management follow it up with visible discipline.

Taking Account of "Chinese Characteristics"

The basic purpose of training is to help local staff to become more effective in their job, not just to gain knowledge for the sake of it. Training cannot be effectively done when it is all about "foreign ideas" taught in the foreign language. Instead, great attention should be given to "Chinese characteristics". First, as placing all Chinese staff in the same training sessions can easily cause unease among Chinese workers, who tend to be concerned with face, separate training sessions should be held for different staff categories, such as supervisors and workers.

Second, when a company uses training resources from outside China, English is by default the language of instruction. But this works only for those local staff whose English is proficient. In cases where the English of local staff is primitive, accurate interpretation becomes vital. In general, since the language of business in China is Mandarin, it is easier for the trainees to apply what they have learnt if training is conducted accordingly. This is especially so when training is interactive, where trainees will be much more comfortable participating in discussions, role-plays and presentations in the local language.

Finally, training effectiveness can be further enhanced when effort is made to take the "foreignness" out of training by using Chinese examples. For example, Xi'an–Janssen has looked back into Chinese history to find appropriate examples, such as Sun Tzu and Mao Zedong, to conduct training in leadership and discipline. Another source of Chinese examples is case studies on local companies, which have been highly publicised in the local press. There are plenty of poorly-run state-owned enterprises. Zhongyuan Pharmaceutical, China's largest ever pharmaceutical enterprise, had to be closed in 1996 because, among other poor practices, when over 100 motors were burnt during commissioning, its directors claimed they could find neither the cause of the problem nor the people responsible for it. There are also a few Chinese companies whose success has resulted from responsible practices from workers all the way to top management, Haier being an outstanding example.

Committing Training Resources

Depending upon the size of the investment a multinational has in China and the amount of training resources it is willing to commit, it can choose from a number of off-the-job training methods and of course use a combination of them. The five main ones are: (1) flying local staff to overseas parent company; (2) flying trainers from overseas parent company; (3) using China-based training providers; (4) developing training partnerships; and (5) establishing own training centre.

Flying Local Staff to Overseas Parent Company

The key advantage of overseas training is the unique chance for local staff to see the real operation of a modern Western company and build a mental picture as to the sort of standards they should strive to achieve once they return to China. Other advantages include motivation and the fact that a Western company can use existing operational staff to tour Chinese visitors around its operation. However, as these programmes tend to be short and the majority of the resources have to be spent on the logistics of getting people around, they can, if not carefully organised, easily turn into tours and sightseeing with the training purpose largely unfulfilled. Of course, if company resources allow, overseas training programmes to last several months or even longer can not only equip the trainees with the necessary professional skills but also help transform their professional personality.

At Tianjin SMG Presses, a German engineering joint venture established in 1992, its first overseas training programme in 1994 was not very successful because local employees arrived in Germany at a time when the parent company was too busy to give them the necessary attention. In 1996, a year into the plant's operation, the joint venture sent another group of eight workers to Germany for three months' intensive training. This time, the programme was more carefully structured, with the trainees only selected from the joint venture's core of assembly technicians. They arrived in Germany at different stages depending on their production skills, with a team of four mechanics and fitters followed by four electricians, and a Chinese foreman acting as a supervisor for the whole period in Germany.

Flying Trainers from Overseas Parent Company

Instead of flying groups of locals to the parent company in the West, multinationals can dramatically cut logistics costs by sending their trainers from the parent company to China to train the locals. Although brought-in trainers may have limited knowledge about and experience of the China context, this approach can be particularly effective in technical training because of its narrow, specialised focus. It can also be used to prepare employee mentality and orientation for on-the-job training. At an automobile joint venture in Shanghai, an American management trainer was brought in to give a lecture to its employees who often were only concerned about pay but not work responsibility. The trainer used the Red Army's Long March in the 1930s to stimulate work spirit. He said: "The Red Army of the Chinese Communist Party was very weak and the life of soldiers was extremely hard but nobody asked for any subsidies. What did they rely on to defeat the powerful enemy? It was belief and spirit!" The lecture made a real impact on the locals.

In some cases, this approach needs to be backed by expatriate coaching or reinforcement for it to be effective. For example, at United Biscuits (China) in Shenzhen, the British-based food manufacturer initially brought trainers in from the UK and so long as they were on site all worked very well. As soon as they left China there was an inclination for local employees to go back to the old ways, including sleeping on the job and not cleaning up around the work area. Since then, it has learned to focus on bringing people from the UK to train the trainers so that when they return to the UK, local trainers can follow up the training results and conduct reinforcement sessions.

Using China-Based Training Providers

Although there is still a shortfall of training alternatives for local staff, the selection of foreign and domestic training providers is rapidly improving. While larger foreign training companies continue to concentrate on sales and basic management training, a host of niche-oriented training firms are now entering China. Computer software, ISO 9000 standards, cross-cultural communication, executive secretarial skills and personal effectiveness are some of the areas being introduced. Monash Mount Eliza of Australia and Schiller of the USA are meeting the rising demand for strategic management training by offering an expanding range of MBA programmes. I Will Not Complain International, an experiential management training company, concentrates on team-building exercises as a means of creating the trust that is required in any co-operative undertaking.

Key criteria to consider when selecting a training provider include experience of China, integrity, ability to customise, cost and sustainability. To cut costs and gain leverage with training firms, multinationals in non-competing areas can also share training resources. In Beijing, Shell has participated in training programmes with both IBM of the USA and German consumer goods firm Henkel. To meet the needs of cost-conscious clients, some training providers, such as Asia East Gate and Learning International, offer train-the-trainer programmes and licensed training courses which together allow a firm to acquire a packaged training programme and use its own instructors to convey material to new corporate recruits. For the general training of local workers, the low-cost services offered by some local Chinese universities and training institutes can be worth considering too.

Developing Training Partnerships

To gain better leverage with the training programmes provided, multinationals can also form training partnerships with local universities or business schools. With a training partnership, a multinational can design the training programme together with the local institution but the training staff and facilities will be from the latter.

At BOC, with the number of joint ventures in China rising to over twenty, it faced an equally sharp rise in the backlog of local staff requiring management training. To cope with the challenge, BOC opted to establish training partnerships with local universities. In 1995, BOC Management College was launched at Fushun Petroleum Institute near Shenyang in the Northeast. Originally the college educated around thirty senior local executives in a ten-month programme. Now it has been restructured as a middle management school. The programme has also been shortened to between three and four months so that BOC can send three or four groups of thirty managers to the college each year. BOC Management Colleges are also being launched at universities in Beijing, Shanghai and the south of China.

To address the leadership and strategic management training needs of the company's senior local staff, BOC has established a training partnership with Nanyang Technical University of Singapore and Beijing University. The "mini-MBA" programme was launched in April 1996 at Beijing University. Taught in Mandarin by business professors from the two universities, the two-week programme employs modern teaching methods and China-based case study materials. The programme was designed to fit the managerial needs of BOC and cost a total of US$90,000 for a group of twenty-three managers over two weeks.

Establishing Own Training Centre

For those multinationals that have established a critical mass of businesses in China, establishing a dedicated training centre for their own employees and for external customers who wish to pay for their training services is probably the most effective training solution. Shell and Motorola, for example, have opted to take full control of the training agenda by setting up extensive in-house training infrastructures using state-of-the-art methodologies such as self-directed learning.

In the case of Siemens China, with more than thirty joint ventures producing high-technology electrical and electronic equipment, the nature of the product means that not only must those producing it be well trained, but also those who are ultimately going to use it. The Beijing Technology Training Centre was set up in 1991 to offer extensive training programmes to its own staff and to its customers' staff. This was a new practice in China, and Siemens had some trouble in introducing it at first. But nowadays, between 4,000 and 5,000 people per year go on courses here that last up to three weeks. Staff members at the training centre have undergone two to three years of specialist training at Siemens' headquarters in Germany before they begin training other people in Beijing. To alleviate the shortage in management training, Siemens has also set up the Siemens Management Institute, where employees of other companies can also pay to go on courses. Of course, the emphasis is on training Siemens' own employees who are already in management positions but are going on the course to gain more knowledge and improve their chances of promotion.

Training to Find and Retain Local Talents

With so many foreign companies in China, there is a huge demand for well-trained staff. You may think that training only leads to poaching from competitors. Yet, it would be a mistake not to train people because without training you will fall into a vicious circle. To overcome the potential problem of trained staff getting headhunted, you can blend training with recruitment, pay, benefits and promotion prospects.

For example, HSBC starts its search for Chinese managers by recruiting from among top students at Chinese universities, with its extensive overseas training being a major lure. Trainees first go to Britain for ten weeks, then three years in Hong Kong. From the start the company emphasises bright promotion prospects for trainees by assuring them that, one day, Hong Kong executives in China will be replaced by PRC executives. Management trainees are also eligible for an alluring housing scheme when they return to China, which allows them to borrow up to 100 times their monthly salary at 2% interest. On top of these attractions, the company must still pay a generous salary. The company wants to offer enough to help ward off poaching from competitors but not so much that it cuts into the bottom line. A final incentive is the repatriation bonus. Every training programme graduate receives a percentage of his or her first year's salary as a bonus on returning to China. After serving one year, the new manager gets another bonus.

LEADING THE CHINESE
THE CHINESE WAY

The superior man has no ordinary mind. He takes as his mind the mind of the people.

To lead the people, follow them.

LAO TZU, *TAO TE CHING*

WHILE THE TRAINING OF LOCAL STAFF IS ESSENTIAL, equally so is the need for Western executives to learn skills for effectively leading the local people. Indeed, leadership skills can help you get the locals on your side and thus bring a complex situation under your control. In this chapter, it is shown that as the Chinese criterion for interpersonal relationships is in contrast with its Western counterpart, you have to learn to lead the Chinese the Chinese way, i.e. employing skills consistent with the Chinese interpersonal criterion. As a pre-requisite to effectively leading others, you also need to learn to manage yourself in the highly challenging China business environment, and in this respect, much can be learnt from ancient Chinese wisdom.

Feelings, Reasons and Rules:
the Chinese Criterion for Human Relationships

Because of the social life orientation contrast as discussed in Chapter 1, the Chinese criterion for human relationships is in contrast with its Western counterpart (see Figure 7.1).

In the West, rules are the most important, followed by reasons that underlie any debate over exceptional situations, with personal feelings being something that one has to take personal responsibility for and thus concerns others least. As such, in any organisational setting, abiding by rules reigns supreme. Those who do not are considered bad, disgraceful or unlawful, and, most importantly, are made responsible. In China, the criterion for interpersonal relationships that has been developed over a period of 2,500 years is the other way round, i.e. feelings, reasons and rules (*qing li fa*). In other words, personal feelings are the most important, followed by reasons that people hold for situations, with rules being the least concerned.

For the Chinese, the "logic" (if, indeed, it can be called logic) behind their interpersonal criterion is as follows. The establishment of any rules in any social context is subject to both external needs and internal intentions, both of which are changeable. Therefore, rules seem to be fixed but are actually alterable with the change of people. To deal with exceptional cases and vague issues, it is necessary to use reasons as the criterion to make a judgement. If things are reasonable, they should accord with the rules; if they are found to be unreasonable but accord

FIGURE 7.1

Interpersonal Criterion Contrast

West		China
Least important	**Feelings** ↑	Most important
	Reasons	
Most important ↓	**Rules**	Least important

with the rules, the rules are considered to be unreasonable and should be revised accordingly. Furthermore, if things are reasonable but are not accepted by people, they are regarded as being against human feelings and still cannot be carried out. As a result, understanding and respecting the feelings of each individual becomes the ultimate goal of the Chinese, and any pursuit of rules at the expense of human feelings is regarded as "attending to trivialities while neglecting essentials".

The Chinese interpersonal criterion of emphasising human feelings while neglecting organisational rules is at the heart of Chinese culture and is based largely on the ancient Confucian social philosophy of human-heartedness (*ren*), righteousness (*yi*) and proprieties (*li*), in that order. As discussed in Chapter 1, *ren*, i.e. human feelings toward other human beings, is what distinguishes humans from animals. *Yi* means being morally good or having just cause, and *li* refers to proper social form and etiquette that make possible and preserve the whole social order. It is important to note that Confucian social philosophy proceeds from neither the society nor the individual, but from interpersonal relations represented by *ren* – *yi* and *li* being its extensions. This is why "human feelings are larger than laws of the kingdom" (*renqing dayu wangfa*) and "no law can punish the masses" (*fa bu zezhong*) have been popular proverbs throughout Chinese history, and why rules and regulations in China are administrative rather than judicial in nature.

As a result of the above contrast, human relationships in the West are impersonal, detached, and mechanistic, whereas in China they are personal, attached, and organic. In the West, if you ask somebody, "Have you eaten?" you are bound to be seen as far too personal, but in China, such a comment is seen as a polite greeting. In the West, when friends go out to eat, each person has to pay for their own portion but this is unthinkable in China, where eating together is in order to be indebted to the host. In the West, the relationship among workers in a factory is of a colleague nature but in China there is a strong sense of "righteous code of brotherhood" among workers. Indeed, a factory in the West exists for the purpose of business results, but in China it is more like a "family", which exists because of relationships. In the West, business transactions are made on the strength of contracts, but in China they are made on the strength of personal agreements. In the West, people do not take business disputes personally, but in China it is hard to separate pure commercial issues from personal issues. In the West, the law is regarded as the primary form of redress when things go wrong, but in China social pressures rather than legal instruments are used to ensure compliance.

In Beijing, there was a retired worker living in a ground floor flat of a residential building, outside which there were several rubbish bins. One day, some school pupils found it great fun to play with these bins by knocking on them. Afterwards, they came and played with these bins regularly, generating terrible noise in the area. Annoyed by the noise, some residents shouted towards the pupils, but the pupils became more excited and made more noise. The retired worker then told them that he enjoyed watching their game and that he would pay them RMB1.00 each time they played. Motivated by this, the pupils returned again and again. A week later, the retired worker told them that he could only afford to pay them RMB0.5. They were unhappy but continued their game. After another week, the retired worker told them that he could now only pay them RMB0.1. They were very upset and shouted towards him: "This is ridiculous! You want us to play for just RMB0.1. No way!" They then all disappeared and never came back.

Had the above story happened in the West, it would have gone like this. Being annoyed initially by the terrible noise, the retired worker would warn them that they were being naughty. When the warning failed, he would tell the pupils that they should stop immediately or he would call the police. End of story!

I cannot imagine that any Westerner could possibly have done what the retired Chinese worker did or that any Chinese would think of referring the case to the police. For the Chinese know that the police are not going to take care of things like this, that referring it to the police will make matters worse, and that they can always find a reasonable solution to the problem between themselves.

Leading the Chinese: Concepts and Skills

Despite its well-known limitations as discussed in Chapter 1, the Chinese interpersonal criterion is deeply rooted and cannot be changed overnight, if at all. To effectively lead the Chinese, you therefore need to learn to employ skills that are consistent with it (see Figure 7.2).

To lead the Chinese, the most powerful skill is to operate at the level of feelings, i.e. appealing to their hearts by addressing their emotional needs. Although this skill is most effective in bringing individuals to your side, it does not necessarily lead to the attainment of business objectives. To address business needs, you need to operate at the level of rules, i.e. leading by setting people an example. Although you can apply this skill almost readily, there is a limit to how much you can do it. Between these two levels, you can lead the Chinese by operating at the level of reasons, i.e. reconciling different viewpoints, which is characterised by taking a highly flexible, harmony-oriented rather than a deadly-straight, "black/white"-oriented attitude and approach.

Leading by Appealing to People's Hearts

According to Mencius in *Mencius*:

> If a sovereign regards his ministers as his hands and feet, his ministers will regard him as their heart and belly. If a sovereign regards his ministers as his horses and dogs, his ministers will regard him as just a passer-by. If a sovereign regards his ministers as sod and grass, his ministers will regard him as their enemy.

FIGURE 7.2

Leading the Chinese at Three Basic Levels

Personal Needs

Level of Feelings: Leading by appealing to people's hearts

Level of Reasons: Leading by reconciling people's viewpoints

Business Needs

Level of Rules: Leading by setting people an example

In the West, many companies have long had the tradition of treating their customers like "transactions" in an economic system, and their employees like "replaceable parts" on a corporate machine, with "ruthlessness" being the driving value of many executives. But in China, you simply have to treat the Chinese as human beings with dignity, a mind and, above all, a heart if you want to lead them, because the Chinese are very tender, very sensitive inside as a result of their valuing of feelings. As such, it is clearly not practical, at least in the short term, for you to develop shared values with the locals. However, you can learn to lead them by consciously addressing the local values while retaining your Western values at heart, because to regard Chinese values as something odd or unworthy, or to impose your external values upon the Chinese, generally drives their heart away from you. To appeal to the heart of the Chinese, you need three critical skills: (1) to respect people; (2) to know people; and (3) to build goodwill.

Respecting People

No matter how much people differ in background or temperament, respect underlies any enduring relationship, and respecting people is simply paying attention to manners when dealing with them, whether you like them or not. In particular, in relationships with the Chinese, the little things are the big things. The little kindness, small courtesies, caring language, appreciative words and understanding attitudes as you have in a family setting are all ways of demonstrating your respect for the Chinese. Simple things like saying "please" and "thank you" and knowing a person's name, and remembering to ask after the person's family can matter a great deal. You can also show appreciation for things Chinese by, for example, flying the Chinese flag for important Chinese visitors. Even things like speaking slowly, and learning or attempting to learn the Chinese language are appreciated gestures. Titles are sometimes down played in the West, but they are very important in China because they reflect status. Respect for people also comes in the sincere apologies, such as "I showed you no respect by embarrassing you in front of your friends. I apologise."

Dr Martin Posth, Chairman of Volkswagen Asia-Pacific, rightly warned his German colleagues in China: "Respect your Chinese colleagues. Even if they are not as capable as you today, they will be tomorrow." Indeed, no matter how incompetent or even "stupid" local staff may appear to be, you should never treat them as inferior because of the significance they attach to face, i.e. the respect and social prestige held by others. You should never use bad words to the face of the Chinese. Criticising or challenging someone fiercely in front of others is also seen as an act of disrespecting them. Given that Western jokes are based on laughing at people's silly behaviour, you need to be extremely careful when joking in China. Yet, you can show your greatest respect for a person by sincerely praising them for even the smallest thing they have done correctly because you are making them feel important.

Of paramount importance is the respect you need to show to the Chinese boss who represents not only himself as an individual but also the Chinese party as a whole. As such, you should never let the Chinese boss lose face in front of other Chinese employees by, for example, criticising him publicly. You can show your respect for him by inviting him to important functions, asking him to make speeches and introducing him to visitors from the West. Other good moves for showing respect for the Chinese boss include keeping him informed and consulting him even if sometimes you know the answer. Equally important is your respect for government officials, who often will only hear what you request if you use subservient language appropriate to your lowly position and humbly ask them to act benevolently towards you. When several officials are present, you should give the right proportional respect to them according to their positions of authority. Other good moves include regularly inviting officials in for visits and consulting them on things like local conditions and culture.

Knowing People

Everyone is unique; one person's mission is another person's minutia. Therefore, it is important to deeply know the individuals you want to lead. Yet, it takes great effort and patience to know the heart and soul of local people, given language barriers, a somewhat insular and alien Chinese culture, and wide gaps in material wealth. To gain insight into people, you need to ensure that you do not take your own views as reality because it is our tendency to project out of our own autobiographies what we think other people want or need or to project our intentions on the behaviour of others. In your interactions with local people, you need to keep your eyes peeled, your ears open, and your mouth closed – well, you need to ask questions, but don't begin to answer them yourself. You need to practice "aggressive observation", which means aiming for the big picture, taking in all the signals, weighing them, and converting them into usable perceptions.

To know your local staff, it is also essential that you go out of your way to connect with them. You should shake hands, eat with employees, learn how they live, and visit them in their offices and homes. Your interactions should have high social and low business content. And instead of trying to get through to people, you should work hard at being with people, listening aggressively, seeing things from their frame of reference, knowing their recent history, finding out their values and needs, understanding how they feel, and discovering the spark of greatness in them. One general manager of marketing for a food and beverage manufacturing operation in Shanghai has started a programme in his company whereby all the company's supervisors visit all their subordinates' families at least once a year. Each supervisor has four or five salesmen reporting to him, and must visit their homes and eat dinner with their families. "It works very well, and helps them get to know each other in a much deeper way," said the general manager.

Of particular importance is the need to be pro-active and regularly spend time with the Chinese boss, such as having lunch with him, so as to know each other on a personal basis. Once you can make him feel that he can trust you as a person, you can then enjoy the support and co-operation you need to carry out your business tasks. Also, you need to spend a substantial amount of time becoming acquainted with officials through regularly meeting them, listening to them about how the government system works and developing an understanding of where the power points lie. I was once asked to speed up the approval process for the feasibility study of a new joint venture. There were a dozen government agencies and several dozen officials involved at various levels, but my dinners with some officials helped me identify who the decision-makers were. With targeted efforts, we soon got the approval.

Building Goodwill

To build goodwill with somebody, it is essential that you make what is important to the other person as important to you as the other person is to you. You may not value face but the Chinese value it dearly; to build goodwill with them, you have to accept their valuing of it even if at heart you value truth. You may expect that a government official should serve you according to rules, but his value for "human feelings" means that when you meet him for the first time and want to spare some of his time you should bring a gift for him. You may want to continue your Western corporate culture by regarding Chinese employees as work colleagues, but the Chinese valuing of personal relationships at a workplace means that you have to treat them as though you are all members of a big family. This is why an expatriate executive of a hotel in Guangzhou said: "If there is anything I've done that works, it's been that I've provided a family atmosphere, a feeling of being at home, with the family, and that this hotel is not just a place where staff come to work. I just try to be fair, to be caring, and to provide a sense of belonging."

You build goodwill with managerial staff by being sensitive to their position and making sure that they do not lose face in front of their subordinates. You build goodwill with competent employees by delegating more, enhancing their responsibility and rewarding their initiative; you build goodwill with incompetent employees by supporting them more and praising them for what they have competently done. You build goodwill with elderly employees by showing understanding and respect for their experience in work and life; you build goodwill with young employees by participating with them in social events, such as discos and sports games. Female employees in China are generally more narrow-minded and dependent than male employees are, and therefore you build goodwill with them through providing even more encouragement, support and caring.

Of course, special effort needs to be made to build goodwill with the Chinese boss, who is looking for both status and money in his dealings with Western companies. You can arrange for him to visit your headquarters in the West. You can sincerely recognise and praise his talents and contributions among the locals and let them pass the message to him. Also, Chinese officials are past masters at getting benefit from the goodwill and favours they bestow, so you must be willing and able to reciprocate. Sometimes, work in this area may not thave any immediate use, but it will certainly be useful for coping with any unexpected governmental demands in the future if only to avoid shock and panic. When BC was developing a new joint venture in Southern China, we were once introduced to a provincial industry official. At dinners, he repeatedly talked about the value and difficulties of sending children abroad for education. We then invited his family to a dinner, at which his daughter bluntly told us she wanted to study in the UK but did not have the overseas connections to do it. Afterwards, we helped his daughter receive education in the UK, and two years later we found we were in a position to benefit from the official's help.

Leading by Reconciling People's Viewpoints

According to Confucius in *The Analects*:

> Superior men seek harmony instead of sameness whereas inferior men seek sameness instead of harmony.

In the West, people have traditionally seen the world as caught between two forces – good and evil – and, as such, the rational right-or-wrong view or the "Tyranny of the OR" pushes people to think that things must be either A or B, but *not both*. In China, such thinking has never prevailed. Opposites are morally neutral, and while they constantly struggle against each other one cannot exist without the other. The Chinese therefore regard right and wrong as something relative rather than absolute. Right or wrong depends on who sees it and when and where. In effect, Chinese-style truth, fairness, and reciprocity are created anew for each situation. Because of this difference, any Western-style, relentless pursuit of the absolute truth on anything or of the "one right way" of doing something under any circumstances generally drives the Chinese away from you. To bring them on your side, you have to learn to reconcile people's different viewpoints. Specifically, you need three abilities: (1) to value different viewpoints; (2) to listen with empathy; and (3) to search for synergetic solutions.

Valuing Different Viewpoints

All too often, many Western executives think they have all the answers and know how to solve every problem but only see the Chinese offended when they try to impose their point of view on the locals. To bring the Chinese on your side, you should recognise that when the Chinese have a different view on a particular issue, you and the Chinese can both be right because both sides have been conditioned to interpret events differently and are speaking from different frames of reference. Forcing the Chinese to accept your idea or decision by completely rejecting the Chinese viewpoint almost always reduces your goodwill with them and also makes the execution of the decision difficult.

In developing the above new joint venture in Southern China, I was once charged by BC with the task of negotiating and agreeing with the Chinese party on the valuation of the items in the engineering store that had been contributed by the latter. Having done all the hard work over a period of time, including checking through the accounts and the actual items together with the relevant Chinese personnel, I got to the stage of discussing and agreeing with the Chinese boss on the final valuation figure. But the Chinese boss asked me first to see the Chinese financial manager and hear his viewpoint. Given that I had to catch a plane to return to Hong Kong that afternoon, I got a bit impatient with this. I went to see the Chinese financial manager but only showed him the summary report. He said, "OK". I then returned to the Chinese boss's office. After he talked to the Chinese financial manager on the phone, the latter came in with a very angry face. He said I cheated him by not asking his full viewpoint. I said that I showed him the report and he replied "OK". He said that his "OK" only meant that he had seen the report. Eventually, the Chinese boss and I reached an agreement on the valuation, but this was achieved two weeks after I repaired the careless damage to my relationship with the Chinese financial manager.

Fundamentally, all people see the world not as it is, but as they are. In China, cultural differences, local conditions, social position, work experience, education and training, family background and self-interest are all reasons why local people view things so differently. Yet, it is the very differences that make a relationship valuable because they add to your knowledge, to your understanding of reality. You will be truly effective if you have the humility and reverence to recognise your own perceptual limitations, to appreciate the rich resources available through interaction with the hearts and minds of local people, and to actively involve local staff in decision making. When you are left with your own past experiences, you constantly suffer from a shortage of data or even have little reality to work with.

Listening with Empathy

One of the most fundamental, most commonly practised human rights in the West is the right to express oneself, with "speaking one's mind" being a frequently used expression. No wonder one of the most common observations that the Chinese have had, about Westerners in general but Americans in particular, is that "they like speaking but not listening". Yet it is listening that gives you the essential information to work with and makes it possible for you to lead the locals.

At the above joint venture, having learnt the lesson, I became ever conscious of the need to fully listen to the Chinese financial manager in my subsequent dealings with him. For example, when I was charged with the task of overseeing the process of obtaining the land use right transfer certificate from the land bureau of the local government, I gave him plenty of time and space to express his viewpoint at every twist and turn. Before meeting various local governmental officials, I listened carefully to his description of their background and characteristics and his introduction to local politics because he had dealt with these officials for years when he was the financial manager of the former state enterprise. As a result, I was able to conduct more engaging conversations with these officials over dinners, which greatly helped speed up their approval and issuance of the certificate.

When we listen to someone from our own culture, it is usually sufficient to concentrate on the words that are being said because we share a similar frame of reference and hold a largely common set of assumptions about things. However, when you as a Western executive listen to a Chinese person, you have to practice listening with empathy because the Chinese person is almost certainly speaking from a very different frame of reference. "Empathy" means the power of understanding, imaginatively entering into, another's feelings. Listening with empathy is not that you agree with the Chinese; it is that you fully, deeply, understand them, intellectually and emotionally.

Also at the above joint venture, an expatriate engineer once asked me for help, complaining that "The Chinese are irrational." He was having a meeting with designers from a design institute in Guangzhou on the design of an administration building. He burst into laughter when he saw that the Chinese had designed each of the four offices for senior managers like a standard hotel room with a bathtub and other toilet facilities. But the local partner insisted the design was good. I had a look at the drawing and carefully listened to each side's point of view. I then explained to the expatriate engineer that, as a tradition, the Chinese layout was meant to signify the status of special people, and to the Chinese that the expatriate engineer was primarily concerned with the functional integration and flow of people and information in the building. Gradually, each side began to see the world the way the other side saw the world. Finally, we worked together and found a synergetic design.

Searching for Synergetic Solutions

A synergetic solution is one that is better than all the solutions originally proposed, about which all the parties feel good. It is based on creative co-operation as well as on valuing the differences – to respect them, to build on strengths, to compensate for weaknesses. Although the process of debating and finding synergy on major decisions takes time, it always works, and it saves you time in the long run because the decision gets implemented with everybody's support. To find a synergetic solution, you need to have a high tolerance for ambiguity and get your security from integrity to principles and inner values, and to open your mind and heart and expressions to new possibilities, new alternatives, and new options. Dr Martin Posth at Volkswagen Asia-Pacific says, "You have to teach your partner and win his support. In a board meeting, if my German managers come up with an idea and I ask, 'Where is the signature of your Chinese partner' and they say 'Pshaw', then I refuse them. We taught our German fellows that you have to sit down together, even if it takes two weeks."

Due to its inherently complementary nature, a Sino-Western joint venture actually presents significant opportunities to observe synergy and to practice it, with the challenge being to have the confidence and capacity to do it. Consider plant construction for example. Truly successful construction should not be to achieve total control by using as much foreign management and materials as possible but to maximise the use of local materials and contractors whilst maintaining international standards of management and quality. This is exactly what US-based pharmaceutical firm Lederle has managed to achieve. While rivals have brought in foreign architects, engineers and construction managers in what are almost turnkey projects, Lederle set out to use local, low-cost resources. The company chose to extract maximum value from its investment, which is at US$12.5 while rivals have laid down multiples of that amount, by using a Shanghai design institute and local construction management where possible. Synergy can also be an effective tool for dealing with bureaucracy. At an express freight joint venture, when the local partner made no headway at the local government, they asked a foreign executive to go with them. They asked him to sit there looking angry while they did the talking. They quickly got what they wanted.

There are of course circumstances in which synergy may not be achievable. If a synergetic solution cannot be found, then it can be worth resorting to compromise, which means give-and-take or 1 + 1 equals 1.5. To compromise is to allow diversity on non-crucial issues instead of giving up critical principles. In reality, unless the underlying issue is of a strictly scientific nature, such as that directly concerning product quality, there is almost always room for some sort of compromise. Of course, compromise is not an optimum solution and can involve risk, but by compromising, you give local staff a chance to take a measured risk and to learn from potential lessons.

Leading by Setting People an Example

The Analects (Chapter 13:1) tells us:

> Zi Lu asked Confucius about the art of government. Confucius said, 'Lead the people by your example; show them that you are hard-working, and the people will work hard without complaint.' 'Anything else?' asked Zi Lu. 'In your efforts to do this, be not weary.'

A popular Chinese saying states: "If the upper beam is not straight, the lower one will go aslant." While the Chinese do not like following rules, they do like closely observing what their leaders do and copy, at least to some extent, their actions and behaviour. Another saying goes: "The actions of the leaders are like the wind, whereas those of employees are like grass; when the wind blows, the grass bends in the same direction." Of course, given the cultural barriers, there are circumstances where it can be difficult to lead by example. For instance, it can be difficult to preach the importance of expense control on your business trips with the locals if you stay at five-star international hotels while the locals stay at much cheaper local hotels. Under such circumstances, you'd better let the locals know that your parent company instead of the joint venture covers your costs. To lead by example, you need three abilities: (1) to see Chinese incompetence as a leadership opportunity; (2) to take a hands-on approach; and (3) to show personal integrity.

Seeing Chinese Incompetence as a Leadership Opportunity

All too often, Westerners only see Chinese incompetence in accomplishing business tasks as a source of irritation, a stumbling block, and wish it would somehow go away. Yet, the very problems create the opportunities to build deep trust that helps you lead the Chinese. Indeed, as soon as you see Chinese incompetence as a leadership opportunity, you will become excited about deeply understanding and helping local people. For example, when a local employee comes to you with a problem, instead of thinking, "Oh, no! Not another headache!" you can think, "Here is a great opportunity for me to really help the Chinese and to make an investment in our relationship." And through offering that helping hand, you are creating strong bonds of trust as the Chinese sense the attention you give to them as well as to their problems.

Taking a Hands-on Approach

To lead by example, you also need to take a hands-on approach. Although this approach requires little emotional attachment to the locals and can be applied quite readily by Western executives, it does require you to get your hands dirty. At Swissotel in Beijing, the German general manager was so fed up with asking staff to paint a door and finding nothing happened that he ordered a tin of paint and a brush with the intention of doing the job himself. He did not have to do it himself because the local staff were then so embarrassed that they immediately started doing it. One of the most vivid accounts on leading by example is given by Jim Mann in *Beijing Jeep* (1997). At Beijing Jeep, when Americans needed a large open space to be cleared in the factory's original body shop but the two different Chinese departments concerned were at loggerheads, they took the initiative to do the work, on their own, at night, and consequently led the Chinese to join their activities.

Showing Personal Integrity

The word *integrity* (from the Latin, *integritas*) literally means wholeness. Personal integrity means an integrated character, a oneness, primarily with self but also with life. Showing personal integrity is making one's actions conform with one's words, i.e. the seizing of responsibility and the willing acceptance of the accountability that comes with it.

Indeed, your character sets the moral tone of leadership. The standards you set become the benchmark for the others; the people you favour become your flag-bearers. You show your integrity by being polite and discreet in your relationships with peers, by being diligent and respectful in serving your employer, by being considerate and fair in managing your subordinates. You show your personal integrity by not second-guessing decisions that have already been made, by not undermining actions already begun, by not assigning blame for errors already made. When faced with difficulties, you show your integrity by being calm and confident, by not sparing yourself at the expense of others, by focusing on doing the best thing in the present moment. You also show your integrity by refraining from doing those things you yourself have prohibited, especially when you are alone, by being loyal to those who are not present. Ultimately, it is the personal power that radiates from your integrity that makes you a leader.

Managing Yourself in China: Inspiration from Ancient Chinese Wisdom

According to Confucius in *The Great Learning*:

The ancients who desired to manifest and shine forth their virtue throughout the empire would first try to govern their own states well. If they want to govern their own states well, they would first try to regulate their own families. If they want to regulate their own families, they would first try to cultivate and discipline themselves. If they want to cultivate and discipline themselves, they would first try to rectify their own hearts. If they want to rectify their own hearts, they would first try to make their thoughts and intentions sincere. If they want to make their thoughts and intentions sincere, they would first try to perfect their knowledge. If they want to perfect their knowledge, they would first try to investigate the nature of all things.

Indeed, to lead others, you first have to be able to manage yourself. Below I present three self-management principles supported by selected gems of ancient Chinese wisdom, which have worked for centuries even under the worst possible conditions and should therefore provide inspiration for you when you feel troubled in the highly challenging China business environment. They are:

- Unlearning, learning and relearning;
- Cultivating a balanced character; and
- Embracing uncertainty.

It is important to note that, according to Chinese philosophy, reality can never be truly described in words because of the limitations imposed by language and man. A piece of Chinese wisdom *per se* therefore does not represent a specific solution to any specific problem. Instead, it is best understood as a catalyst for the mind of the reader, triggering insights into the nature of reality. As such, you will learn most effectively as you read the following passages if you participate in creating meaning in them by conducting thought experiments or mental exercises and, as a consequence, find your own solution to your own problem.

Unlearning, Learning and Relearning

According to an expatriate executive in a hotel management chain:

> If you want to cross any culture, it is best to forget about yourself and be open-minded. If your head is already full of ideals, values and principles, then you are full of yourself, leaving no space for others. When you go some place, you'd better leave your luggage behind and be empty in a positive way. You must be available and not full of opinions.

While learning is the essential fuel for any leader, the significance of learning in the China business environment increases exponentially. "In a year in China, you can learn more about international business, about leading people and about managing yourself than in a decade anywhere else," reflected an expatriate. To most Westerners, China is a completely different world. Without an insatiable desire to learn, you easily miss critical information, key people and important relationships that are essential to your business success in China. You also need to actively seek out those unfamiliar areas of knowledge and skills, an ignorance of which can lead to disaster.

To learn effectively, you first of all need to unlearn. This requires suspending your prior beliefs, dropping your expectations, discarding your pre-conceived ideas and abandoning any method of knowing that might limit your horizons in order to clear the way for new information, new possibilities and new paradigms.

Ancient Chinese wisdom teaches us that language and words are merely symbols with which to express truth, and that the insight of others is always theirs and can never be made yours unless you can have your own perception. Therefore, instead of staying as long as possible in a hotel room, you should immerse yourself in the local culture by walking the streets, venturing out into markets, stores and museums, and reading local papers so as to learn the feel of the very texture of the new place. You should pose penetrating questions to people about their culture and history, and consider others' tough questions as starting points for dialogue and understanding, rather than for argument and persuasion. You need to observe, deliberate, and ponder so as to develop a sophisticated understanding of the way things are in China.

Once learnt, your new knowledge needs to be relearned through your own practice because if knowledge goes beyond worldly matters and runs deep into the self, wisdom will grow. British philosopher A. N. Whitehead has said: "In a sense, knowledge shrinks as wisdom grows: for details are swallowed up in principles. The details of knowledge which are important will be picked up ad hoc in each avocation of life, but the habit of the utilisation of well-understood principles is the final possession of wisdom."

To love to learn is to approach wisdom. To work hard at doing what is good is to approach human-heartedness. To know shame is to approach fearlessness. He who knows these three things knows how to cultivate himself. He who knows how to cultivate himself knows how to rule men. He who knows how to rule men knows how to govern an empire.

CONFUCIUS, *THE DOCTRINE OF THE MEAN*, CHAPTER 20

To love human-heartedness without loving learning may lead to ignorance. To love cleverness without loving learning may lead to misconduct. To love honesty without loving learning may lead to harm. To love uprightness without loving learning may lead to rashness. To love courage without loving learning may lead to misfortunes. To love mightiness without loving learning may lead to brashness.

CONFUCIUS, *THE ANALECTS*, 17:8

Without expectation, one will always perceive the beautiful whole; and with expectation, one will always perceive artificial boundaries.

LAO TZU, *TAO TE CHING*, PASSAGE 1

The superior man is impartial and is not biased, whereas the petty man is prejudiced.

CONFUCIUS, *THE ANALECTS*, 2:14

Perfecting knowledge consists in scrutinising the nature of all the things we come into contact with and investigating their cause and principle. For the mind of man is certainly formed to know and all things under Heaven are not without cause or principle.

CONFUCIUS, *THE GREAT LEARNING*, COMMENTARY 5

Reading and studying without thinking is futile labour; and thinking without reading and studying is perilous.

CONFUCIUS, *THE ANALECTS*, 2:15

When I'm walking in the company of two other men, there is always something I can learn from them. Their strengths I pick up. Their weaknesses I use for self-correction.

CONFUCIUS, *THE ANALECTS*, 7:19

"Men who possess virtue and wisdom are often those who have been through sickness or troubles. (. . .) Through this type of experience, they acquire understanding and insight into human relationships.

MENCIUS, *MENCIUS*, THE CHAPTER ON JIN XIN

To pursue the academic, add to it daily. To pursue the Tao, subtract from it daily. Subtract and subtract again, to arrive at non-action. Through non-action nothing is left undone.

LAO TZU, *TAO TE CHING*, PASSAGE 48

Cultivating a Balanced Character

According to Warren Buffett, the "world's greatest investor":

When looking for managers, I basically look for three things: integrity, intelligence, and energy. The problem is that if they don't have the first, the other two will kill you because if they don't have integrity, you really want them to be dumb and lazy. It is only if they have the first that the second two really count.

Through unlearning, learning and relearning, you acquire new knowledge and develop wisdom about how to operate in China. But to manage yourself, you also need to cultivate other qualities. Apart from wisdom, Sun Tzu prescribed sincerity, human-heartedness, courage and strictness as the key qualities of a military commander, which are equally applicable to today's business leader. Indeed, you need to be sincere toward your subordinates and business partners so as to gain their trust. You need to have love for mankind so as to sympathise with others. You need to be brave and decisive so as to engender others' confidence in you. Finally, you need to be self-disciplined so as to command the respect of others. Sun Tzu also highlighted five character flaws that should be avoided, i.e. recklessness, cowardice, quick temper, sensitivity to honour, and over-compassion to people. As a result, central to character is the cultivation of a balanced set of qualities. If you take one or two qualities to an extreme or are too weak in one or two areas, you will find yourself significantly ineffective or even handicapped under certain circumstances.

To cultivate yourself, you need to know yourself, limit your desires, and rectify your heart. "History is a mirror." One of the best ways to know yourself is to reflect on your experience, i.e. to look back with honesty. Reflecting leads to understanding. Nothing is truly yours until you understand it – not even yourself. When desires are under control, internal growth begins. You need to be free of the desire for superfluous possessions, free of the desire for praise or the fear of blame. Those who have strong uncontrolled desires have limited possibilities in life, while those who are attached to little experience all. You also need to be candid, open and integrated in your environment, and serve as a conduit, not an accumulator of goods, services and information. In this way, you are ever replenished with the new and vital as you continue to grow inner strength. To rectify your heart is to use your inner strength to rise above the excesses of emotions in your response to things and circumstances rather than to allow yourself to be ensnared by them. If you are filled with anger, terror, joy, worry or grief, you will not be able to function effectively.

A virtuous man is never lonely.

CONFUCIUS, THE ANALECTS, 6:25

The heart of a superior man is calm and serene, whereas the heart of a petty man is fretful and ill at ease.

CONFUCIUS, *THE ANALECTS*, 7:36

The superior man's action is consistent with his situation in life. He does not desire to go beyond this. (. . .) We may compare the superior man to an archer. When the archer fails to hit the target, he blames himself for being unskilled.

CONFUCIUS, *THE DOCTRINE OF THE MEAN*, CHAPTER 14

Those who know others are intelligent; those who know themselves have insight. Those who master others are powerful; those who master themselves have strength. Those who know what is enough are wealthy. Those who persevere have will power. Those who do not lose their root endure.

LAO TZU, *TAO TE CHING*, PASSAGE 33

Superior men avoid extremes, extravagance and excess.

LAO TZU, *TAO TE CHING*, PASSAGE 29

Superior men put themselves last and yet they are first; they put themselves outside and yet they remain. Is it not because they are without self-interest that their interests succeed?

LAO TZU, *TAO TE CHING*, PASSAGE 7

The wise is never confused; the human-hearted is never worried; the courageous is never afraid.

CONFUCIUS, *THE ANALECTS*, 9:29

Artful words may confound moral virtues. Lack of patience in small matters may confound great strategy.

CONFUCIUS, *THE ANALECTS*, 15:26

Sincerity is the beginning and the end of all things. Without sincerity, there would be nothing.

CONFUCIUS, *THE DOCTRINE OF THE MEAN*, CHAPTER 25

Fan Ci asked Confucius: 'Master, how can one live a moral life?' Confucius replied: 'Be humble in daily living, be serious in business, and be sincere in relationships. Even when you live among foreigners, you cannot abandon these principles.'

CONFUCIUS, *THE ANALECTS*, 13:19

Embracing Uncertainty

According to Irene Wolinski of General Motors in Beijing, as quoted by Stephanie Jones in *Managing in China*:

> I used to have firm goals for every project completion, for every plan I was working on, as I did in the USA. But it just didn't work here. I just got more and more frustrated and felt under more and more pressure, but I couldn't do anything. So I gave up having such fixed objectives. I still make goals, but I tend to keep things much more fluid. It's impossible to know what will happen from one day to the next, and you have to keep yourself open for new possibilities.

When you arrive in China, the odds are that everything can go wrong. Indeed, the China business environment is full of "the strange, the bizarre and the weird", and above all of tremendous uncertainties. Having got used to operating in a more predictable business environment in the West, you can easily get frustrated due to the lack of control in the face of these uncertainties. To effectively manage yourself in China, you therefore need the ability to embrace uncertainty, i.e. to learn to live with uncertainty and to employ "subtle powers", as advocated by Lao Tzu whose wisdom is perhaps the world's most profound.

To live with uncertainty, you need to expand your mindset from a linear, analytical, structured orientation to one that also has a broad, intuitive, fluid orientation, and to give up the compulsion to control. First, reality is like "muddy water" – you should harmonise with its subtle unity and intuitive impressions because seeking to arrive at complete clarity is an invitation for trouble. You should drop inflexible expectations about the results you can achieve by specific dates, and about your lifestyle or anything in China, and instead, take each day as it comes and focus on creating and directing the flow of events. Second, your environment is not made for you to control. It is simply an illusion that you can find all the answers and be in control. The truth of the matter is that often when you give up control, the answers will find you. To stabilise your position within the flow of people and events, you should dispense what you have so that more might flow through your hands.

Although you cannot control the uncertain world, you can achieve your goals through the use of "subtle powers". Just as large ships are steered with small rudders, the subtlest effort can yield the most effective result – a result that will not bring along a new set of problems. When influencing an ongoing process, it is most effective that you direct your energy toward its weakest and most receptive areas, such as the origins of events. As you are subtle and your actions are appropriately restrained and do not interfere with the natural cycle of events, you avoid counter-reactions and achieve your goals with least effort.

Keep your mind alert and free without abiding in anything or anywhere.

HONG-REN, THE FIFTH PATRIARCH OF THE CH'AN BUDDHISM

A man who does not think far ahead in whatever he does is sure to be troubled by worries much closer at hand.

CONFUCIUS, *THE ANALECTS*, 15:11

Who can harmonise with muddy water, and gradually arrive at clarity? Who can move with stability, and gradually bring endurance to life? Those, who can, do not desire to become perfect. Indeed, since they are not perfect, they can be changed and renewed.

LAO TZU, *TAO TE CHING*, PASSAGE 15

Those who would take hold of the world and act on it, never, I notice, succeed. The world is a mysterious instrument, not made to handle. Those who act on it, spoil it. Those who seize it, lose it.

LAO TZU, *TAO TE CHING*, PASSAGE 29

The only thing people know about the best leaders is that they do exist; the next best are loved and honoured; the next are feared; and the next are ridiculed. Those who lack belief will not in turn be believed. But when the best lead from afar and the work is done, the goal achieved, people say, 'We did it ourselves.'

LAO TZU, *TAO TE CHING*, PASSAGE 17

Produce but do not possess. Act without expectation. Advance without dominating. These are called the subtle powers.

LAO TZU, *TAO TE CHING*, PASSAGE 51

You might force people to act according to a certain principle, but you won't be able to force them to understand it.

CONFUCIUS, *THE ANALECTS*, 8:9

What is at rest is easy to hold. What is not yet begun is easy to plan. What is brittle is easy to shatter. What is small is easy to disperse. Deal with things before they emerge. Put them in order before there is disorder. A tree of many arm spans grows from a tiny shoot. A tower of nine stories is raised from a pile of earth. A journey of a thousand miles begins by taking the first step.

LAO TZU, *TAO TE CHING*, PASSAGE 64

Governing a large country is like cooking a small fish.

LAO TZU, *TAO TE CHING*, PASSAGE 60

8

BALANCING MANAGING AND LEADING

When the State is in order, ministers are the key; when the State is in crisis, generals are the key.

DECREE COLLECTION OF TANG DAZHAO, VOL. 25, TANG DYNASTY OF
CHINA (618–907)

You can manage inventory, you can manage things, but you must lead people if you want to tap their full potential.

H. ROSS PEROT, AMERICAN FOLK HERO OF BUSINESS

WHEN WESTERN EXECUTIVES equipped with modern management techniques have come to operate businesses in China, the single biggest resistance from local partners and employees has been the claim that these techniques are not applicable to China. In this chapter, I demonstrate that management techniques developed in the West are actually essential to long-term business success in China but their effective application needs to be balanced by the exercise of leadership skills. Indeed, the ultimate key to successfully operating a Sino-Western joint venture lies in balancing managing and leading.

The Myth of Western Management Techniques' Inapplicability to China

Given the inherent conflict between rules-based management techniques and the connection orientation of the Chinese, the process of applying modern Western management techniques in China is arguably the most difficult in the world. But this does not mean that China does not need them or that they are inapplicable to China. In any case, the issue is when rather than whether or not these techniques should be introduced and applied to businesses in China.

China's Desperate Need for Management

Today's Western management methods have evolved since the industrial revolution in the 18th century. As the centuries went by and modern science and technology remade the Western world, China was wracked by internal discontent and strife with its economy predominantly based on family-farmer agriculture. From 1949 to 1979, during the period in which management developed into a science in the capitalist West, China was a centralised economy, in which only administrators were needed to allocate resources. As such, it was not until 1979 that China finally broke with the past and took the first bold steps toward creating a market economy where management is a necessity. Yet, despite the call of China's late supreme leader Deng Xiaoping in 1979 that "we should introduce not only advanced foreign technology from abroad but also advanced foreign management methods," the process for the Chinese to embrace Western management has not been easy.

One of the most outstanding examples demonstrating China's poor management capability at the outset of the opening-up was the US$5 billion Baoshan Iron & Steel Works, which China began constructing in December 1978. It soon turned out that in the rush to modernise, China had not even done the feasibility study and the financial planning that such a project required. This led China in 1980 to suspend its plan for the second phase of the mill and cancel contracts that had already been signed with foreign companies. Two decades later, frequent reports of major financial scandals and collapsed civil structures still overshadow China's ability to manage large projects. By the end of 1998, the inspection authority had discovered ninety-five embezzlement cases related to the Three Gorges Dam project. In January 1999, a three-year old bridge in Chongqing collapsed causing forty deaths because an official had offered the project to an unqualified contractor after accepting bribery of RMB130,000. Half a year later, a one-month-old bridge in Gansu province collapsed causing fourteen deaths because an engineer with only a primary school education had designed it.

The biggest managerial headache though has been with some 100,000 existing state-owned industrial enterprises, which all suffer the "three no difference" syndrome – it makes no difference whether one works more or less, no difference whether work is done well or poorly, and no difference whether one works or not at all. But at the heart of the problem have been unaccountable management and nepotism. Following various reform measures over a period of two decades, over half of the state-owned industrial enterprises are still operating in the red or have negative net assets, according to official reports. Although flexible and responsive, most of the newly established collective and private businesses are tiny, with most entrepreneurs having little idea as to how to establish a modern management system to keep things in order when their businesses grow to a certain size. As a result, many succeed quickly and then get into trouble quickly, and are largely responsible for much of the 50% "substandard" of all Chinese output reported by the official *People's Daily* on 21 January 1998.

Managerial frustration at foreign-invested businesses is abundant throughout China. John Marshall, who has had twenty years of experience in spearheading 3M's efforts in China, best summarises it:

> Even Thailand, Malaysia and Indonesia have economic systems in place that, in varying degrees, are akin to those in the West. Their private sectors understand profit motives, balance sheets, unit costs, quality control, how to develop export markets, advertising, market-

ing, promotion, customer trust and all those things that are second nature to us. None of these apply universally to China; only some are now slowly developing in the more advanced regions.

Recognising China's desperate need for management, Chinese Premier Zhu Rongji wrote in 1997:

> With respect to modern business management, the West is of course leading. Without modern finance, cost and quality control, and scientific decision-making, an enterprise cannot operate in a market economy. We need to emphasise that management science and management education is the fundamental way to prosper China. I suggest that we should bring about an upsurge in learning management and strengthening management training.

Western Management Techniques Applied to Businesses in China

Not only does China desperately need Western management techniques, but these can also be successfully applied to businesses in China. A few Chinese businesses of international competitiveness, such as the Qingdao-based conglomerate Haier Group, can attribute much of their success to the application of management techniques to the functions of operation, finance, personnel, and marketing.

Operations Management

One of the first things that successful Sino-Western manufacturing joint ventures do is to use philosophies, tools and techniques of quality management to improve product quality and production efficiency. After nearly six years of endeavour, Boqing, a British Sugar's joint venture in Guangxi province, was credited ISO 9000 status in 2000 with its operating techniques largely transferred from Britain. A few manufacturing joint ventures in the automotive industry have successfully applied JIT philosophy and its associated practices to improve production planning and control. For example, GM Shanghai has applied manufacturing techniques learned at their plant in Eisenbach, Germany. The Eisenbach plant, operated by GM's European division, Opel, learned its manufacturing techniques from NUMMi, a GM-Toyota joint venture in Fremont, California, which was set up in 1984 to help GM learn Toyota's lean manufacturing techniques.

The application of basic service management concepts and techniques, such as service package, layout and queue system design, and capacity management, by multinationals like McDonald's in China has been as successful as in the rest of the world. Since entering China in 1990, McDonald's has achieved impressive results based largely on the same QSC&V (i.e. quality, service, cleanliness and value) service concept. The trademark uniformity of McDonald's more than 300 outlets in China – down to the floor tiles, the hand dryer and the French fries – has been striking. McDonald's highly efficient service and management, spotless dining environment and fresh ingredients have featured repeatedly in the Chinese media as exemplars of modernity.

Given the prevalence of fake and inferior goods and kickbacks in China, purchase management is of particular importance. The general manager of a European mail order business in China commented: "If you have a clean purchasing function and an independent quality control function, then you much reduce the offering of kickbacks from suppliers. Three quotations must be received before any supplier is chosen for an item over a certain amount. You should always keep the accounting person separate from the person who authorises payments. Cash transactions should be minimised by using a bank transfer system. You must have checks to make sure that nothing deviates from the standard procedure. Doing so actually protects people and enables the company to trust them to do jobs on their own."

Haier's success also originated from the implementation of strict operational control procedures at the former Qingdao Refrigerator Factory. After Zhang Ruimin became its director in 1985, he observed that the ratio of output over input was too low because of the lack of detailed control of processes. To improve the ratio, he initiated strict management by establishing the "13 Rules" – one rule being that "urinating on the factory floor is prohibited". In Haier's exhibition room, there is a big hammer Zhang used to smash seventy-six refrigerators with defects in the first month of his appointment. He has since then changed the conventional rule that products could be classified into different grades to one that only a grade-1 product was acceptable. On the refrigerator line, all the 156 process stages and the 545 responsibility areas are designated to specific employees. Even the 1,964 pieces of window glass in the refrigerator warehouse have dedicated cleaners and independent inspectors to check their cleanliness.

Financial Management

On 1 July 1993, sweeping change began with the government's promulgation of *Financial Rules for Enterprises and Accounting Standards for Enterprises*, which signified the beginning of the end of government accounting in China and the migration of Chinese accounting standards towards international standards. According to Coopers & Lybrand, the international accountancy firm, there are now few material differences between Chinese accounting regulations and international standards although the former is not as broad as the latter yet. Therefore, it is up to the Western investor to ensure that financial management tools, such as financial reporting and management accounting systems, are well used. Of particular importance in the connections-based China business environment are financial control procedures. The general manager of a subsidiary of a diversified American technology and manufacturing conglomerate commented: "At my joint venture in interior China, overheads threaten to consume all capital resources before they can be used for reinvestment. Keeping overheads, including wage bills, non-wage obligations that can be as high as 50% of wages, 'consulting fees', electricity and water supply assessments, and all sorts of other expenses, down is thus the number one challenge to productivity."

The "Hangang model" below demonstrates both the seriousness of financial management problems at Chinese businesses and the huge benefits that can be realised through the application of basic financial management techniques like budgetary planning and control. In 1990, the Handan Iron and Steel Works (*Hangang*) in Hebei province was on the brink of bankruptcy. Director Liu Hanzhang saw high costs as the problem and pioneered the Hangang system to bring costs under control. At the apex of the Hangang system was the accounts department that ensured that budget discipline was imposed throughout the business. By checking market prices for its steel products, the accounts department determined budgets for every stage of the business process, from the raw materials yard, the six blast furnaces, the rolling mills, through to storage and delivery. It then passed budgets down to sections, sub-sections and the 28,000 individuals, and then rewarded them for budget savings and penalised them for budget overspend, with 40% of cost savings passed on to, and 20% of cost overruns deducted from, the company's bonus pool. In 1996, the company posted a pre-tax profit of RMB700 million (US$84 million), which amounted to 14% of the revenue, a fine performance by any company's standards, and was confirmed as a "national model" of state enterprise management at a conference presided over by deputy premier Wu Bangguo.

At Haier, it is strict budgetary planning and control that provides the necessary robustness to the business. To ensure that what everybody does contributes to the achievement of overall business objectives, these objectives are broken down into departmental objectives, which are further broken down into specific objectives for each employee at the planning stage. To ensure the attainment of these specific objectives, Haier has developed the "daily control and clearing mechanism" by which everything on a day must be resolved or a responsibility fixed. If objectives are met consistently for a certain period of time, higher ones will be set. To support the implementation of the above planning and control mechanisms, the company has also developed a motivation mechanism that links contributions directly with rewards.

Personnel Management

According to a recent survey of local managers, Western personnel management practices are generally regarded as effective in attracting highly qualified people and motivating employees. The effectiveness is attributed to their systematic methods in performance appraisal, performance-related pay and promotion, and an emphasis on the long-term development of an employee's career. Many like to use terms such as "scientific", "fair", and "objective" to label Western methods. Of course, difficulties do arise in implementing these practices in some situations. For example, while employees in coastal cities, such as Shanghai or Guangzhou, are receptive to individually based pay, people in northern or central China may still be in favour of collectively based pay. In any case, the issue is when rather than whether or not these modern personnel management practices are introduced to businesses in China, as noted by an expatriate human resource manager: "All these aspects are very new in China. You have to be patient, that's for sure, because it will take a lot of time to implement them successfully."

Central to personnel management is recruitment. Existing employees of a local partner can provide the venture with a quick way to start. Due to an established home base, they are generally more loyal, but they also bring the old organisational culture to the joint venture. While recruitments from external sources, such as labour markets, personal contacts and head-hunters, enable the business to select the best candidates and create a new and better organisational culture, these employees can lack loyalty. Increasingly, multinationals like Motorola, IBM and GE are finding ways, such as establishing scholarships, to recruit top graduates from local universities who are often ambitious, open to Western-style thinking, and prefer to work in joint ventures both for prestige and for fatter pay. Proper recruitment has to be backed by other personnel practices. One American joint venture has developed monthly appraisal of service operators by supervisor in terms of job quality, service attitude, labour discipline, and job efficiency. Another has focused on the introduction of reward systems to develop employee loyalty to the business itself instead of the foreign partner or the local Chinese partner.

At Haier, it is personnel management centring on finding, using and rewarding talents that gives vitality to the business. The company has established a "horse racing court", where it regularly announces job vacancies and encourages people to apply, and as a result many talents have come out of the crowd with the average age of managers at Haier being only twenty-six. Haier believes that "running water is never stale." It has a managerial job rotation system where section managers can maximally stay on their job for two years and division managers for four years. When a manager's term expires and his performance is accepted, he will be moved to a different job at the same managerial level or be encouraged to compete for a more senior position, otherwise he has to step down. Haier has also developed the "co-existence and dynamic transformation of three grades" system, where workers are graded as "excellent", "accepted" or "probationary". If somebody cannot meet the work standards of a particular grade, they will be dropped to a lower one with poorer financial benefits, and vice versa.

Marketing Management

Successful Western companies in China, such as Procter & Gamble (P&G) and Pepsi, can attribute their success as much to their superior marketing capability based on the application of marketing management techniques, such as market research, STP (i.e. segmentation, targeting and positioning) and marketing mix tools, as to their quality products. At P&G, armies of researchers regularly hit neighbourhoods to find out exactly what consumers want. It then tries to develop product concepts that address consumer needs. These are then tested in focus groups and with questionnaires, refined, re-tested and refined again. Over the past decade, P&G have amassed a huge database, which is proving invaluable in defining strategy and brand decisions. The diverse nature of the China market also makes the application of STP hugely important. Pepsi-Cola itself is aimed at young adults, but Pepsi has introduced Fruit Magix purely for Chinese children, which is a still fruit drink that comes in Tetra-Packs and is consumed during break times at school.

To uncover conflicts between global product positioning and local consumer habits, multinationals have used concept testing. Oral B is sold throughout the world as the toothbrush dentists recommend most, but most Chinese people do not visit dentists; Kraft had to reposition its coffee after it became clear the "wake-up" message would not work since most Chinese who drink coffee drink it in the evenings. While McDonald's succeeded with a skimming pricing policy upon entering the China market and later by reducing its premium to support continued brand growth, Tambrands succeeded through an initial low pricing to attract consumers and introducing price increases after the market was opened up. To distribute its products nation-wide, Pepsi relied on building joint venture bottling plants in major cities throughout China as well as deliveries direct to retailers using both its own lorries and the railways, and sales to wholesalers.

Possibly as huge signs and posters have long been a part of the urban landscape, billboards remain an effective advertising medium for Pepsi and Coca-Cola. Mary Kay, on the other hand, has successfully relied on newspapers and magazines to advertise its mail order business. In the case of P&G, its nation-wide TV advertisements have to be supplemented by "road show" campaigns in the rural areas, consisting of demonstrations, consumers' own tests, sample packets, discount sales and prize draws, because rural consumers are straightforward and believe more in what they actually experience than TV advertisements.

Given the network nature of Chinese society, PR tools including lobbying, press relations, product publicity, and corporate communication all work well in China. For example, having developed very close relationships with the central Chinese government through highest-level lobbying activities, Siemens has achieved notable success in China. In the case of McDonald's, its restaurants actively participate in community affairs and have established special relationships with local schools and neighbourhood committees.

At Haier, it is the application of modern marketing techniques like STP that has ensured its marketing success. In 1988, Haier noticed that the same refrigerators that sold very well in Beijing were not well received in Shanghai. Following investigation, it found that very small refrigerators priced under RMB1000 were what Shanghai people wanted because most of them lived in very small apartments. Haier thus designed the "Little Prince" refrigerator, which enjoyed a 40% share of the total Shanghai market for refrigerators. In 1997, Haier very successfully launched ten clusters of refrigerators targeting consumers in ten different regions in China, based on a comprehensive study of their very different income levels and consumption needs and habits.

Balancing Managing and Leading
at a Sino-Western Joint Venture

That China desperately needs Western management techniques does not mean that the Chinese will readily embrace them. To be successful in applying them, Western executives need to balance their application with the exercise of leadership skills.

Western Executives' Preoccupation with Managerial Thinking

According to a French general manager at a Sino-French joint venture in China:

> Managing a joint venture in China is like dealing with a big locomotive train. Just imagine an old Chinese train, it has an engine and five cars. It chugs along the track at one speed. It cannot go faster, it just goes at that speed. So a foreign manager like me comes here and has a lot of energy, really wants to make the train go faster. So I get behind the train and push, and push, and push. Eventually you realise no matter how hard you push the train will not go any faster. So, you stop pushing and just jump on board and go along for the ride. You know that there is no point expending your energy!

The "push" or managerial mentality reflected in the above account is not accidental. In fact, many Western executives come to China with a managerial mentality initially developed in the rules-based, more predictable Western corporate world where, in parallel to China's desperate need for management since 1980, there has been a search for leadership. Publication of books on leadership has been a high growth industry in the West. In *A Force for Change* (1990), John Kotter, Harvard Business School professor, states that thousands of American companies are "over-managed" and "under-led" because too few executives, while managerially competent, have a clear understanding of what leadership is. In *The New Leaders* (1995), Paul Taffinder concludes that the Western business world has "neglected" the concept of leadership or "mistaken" management for leadership. In *Managing People Is like Herding Cats* (1997), Warren Bennis, the "Dean of Leadership Gurus", asserts that the American business community has been managed to "the edge of ruin" and that it is now in desperate need of leaders.

The reason that there is a lack of leadership thinking among executives is that they have typically been trained with a specialist or technical background. They concentrate on facts and figures and are not too concerned about the wider, longer-term implications. Many are simply driven by management fads, and do not have an adequate capability to place a particular management idea into the context of their business situation and develop an appreciation of its merits. They view an organisational change like a replacement part on a machine, having little understanding of its human implications. Too much attention is given to the use of historical data to forecast future trends, losing sight of key human-related drivers behind any developments. Inside an organisation, most managers only pay lip service to things like "people are our most important assets", with little genuine attention paid to the individual characteristics of employees.

In China, where an adequate managerial infrastructure is yet to emerge, like the French general manager, many Western executives have painstakingly continued their preoccupation with managerial thinking. As relationships take time and provide benefits that are difficult to quantify, executives who focus on short-term results see little value in establishing lasting relationships. Some are too proud to go through the relationship-building process, particularly when it comes to interactions with low-ranking employees in the venture. They show little interest in local people – in some cases, they actually "hate" them. They just seem eager to finish their assignment and go home. They see their job responsibilities as neatly defined and task achievement as a linear progression from A to Z. They become like the manager who is good with a hammer, who sees every problem as a nail. But the more hammering they do, the more problems there are; the harder they push, the stronger the resistance.

Achieving Five Balances between Management and Leadership at a Sino-Western Joint Venture

As the mere application of "push" or management techniques can be very difficult in China, Western executives need to achieve five balances between management and leadership that are key to the successful operation of a Sino-Western joint venture:

- Training local staff versus learning leadership skills
- Driving for business results versus nurturing partner relationships
- Maintaining business entity integrity versus obtaining governmental officials' support
- Meeting managerial requirements versus satisfying personal needs
- Achieving short-term profitability versus keeping long-term commitment

The Balance between Training Local Staff and Learning Leadership Skills

Given that most local employees do not have the necessary professional quality and that the Chinese are very different from Westerners, there is a fundamental need for both the Chinese and Westerners to learn at a Sino-Western joint venture. Local employees need to be trained to improve their professional personality and skills, while Western executives need to learn to lead the Chinese the Chinese way. Due to their strategic importance, the issues of training local staff and of leading the Chinese have been dealt with in depth in Chapters 6 and 7 respectively.

Through training local staff, management techniques can be more readily applied, and this not only makes life easier for you but also leads to improved organisational performance. Through learning and applying leadership skills, you can get the locals on your side and this helps get things done your way.

The Balance between Driving for Business Results and Nurturing Partner Relationships

Western executives come to China with a natural drive for business results. To deliver them, they set business objectives, plan business activities and push people to accomplish challenging business tasks. Yet, such a single-minded drive is unlikely to lead to the effective attainment of intended results simply because the Chinese may not be ready, both emotionally and intellectually, to follow their relentless drive. If you push too hard you will begin to damage your relationship with your partner, and without a good relationship, your partner may hinder rather than support your effort to deliver business results. Thus, you must have the twin goals of delivering business results and of nurturing partner relationships. One expatriate discovered: "The best way to deal with your Chinese partner is to be flexible, go along with them, give them face, let them take the lead, help them get what they want – as long as your profit is not adversely affected."

On the one hand, your Chinese partner has the potential to make or break you, so you need to be very careful about your relationship with them. It pays to work with your local partner and use them to help the business. You should demonstrate sensitivity and understanding so as to gain the trust and respect of your Chinese partner. In particular, you need to build a good relationship with the principal representative of your local partner. On the other hand, you should not make decisions based on personal relations to the exclusion of the interests of the business. From time to time, relationships have to be subordinated to business needs – for example, you cannot afford to always support excuses from the local partner when things do not happen.

The Balance between Maintaining Business Entity Integrity and Obtaining Government Officials' Support

In the West, the government has an obligation to support and serve a business but it is in no position to intervene in its operation. In China, the government has a far greater impact on business. It can deny approvals for proposed projects or withdraw licenses from existing ones; it has control over state-owned enterprises, which multinationals often have to choose as joint venture partners or inevitably as suppliers or customers. Although the central government is advocating the separation of politics from business, in reality, especially in regions other than major cities, businesses can never stay away from the direct and indirect intervention of all sorts of local government bodies. It is widely expected that this situation will continue possibly for generations to come, given China's cultural and political burdens.

Thus, in China, trying too hard to maintain the business entity integrity of your venture or expecting governmental bodies to provide professional services for you is equal to asking for frustration and disappointment. On the one hand, you need to minimise negative interventions of some local government officials, such as securing positions for friends, and manage fees and taxes that government agencies may individually create and promote. On the other hand, you have to work at obtaining the support of government officials because in matters like approvals and licenses, your relationship with them can mean the difference between success and failure. Besides, "through good relationships with regulatory officials, it is possible to influence the development of regulations as well as their interpretation, to the benefit of the business," advised a China consultant.

The Balance between Meeting Managerial Requirements and Satisfying Personal Needs

To meet the managerial requirements of a business, Western executives have to design an organisational structure, staff jobs with qualified individuals, and plan and control their activities. Without such managerial efforts, people's efforts will not pull in the same direction and their contributions will not fit together to produce a whole that satisfies customers. Yet to make such efforts work in China, they also need to pay attention to satisfying the personal needs of individual employees, suppliers and customers. Specifically, they need to achieve five sub-balances: (1) formal organisational structure versus informal human network; (2) meeting job requirements versus tapping into individual skills; (3) managerial control versus caring for people; (4) transactional purchase versus supplier relationship building; and (5) rational selling versus customer relationship building.

Balancing formal organisational structure and informal human network. A formal organisational structure pre-defines how people should work together in a business, whether it is a hierarchical structure concerning managerial responsibility and authority, a functional structure concerning separate specialist work or a horizontal structure concerning collective teamwork. It is necessary to keeping things running in an efficient and orderly manner. In China, as local employees want to feel a sense of personal dependence on each other, you need informal webs of influence as well as "solid" authority and rules to be effective. An informal human network may be likened to lubricant to a formal structure and is particularly important when introducing managerial change. You can build informal human networks through spending time with local employees and seeking out rich personal relationships. At a joint venture in Southern China, I once got a trade union leader involved when introducing financial control measures. The union leader had become a local "friend" of mine after my networking work, including regular consultations, and he helped ensure that the walls came tumbling down at a rallying dinner attended by all the relevant employees.

Balancing meeting job requirements and tapping into individual skills. In the West, executives are used to appointing competent people to professionally defined roles and then leaving them unsupervised for long periods. In China, the shortage of professionals means that it can be difficult to appoint local people to fit prototype professional roles. As what will usefully be done is what people can usefully do rather than what you think is needed, you need to pay particular attention to tapping into individual skills. A Shell executive observed: "Leadership is about getting people to focus on what they are good at, not destroying it. In China, we need to blend Chinese savvy with our processes." To tap into individual skills, you need to develop a thorough understanding of local individuals so as to define roles that fit their capabilities. Often, many of the roles you assume for professionals may need to be broken up into smaller ones. One Sino-American joint venture has succeeded to improve quality by breaking the process of quality down, and making it measurable and workers accountable. Of course, you also need to keep up with the development of their capabilities, and review and redefine their roles when necessary.

Balancing managerial control and caring for people. Managerial control is necessary to bringing people's behaviour in line with managerial needs. It focuses on monitoring people's activities and reprimanding people for any deviations. But for reprimand to be effective, trust has to be established between you and your employees in the first place through your caring efforts, as Sun Tzu says in *The Art of War*: "If the commander punishes his soldiers before they have trust in him and are attached to him, they will not be submissive and consequently it will be difficult to employ them. If discipline is not enforced after the soldiers have become attached to him, they will not be able to fight well. Therefore he should make the soldiers submissive with favour and keep them under control with discipline to ensure victory." You can use gift giving and social occasions to show yourself as a human being to them and your sense of personal commitment in giving your time, and that you care about them. But you need to make sure that they see you clearly, i.e. your caring for them is in the appropriate proportion to preserving discipline, so that they do not become "spoiled children".

Balancing transactional purchase and supplier relationship building. In the West, given the maturity of the business environment, it is usual for companies to frequently switch between suppliers based on transactional benefits. In China, people like to do business with those whom they trust and have developed goodwill with. As such, while you should warn your suppliers very clearly about the high standards they must meet, a commitment to a good and long-term supplier relationship and to the obligations arising from such a relationship can not only ensure quality and reliability but also help you to survive market changes. In the early 1990s, the cashmere supplier of a Beijing-based joint venture had funding problems. The joint venture, a producer of cashmere knitwear, decided to help. In the mid-1990s, when the market for cashmere knitwear heated up and the price of cashmere rocketed, the supplier helped the joint venture by supplying cashmere at below market price. The joint venture not only survived the price rise in cashmere but also captured the market that their competitors left.

Balancing rational selling and customer relationship building. In the West, you can identify customers' needs, priorities and objections, and make an initial sales presentation in a brief meeting with them because business rarely mixes with personal matters. But in China, it can take many visits to the customer to even get to the first stage of finding out their needs, and then, a number of banquets and social occasions to get the same results because people are used to mixing business and personal matters. "If you appear to be in a hurry, you are seen as insincere," advised a US marketing executive. Ericsson uses local staff to build the customer relationships it needs in China. In an interview with CNBC News, John Gilbertson, Ericsson's managing director for China, said: "The local staff are the ones with the relationships. They open doors for me. I just walk in behind them." Of course, local sales people tend to take customer relations too far. Managerial measures thus have to be set covering budgets for customer entertainment, record-keeping for all expenses and reporting of kickbacks, otherwise "your budget can go through the roof," warned an expatriate executive.

The Balance between Achieving Short-term Profitability and Keeping a Long-term Commitment

Western investors make investments in China in order to make money and, naturally, they want to make money as soon as possible. Typically, after a joint venture is formed, head office would set short-term profit targets for its executives on the ground and expect them to get some major things accomplished by a deadline. Too often, when profits take longer to materialise and the forecasts in the business plan are not met, head office tends to forget the peculiarities of the China operating environment and make too swift changes to its China management team. Or, more recently, to reduce costs in a dramatic way, some head offices have regarded "localisation" as the panacea and left important responsibilities to unreliable and incompetent local personnel. Or, in some cases, Western investors have reacted too quickly to relationship problems by pulling out from their China ventures.

Yet, it takes time for both Western executives and local staff to learn and for two very different cultures to work together. Shanghai Volkswagen, established in 1985, is currently one of the most successful Sino-Western joint ventures, which only repatriated profits for the first time in 1993. As such, to maintain the pace of the joint venture in the desired direction, it is absolutely essential to balance the desire to achieve short-term profitability and the need to keep a long-term commitment. You need a longer and wider horizon to give you the big picture and the confidence in investing in China, but you also need the short-term action orientation to tackle the immediate steps along the way and overcome current barriers and crisis. Too much focus on one, to the detriment of the other, inevitably leads to either a slowing down of progress or a preoccupation with inessentials.

Toward Management-Leadership Unity: The Ultimate Secret of Business Success

It is tempting to assume that the above balances are solutions to the problems of operating a Sino-Western joint venture. In reality, however, they are not. First, these balances never stay unchanged, and as circumstances change, they need to be adjusted. Next, new balances arise while others fade as business situations develop, and therefore these balances are not the entire story. As it is shown below, they are in fact part of the more fundamental balance for a business, i.e. the balance between management and leadership, which represent the two opposites of the same unity and cannot exist without each other. Thus, to be successful, each business must find and continually evolve the right set of balances between management and leadership for its own circumstances.

Management and Leadership Revisited

The Chinese word for management is made up of two characters, i.e. *guan li*, where *guan* means to bring things under control and *li* to put things in order. By contrast, the Chinese word for leadership is made up of two other characters, i.e. *ling dao*, where *ling* means to take somebody forward and *dao* to guide somebody. As can be seen literally from the Chinese wording for management and leadership, the focal point for management is things whereas the focal point for leadership is people. In *The Classic of Opposites* (or *Fan Jin* in Chinese), which has absorbed the wisdom of many earlier classics, author Zhao Zhuo of the Tang Dynasty (618–907) states:

> In *Ren Wu Zhi* by Li Shao, philosopher of the Three Kingdoms, it was said, 'The responsibility of a minister is to use one taste to co-ordinate with other tastes whereas the responsibility of a ruler is to use the tasteless to reconcile all the tastes. Being competent in doing a job is the capability of a minister whereas being good at using people is the capability of a ruler. Planning and talking is the capability of a minister whereas being good at listening to the people is the capability of a ruler. Practising what one preaches is the capability of a minister whereas properly rewarding and reprimanding people is the capability of a ruler. It is because the supreme ruler is not good at doing every job that he can lead talented people.' Thus, knowing people is the way of a ruler; knowing matters is the way of a minister.

Again, management, the capability of a minister, is in contrast with leadership, the capability of a ruler. Drawing on the ancient Chinese wisdom on governance and command, and the recent research results on leadership in the West, Table 8.1 shows the contrast between management and leadership. This list is by no means exhaustive. But from it, we can clearly see that management and leadership represent two opposite ways of thinking and acting.

TABLE 8.1

Management and Leadership Contrasted

	Management	Leadership
Theoretic foundation	*Science*. Management is founded on principles of a scientific nature, such as analysis, exactness, and factualness.	*Art*. Leadership is founded on principles of an artistic nature, such as expressiveness, imaginativeness, and intuitiveness.
Purpose	*Organisational results*. Management exists for the purpose of achieving organisational results, which are typically expressed in quantitative terms, such as profitability, sales revenue, and production output.	*Personal interests*. Leadership exists for the purpose of serving the interests of relevant constituents, including shareholders, employees, customers, suppliers, local communities, and government.
Focus	*Things*. Management focuses on things or business issues. It is primarily concerned with understanding and controlling the business logic.	*People*. Leadership focuses on people or human issues. It is primarily concerned with understanding and influencing human motives.
Activities	*Formal*. To achieve organisational results, management relies on a formalised system of activities, such as analysis, planning, implementation and control, in that sequence.	*Informal*. To serve personal interests, leadership relies on a variety of informal activities, such as investigation, networking, motivation, inspiration, coaching, persuasion, and negotiation.
Means	*Impersonal*. Management uses formulaic organisational rules, formal structures, quantitative techniques, and facts. It sees people as a set of skills that have to fit the organisation's requirements.	*Human*. Leadership relies on emotional human relationships, informal skills, qualitative approaches, and intuition. It sees people as having their own values, strengths and weaknesses.
Hallmark	*Stability*. Management seeks to legitimise the norm and to reinforce the routine in order to maintain stability.	*Change*. Leadership goes beyond the norm and challenges the status quo in order to bring about change.
Source of power	*Organisational*. Management derives its power from the superior-subordinate organisational relationship.	*Personal*. Leadership derives its power from the personal trust and goodwill earned from the followers.
Context	*Certain*. Management is called for by a context that is certain. It follows a course of familiarity and seeks to avoid any risks.	*Uncertain*. An uncertain context is the birthplace of leadership. It involves risk-making and risk-taking.
Way of thinking	*Logical*. Managerial thinking is largely logical thinking, which operates on a Yes/No progression of alternatives, seeking always the solution that is right. It is characterised by continuity.	*Lateral*. Leadership thinking is largely lateral thinking, which proceeds by provocative leaps in unlikely directions, seeking what can be used in an idea. It is characterised by discontinuity.
Attention	*Operational details*. Management involves studying and paying attention to operational details so as to improve operational performance.	*Strategic forces*. Leadership involves sensing and paying attention to strategic forces so as to master the situation as a whole.
Decision-making	*Analysis*. In management, decision-making is based on research and analysis, driven by models.	*Intuition*. In leadership, decision-making is based on judgement and intuition, driven by principles.
Attitude	*Straight*. Management is the unyielding battle for what is right. It is the removal of the many masks people wear to hide or deny their imperfections.	*Flexible*. Leadership is not black or white, but it is made of black and white. It is the flexibility of adapting to different and changing circumstances.
Capability	*IQ*. A high intelligence quotient (IQ) is required of a manager, emphasising knowledge and ability to think and reason.	*EQ*. A high emotional quotient (EQ) is required of a leader, emphasising experience and ability to feel and act.

Orienta- tion	*Inward.* To manage, you need to look inward and be "professional", i.e. work within the constraints predetermined by rules, regulations and procedures.	*Outward.* To lead, you need to look outward and be "entrepreneurial", i.e. take initiatives, break the rules, reach out and do the "impossible".
Develop- ment	*Training.* Management techniques can be taught at educational institutions.	*Learning.* Leadership wisdom is largely born out of self-reflection of practice.
Cultural sensitivity	*No.* Management is culturally insensitive because it is about organising things.	*Yes.* Leadership is culturally sensitive because it is about dealing with people.

Uniting Management and Leadership through the Concept of *Yin Yang*

The *Yin Yang* symbol has become the most prevalent Chinese symbol in the West. With its vivid flowing black and white swirls, each has a dot of the other at their centre. It captures within it the quintessential essence of balance, harmony and equality. Each one, yin and yang, gives way to the other in flowing lines and thus they complement each other. Yet their balance is not a passive one; it comes from dynamic tension, from the constant struggle of the one to overcome the other. They each wish to eradicate the other and be supreme, yet they cannot do this because nature has placed a part of one at the heart of the other. Thus, as they reach their zenith, they peak and begin to decline, allowing the other to rise. Yin and yang are not gods, nor are they good and evil spirits. They simply are, and as a result the cosmos is.

Given the contrast between management and leadership, I have developed the management–leadership unity logo (see Figure 8.1), based on the concept of *Yin Yang*. The basic interplay between management and leadership in the management–leadership unity consists of two aspects, i.e. universality and particularity.

Universality. The universality of the balance between management and leadership means that management and leadership not only complement each other but also combat each other. On the one hand, both management and leadership are needed to make a viable business. Management is needed to make it an organised entity but leadership is needed to free it from rigidity. Management is needed to develop people's work

FIGURE 8.1

Management-Leadership Unity

discipline, but leadership is needed to bring people's potential fully into play. Although the world is changing fast and we need to change, we also need to be stable while we do so. On the other hand, management and leadership do not lie side by side in peaceful co-existence. They are in constant contest and combat, producing the fundamental conflict between the need for discipline so as to meet organisational requirements and the need for freedom to meet the personal expectations of people. Indeed, it is the dynamic tension between them that gives life to a business. Strong leadership can disrupt an orderly planning system and undermine the formal hierarchy, while strong management can discourage risk taking and the enthusiasm needed for innovation.

Particularity. The particularity of the balance between management and leadership means that in any given situation, either management or leadership should be the principal aspect, which determines the nature of the situation, and that as the situation changes, the principal and the non-principal aspects transform themselves into each other. On the one hand, management and leadership should not be treated as equal for any given situation. When you focus on specialisation, fitting people to jobs, and compliance to rules, you necessarily divert your attention away from integration, tapping people's potential, and taking initiatives. When you emphasise operational details and control, you de-emphasise strategic issues and autonomy. When you endeavour to solve internal problems, you increase your chances of missing external opportunities.

On the other hand, the balance between management and leadership is not static. When too much management is present, bureaucracy, suppression, inertia and order keeping for the sake of order keeping arise and the voice for leadership gets louder; when too much leadership is exercised, personality cults, flashiness, obsession for change and innovation without a conscious direction become present and the call for management begins to grow.

Achieving Management–Leadership Unity

In the West, business study and practice have been largely characterised by the search for the *one right solution* to business problems. For example, for more than a century, there has been the search for the "one right organisation" and the "one right way to manage people". Since the 1980s, the search for the "one right solution" has effectively created a "guru industry", in which gurus are believed to have all the answers. In particular, the widespread adoption of the best practices of "excellent" companies has allowed executives to rely on ready-made answers.

Yet, although these ideas have merits, they often represent only *particular* truths. Nowhere can this be more clearly seen than in the fact that two-thirds of the "excellent" companies quoted in *In Search of Excellence* have subsequently fallen from grace. Indeed, universal answers rarely meet particular needs. As every business is unique, it must follow its own path, develop its own culture and retain its own individuality, as defined by its own distinctively right balances between management and leadership. To realise such business-specific, evolving management–leadership unity, you need to undertake two tasks: (1) combine theory and practice; and (2) adjust the balances dynamically.

Combining theory and practice. At the heart of the above managerial trend in the West has been an imbalance between theory and practice, where theory has mistakenly been regarded as higher than practice. According to Mao Zedong in *On Practice*:

Theory is based on practice and in turn serves practice. The truth of any theory is determined not by subjective feelings but by objective results in social practice. Only social practice can be the criterion of truth.

To combine theory and practice, it is imperative to avoid both dogmatism and empiricism. With dogmatism, one takes established theories as panacea and refuses to combine them with real situations. Yet all things have both general and particular characteristics. General characteristics, general law and theory are the guide for knowing and solving the same categories of problems, but they cannot provide specific solutions to specific problems. With empiricism, one takes specific or partial experience as something universal or absolute, or mechanically relies on past experience to deal with new situations. Vulgar "practical men" respect experience but despise theory, and therefore they cannot have a comprehensive view of an entire objective process, they lack a long-term perspective and clear direction, and are complacent over occasional successes and glimpses of the truth. If they direct a business, they will lead it up a blind alley.

Thus, instead of subscribing impulsively to fads, you should start with practice, i.e. with your particular circumstance. You should have a thorough knowledge of your business' constraints with respect to finances, history, relationships, and employees' ability to learn. Without an insightful understanding of your problems and the associated context, you can never expect to find the right solution. Next, you should assess and carefully choose the management ideas that promise to be useful. You need to bear in mind that a management idea that worked in one context could just as easily fail in another. Finally, you should adapt the chosen idea rigorously to your particular situation or use it as a guide for working out your own solution. Even when a complete programme is adopted, you still need to consider how best to implement it by taking human or leadership factors into account.

Adjusting the balances dynamically. Today's formula for success contains the seeds of decay for tomorrow; a solution that works today can easily fail tomorrow. As changes take place in its environment, a business must dynamically adjust its management–leadership unity in order to prosper or even to survive. In a time of change, there can be many balances that need to be adjusted, but of particular importance is the need for business leaders to master the new principal balance, which determines the direction a business takes.

According to Mao Zedong in *On Contradiction*:

> If in any process there are a number of contradictions, one of them must be the principal contradiction playing the leading and decisive role, while the rest occupy a secondary and subordinate position. Therefore, in studying any complex process in which there are two or more contradictions, we must devote every effort to finding its principal contradiction. Once this principal contradiction is grasped, all problems can be readily solved.

A business is originally born from a leadership idea, which captures the imagination of, and promises unique value to, customers. To make it happen, management is needed to organise resources, systematise the work, and efficiently produce and deliver quality products to customers. Without management, quality and efficiency cannot be achieved. On the other hand, even during smooth, steady operations, innovation efforts and leadership initiatives should always be encouraged in the business so that the whole system can be fine-tuned, leading to continuous performance improvement.

Over time, fundamental changes in competition, technology, the power of customers, the power of suppliers and regulations will inevitably occur, and these require the business to adapt. Typically, change needs to be introduced to the business itself through a major leadership effort. To make a change happen successfully, it is essential to make it meaningful to people. Also, people need to be made aware of what they should hold on to so as to balance the natural anxiety associated with change. If people do not understand and accept the change wholeheartedly, the outcome of the change campaign will deviate from what was originally expected. Once people are in a position to embrace the change, management effort is again needed to link the changed with the unchanged and finally to systematise the whole.

PART III

THE BIGGER PICTURE

China's accession to the WTO is a win-win situation for everyone. It is good news for Chinese consumers. It is good news for Chinese businesses. It is good news for international companies wishing to invest in China.

ZHU RONGJI, THE THEN CHINESE PREMIER, 2000

9

MAKING A SUCCESSFUL INVESTMENT IN CHINA

Successful business strategies result not from rigorous analysis but from a particular state of mind. In what I call the mind of the strategist, insight and a consequent drive for achievement, often amounting to a sense of mission, fuel a thought process which is basically creative and intuitive rather than rational. Strategists do not reject analysis. Indeed they can hardly do without it. But they use it only to stimulate the creative process, to test the ideas that emerge, to work out their strategic implications, or to ensure successful execution of high-potential 'wild' ideas that might otherwise never be implemented properly. Great strategies, like great works of art or great scientific discoveries, call for technical mastery in the working out but originate in insights that are beyond the reach of conscious analysis.

KENICHI OHMAE, *THE MIND OF THE STRATEGIST*

Success means accomplishments as a result of our own efforts and abilities. Proper preparation is the key to our success. Our acts can be no wiser than our thoughts. Our thinking can be no wiser than our thoughts. Our thinking can be no wiser than our understanding.

GEORGE S. CLASON, AMERICAN PUBLISHER AND AUTHOR OF *THE RICHEST MAN IN BABYLON*

DESPITE THE BENEFITS China's WTO accession promises to bring about, it remains no easy task for multinationals to make a successful investment in China. To succeed, they need to understand the strategic forces that determine the success of a business and craft a business strategy of advantage. More fundamentally, Western executives need to enlarge their worldview beyond the things-oriented, divided tradition and broaden their understanding of the nature of business beyond the notion of rationality.

Crafting a Business Strategy of Advantage

Although they have influenced generations of business people and students, classical Western strategy theories have serious limitations in serving the strategic needs of multinationals in the complex, dynamic China business environment. Fortunately, much can be learnt from ancient Chinese strategists and philosophers like Sun Tzu and Lao Tzu whose wisdom is as real today as it was 2,500 years ago.

Five Forces Determining the Success of a Business

When it comes to strategic study, Michael Porter's five-force model, i.e. the forces of new entrants, suppliers, customers, substitute products and existing competitors, has been the most influential. But the model is of limited help when dealing with the China investment challenge. First, it is narrow. It considers only the forces in the microenvironment of a business, ignoring significant forces, such as governmental regulation and business location. Second, it is purely economic. It focuses on competitive analysis from an economic point of view, ignoring how cooperation, social and cultural factors work. Third, it is static. Apart from recognising the threat of new competitors, it does not encourage the development of critical insight into how business climate might evolve over time. Last but not least, it fails to recognise the role of leadership. Let's see what we can learn from Sun Tzu's *The Art of War*:

> War is a matter of vital importance to the state. It concerns the lives and deaths of the people and affects the survival or demise of the state. It must be thoroughly studied. And it should be studied on the basis of five factors. (. . .) The five factors are moral influence, weather, terrain, commander, and doctrine.

In essence, the above five factors represent the moral force, the temporal force, the spatial force, the command force and the organisational force of a war situation. For a business, although there are many forces in its environment, the forces represented by business purpose, business climate, business location, business leader, and business organisation are of a strategic nature and determine its success (see Figure 9.1).

As shown in the diagram, the business leader plays a pivotal role in ensuring success because it is the business leader who is in a position to wisely harness all the other forces influencing the business, as confirmed by Sun Tzu in *The Art of War*:

FIGURE 9.1

Five Forces Determining the Success of a Business

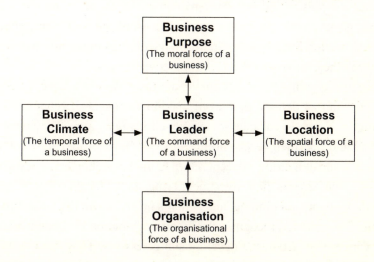

The commander is the pillar of the state. The state will prosper if the command is competent; the state will decline if the command is incompetent. (. . .) The commander who advances without seeking personal fame and glory, who retreats without fear of being punished, but whose main concern is for the welfare of the people and the interests of the state, is the precious gem of the state.

Business Purpose

According to Sun Tzu in *The Art of War*:

By moral influence I mean that which causes the people to be in harmony with the leader, so that they will accompany him in life and unto death without fear of mortal peril.

Business purpose defines the institutional role of a company in society by recognising that virtue is the root and wealth is the consequence. It is the sense of meaning, which all those related to the company could identify, in which they share a feeling of pride, and to which they are willing to commit themselves. It represents not only value to shareholders but also value to other parties including employees, customers, suppliers, government, community, natural environment, and even competitors. A well-defined business purpose thus brings maximum harmony between the business and its operating environment.

To succeed in China, multinationals must therefore have a vision larger than that defined as a profit-maximising agent of economic exchange and seek to enhance society's well-being at large. They need to understand that their responsibilities extend beyond obeying the Chinese law and delivering a decent return to their shareholders. They need to value the benefits their investment brings to the local economy, such as employment and training, and benefits up and down the local supply chain. They need to recognise the broad contribution they can make to the Chinese government's development objectives. They need to have high environmental standards. In short, they need to be committed to operating in a socially responsible and sustainable way.

Motorola, for example, has been one of the most successful foreign investors in China, and one of the secrets behind its success has been its endeavour to integrate its business activities into Chinese society. For example, it has striven to localise its operations by investing heavily in training up local staff while reducing the number of foreign employees. By now, all members of the Motorola (China) board of directors are of Chinese ancestry. In April 1997, Motorola signed an agreement with the State Planning Commission, under which Motorola would spend US$10 million over a five-year period on management training for 1,000 state enterprises. It has established the unique Motorola Co-operation Committee, consisting of senior Motorola executives and relevant government officials. The committee regularly discusses topics, such as the Chinese economy, industrial developments, problems and solutions in Motorola operations, recommendations made by local suppliers, Chinese government requirements, and Motorola's suggestions for government policies. Motorola also does extensive co-operative research with government agencies, universities and research institutes, participates in various educational assistance programmes, and contributes generously to local community charities.

Through these kinds of co-operation, Motorola has turned many state enterprises into its suppliers, supported the growth of related industries, and consequently enjoyed favourable government policies when expanding its businesses in China. And by recognising that money is a by-product of satisfying customer needs and enhancing Chinese society's well being, Motorola has made a lot of money in China.

Business Climate

According to Sun Tzu in *The Art of War*:

> By weather I mean day or night, overcast or sunny, severe cold or intense heat, and the seasons of spring, summer, autumn and winter.

Business climate is made up of dynamic factors that influence a business, including political stability, economic prosperity, changes in governmental regulations, trends in consumer values, competitive dynamics, shifts in industry structures, and development in technology. It determines when to invest in China and also dictates the need for adjustment in business direction and strategy over time.

Although China's future political stability and economic prosperity can be predicted with certainty because of its unique cultural centrality and huge development potential, business climate in China will continue to be characterised by constant changes in governmental regulations, consumer expectations, competitive situation, industry structures and technology. To take advantage of such changes, foreign investors need to work with the government and, through good relationships with governmental officials, shape the regulatory environment, influence the emergence of technical standards and control intellectual property rights. They need to identify and aim for the emerging patterns and underlying trends in customer values, and avoid conclusions based only on symptoms. They need to closely monitor as well as anticipate changes in industry structures and competition. They need to keep up with the development of new technology. Above all, they need to constantly review and, if necessary, adjust their direction and strategy.

The impact of business climate upon a business can be illustrated by the case of Motorola in China. The company had ruled mobile telephony in China since it arrived in 1987. It entered the China market at a time when the Chinese government encouraged mobile telephony because mobile networks were cheaper to install than fixed line ones and could be deployed more quickly. Additionally, combining two irresistible virtues – efficiency and status – mobile phones were highly attractive to the tens of millions of consumers in China's major urban centres who had growing incomes. Consequently, Motorola had more than 70% of the mobile phone market and margins were fat. By 1993, the company broke the billion-dollar revenue barrier while its multinational competitors were still trying to figure out their entry strategies.

Then came the Global System for Mobile Communications (GSM), a better technology, of European origin, which gobbled up market shares around the world at the expense of the analogue system with which Motorola had been so successful. In China, sales of GSM handsets were 15% of those of analogue handsets in 1995, 35% in 1996, and 200% in 1997. In 1997, Sweden's Ericsson displaced Motorola as China's dominant supplier of mobile telephony and Finland's Nokia came from nowhere to grab a big chunk of the market. As part of its strategy to fight back, Motorola sought to convince China of the need for a new, competing technical standard – the US-developed Code Division Multiple Access (CDMA). The company even looked to President Bill Clinton's visit to Beijing in June 1998 to produce results for CDMA. In March 1999, China decided to embrace CDMA. But the competitive arena for mobile telephony remained challenging for Motorola, because provincial Post and Telecommunications Administrations had spent hundreds of millions of dollars on GSM infrastructure and 99% of China's 45 million mobile subscribers were already using GSM networks.

Business Location

According to Sun Tzu in *The Art of War*:

> By terrain I mean high or low land, faraway or nearby location, dangerous or flat place, large or small ground, and fatal or advantageous spot.

Business location is concerned with where to invest in China. It determines accessibility to the target market, proximity to supply, quality and cost of labour, government support, cost of land and availability of infrastructure facilities, such as telecommunications, transportation, water and power supply. In particular, once a location is chosen, an investor has to face the associated consequences, such as working with the local people even if they are not competent. Business location thus dictates to a great extent the operation and logistics of a business and can constrain the strategic stance that it can take. As such, investors should spare no expense in studying the characteristics of a potential location. At times, it is not possible to have all the location factors in your favour, in which case it is important that you find ways to resolve the difficulties posed by the unfavourable.

In the past, some foreign investors hurriedly invested in certain geographical regions of China and then found that they could not cope with the infrastructure constraints of the location. One notable example is British Brewery Bass, which had to pull out of China in April 2000 after its joint venture in Siping – a remote town in Jilin province – proved to be located in the wrong place. In the case of Shenyang Tambrands, a Sino-American joint venture manufacturing feminine hygiene products, it found that the location added significantly to the cost of sales, eroding profitability. Shenyang is far away from the cotton-growing region. The region's concentration of heavy industry often caused power and water supply shortages. Shenyang is also distant from the major markets in central, east, and south China, and the poor transportation network made it difficult to distribute the product through large state-owned agencies and wholesalers, or directly to retailers.

China, of course, is not short of excellent investment locations. Consider Shanghai and Tianjin. On 27 October 2000, IBM Corp announced that it was to build a US$300 million computer chip packaging plant in Shanghai, which was chosen over ten other cities in four countries. Equally attractive is the Tianjin Economic-technological Development Area (TEDA), rated by *Business Asia* in the 1990s as the best-managed investment zone in China. TEDA has long been renowned for local governmental support, excellent infrastructure, and low-cost and qualified labour, and is home for over 3,900 companies including Motorola.

In any case, great caution needs to be exercised when it comes to choosing a location. Since 1990, McDonald's has set up 337 restaurants in China (all of which are 50:50 joint ventures), but most of them are located in roughly 40 coastal cities. It only opened its first restaurant in southwestern China, i.e. Chengdu, in 2000 after a three-year study of the local market; it was not until 2001 that it opened its first restaurant in northwestern China, i.e. Xi'an. Although McDonald's has an ambitious expansion plan in China, it insists that if ideal management and locations cannot be found, it would rather slow down its expansion.

Business Organisation

According to Sun Tzu in *The Art of War*:

> By doctrine I mean organisation, control, assignment of appropriate ranks to officers, regulation of supply routes, and the provision of principal items used by the army.

Business organisation is made of skills and resources, including managerial know-how, functional assets and human resources, necessary to serve the defined business purpose, including the primary task of profitably producing and delivering product and services to customers. An effective joint venture organisation rests on both finding a suitable partner and working harmoniously with the partner.

Finding a suitable partner requires, above all, time commitment and large doses of patience. Several potential partners should be approached with the help of reliable China guides, and assessed from the perspective of motives, credibility and capability through both formal introduction and informal investigation, and where possible, real engagement. In selecting a partner, it is important to go through the process of jointly defining the business philosophy and identifying complementary skills and resources, with the final decision made on the basis of both financial numbers and qualitative factors. The two partners must also negotiate, bearing in mind the differences in their negotiating philosophies, so as to reach a win-win position represented by both a mutually beneficial contract and sufficient mutual trust.

Working effectively with the partner requires harmonising cultural differences and learning on both sides. Communication gaps between Western and local staff, between expatriates and their headquarters need to be bridged. While local personnel need to be trained to meet managerial needs, Westerners need to learn skills for leading the Chinese. Above all, an effective business organisation requires continually evolving its right set of balances between management and leadership – management is about rationality, systems and control, while leadership is about capturing hearts and minds, building consensus around goals larger than individuals, and releasing energy.

Suzhou Capsugel, a 50:50 joint venture making two-piece gelatine capsules for drug packaging made a profit in its first year of production, 1989, and paid down its original investment in just four years. Capsugel found China National Pharmaceutical Foreign Trade Corp., a unit of the State Pharmaceutical Administration, willing to invest cash in a green-field site and thus share Capsugel's interest in paying down its investment as quickly as possible. With its clout, the local partner enabled the venture to sell direct to all clients and have few problems with receivables. In addition, Capsugel's willingness to invest in reliable distribution in its start-up phase won it much business because refrigerated distribution is necessary for gelatine capsules. Good management relations and workforce loyalty have also been its key strengths. Both the expatriate general manager and the Chinese deputy general manager have been with the joint venture since the planning stage. The workforce has been stable too, with demands for housing – small apartments typically cost 15 times a worker's annual salary – being met by payments to the factory's labour union.

Business Leader

According to Sun Tzu in *The Art of War*:

> By commander I mean the general's virtues of wisdom, sincerity, human-heartedness, courage, and strictness.

When a business fails, executives routinely point to causes, such as partner relationship problem, poor quality employees, low demand and fierce competition. These can be facts, but it is the leader's responsibility to develop the business purpose that creates shared destiny relationships between partners, and also with other players in the business venture's environment. It is the leader's responsibility to devise effective policies that motivate employees under new working conditions and improve their quality through investing in training and leading by example. It is also the leader's responsibility to anticipate the changing market situation and adjust the direction and strategy of the business so as to adapt to the new reality. Thus, while it requires everything to be right for a business to succeed, a business leader of poor quality or competence is bound to fail the business.

In the past, poor choices of China executives have led to many problems. Senior executives dispatched from Western headquarters are usually either at the age of retirement or have little experience. The older executives consider China the last stop of their career and tend to follow the beaten path without any pioneering passion. The green hands, with little experience in running large businesses, do not have the tools to deal with the complex China business environment. Some multinationals prematurely rely on "experienced" directors of state-owned enterprises, but many such directors have no virtue or abilities to speak of. They assume personal command of one aspect of the business and forget to devote any energy to other aspects; they are astute in the political arena but negligent in business. In addition, frequent reorganisation in the top management ranks initiated by head offices can significantly hinder the building of new learning and consequently the successful development of businesses in China.

"The most difficult job in the world is being the general manager of a joint venture in China," says Kent Watson at PricewaterhouseCoopers China. As such, it does not make sense to send anyone but your most capable executives to China to head your China operations. To succeed, your China executives need to have a balanced character and be multitalented. They need to be persistent, patient, and flexible. They need to be able to bridge the gap in the differing expectations of the local partner and the Western head office. They need to have not only adequate industry knowledge and experience but also a strong ability to emotionally connect with people. They need to have not only skills to analyse business situations, plan business activities, and control business results but also the ability to appeal to the heart of locals, reconcile their different viewpoints, and lead them by example.

Above all, given the complex and dynamic nature of the China business environment, China executives need to have an insatiable love of learning so as to maintain a sharp personal edge and develop an enduring reservoir of knowledge and skills, with which they can see things that others miss, sense patterns where others find only confusion.

Four Levels of Strategic Advantage to Pursue

In the Western corporate world, there is much confusion about what strategy is. Three problems are evident. First, "competitive strategy" is often used as a synonym for "business strategy". Most strategy models overemphasise competition and overlook co-operation and creation, i.e. encouraging companies to claim a bigger share of the same pie while losing sight of the strategic task of creating a bigger or a new pie.

Second, strategy has unfortunately been formalised into a planning discipline, i.e. "strategic planning", which is decomposition by nature, producing even functional strategies, such as operations strategy. Strategic planning overemphasises rationality (e.g. the linear progression from "strategy formulation" to "strategy implementation"), analysis (e.g. over-reliance on hard data), rigid timeframe (e.g. five- or ten-year strategic plan), and concrete steps (e.g. a timetable of actions that must be implemented). But strategy is essentially the opposite of the planning discipline. It is integration by nature, concerned with the situation as a whole. It is primarily a creative thinking process, emphasising informality (i.e. organically integrated with practice), intuition (i.e. valuing hands-on experience and qualitative information), flexible timeframe (i.e. dependent upon the characteristics of the industry and the leader's foresight), and guiding principles (i.e. adaptable to reality).

Perhaps the most misleading is the prescription of "generic strategies" which are claimed to be formulary solutions to competitive problems. The true meaning of strategy is the one that is right for you, and is the result of combining theory with practice and cannot be produced without your insightful understanding of your particular circumstances. Therefore, the essence of strategy is uniqueness rather than generality, and the power of strategy is creativity rather than stereotyping.

Let's see what we can learn from Lao Tzu and Sun Tzu. Lao Tzu's *Tao Te Ching* is perhaps the world's wisest book ever written, emphasising the power of "not competing" in 9 passages of all 81 passages. For example, Lao Tzu states in passage 66:

Because superior men do not compete, the world cannot compete with them.

Equally profound is Sun Tzu's *The Art of War*, which is the world's earliest book on military strategy. But even in war, Sun Tzu does not advocate direct confrontation:

> Winning battle after battle is still not good enough; it is better to win when your enemy surrenders without giving you a fight.

> A skilled commander will subdue the enemy without fighting, taking the walled cities without storming them, and capturing the enemy state without a protracted war. He will seek to gain the world through no destruction, and this way no army will fight to death but total benefits can be achieved: this is the art of strategy.

> The best war policy is to attack the enemy's strategy. The next best is to disrupt his alliances. The third best is to conquer his army. The worst is to besiege his cities. Besiege cities only when there is no other alternative.

Drawn on the above ancient wisdom and given that the fundamental purpose of business is value creation rather than competition, strategic advantage in business can be pursued at four levels (see Figure 9.2).

FIGURE 9.2

Four Levels of Strategic Advantage

Innovation	▲	Minimum Competition	(Focusing on creating a bigger or an entirely new "pie")
Alliance			
Differentiation			
Excellence		Maximum Competition	(Focusing on claiming a bigger share of the same "pie")

These four levels of strategic advantage vary in the relative attention given to competition and creation. Competition represents quantitative thinking – to compete is to divide an existing pie. Creation represents qualitative thinking – to create is to enlarge the existing pie or make an entirely new one. The four levels also differ along other dimensions of strategy, each demanding different industry conditions, requiring different organisational capabilities, involving different risks and rewards and, ultimately, suiting different business circumstances. Besides, the four levels are not only distinctive but also connected because a higher-level advantage can be seen as having evolved from the lower-level ones. In the West, companies used to focus on pursuing excellence- and then differentiation-based strategic advantages, but increasingly they have to learn to pursue alliance- and innovation-based strategic advantages (see Table 9.1).

It is vitally important to note that the above framework only serves as a guide for strategic thinking because a true, creative, successful strategy cannot be produced without your insight into and intuition about your particular business circumstances. The four levels are not mutually exclusive and do not represent black/white "trade-offs" that a company must choose because it can creatively pursue a combination of them. In fact, the most successful companies are good at achieving all levels. Besides, strategic advantage is not a static position but a *moving target*. For example, a company that has pursued a particular innovation may sooner or later face challenges from rivals and, unless it launches a new innovative effort, its existing innovation-based strategic advantage will erode. And then it will have to pursue alliance-based advantage or begin competing with rivals on the basis of differentiation or even excellence. This of course will lead to diminishing margins and returns. Below, I illustrate and discuss the four levels of strategic advantage in the China business context.

Excellence-Based Strategic Advantage

Excellence means performing similar activities better than rivals perform them. It is important in a head-to-head, zero-sum competitive situ-

TABLE 9.1

The Evolving Nature of Strategic Advantage

	Scope	Focus	Capabilities	Consequences
Excellence	Within the boundary of the existing segment	Achieving lower total cost than competitors through operational improvement	(1) Eliminating inefficiencies. (2) Employing more efficient technology, such as information technology. (3) Motivating employees better, and improving customer satisfaction.	(1) For one or two potential winners, involving highest rewards as well as highest commitment and cost. (2) For all the potential losers, involving lowest commitment and cost and highest risks.
Differentiation	Within the boundary of the existing market	Taking customers from competitors through finer segmentation and targeting	(1) Understanding customer needs more deeply. (2) Segmenting the existing market more finely. (3) Offering products/services with add-on values for specific market segments.	(1) Involving low commitment, cost, risk and rewards. (2) Suiting a large number of niche players.
Alliance	Within the boundary of the existing industry	Influencing industry dynamics through partnering with other players	(1) Selecting the right supplier, customer and/or competitor in the same industry as allies. (2) Eliminating inefficiencies and exploiting synergy. (3) Balancing competitive and co-operative agendas over time.	(1) Involving high commitment, cost, risk and rewards. (2) Suiting those with shared motives and complementary competencies.
Innovation	Beyond the boundary of the existing industry	Creating a new market through creating new concepts that rewrite industry rules	(1) Developing new industry foresight. (2) Building and deploying new competencies. (3) If necessary, partnering with players in other industries and with governmental agencies.	(1) Involving highest commitment, cost, risk and rewards. (2) Suiting market and product leaders.

ation, where customers can find little difference in the value delivered by the players and the market largely sets the product price, depending on the perceived balance between demand and supply. A company that is able to get more out of its inputs than others can achieve lower costs, and often better quality too. Lower costs of course lead to better profitability. Excellence-based advantage can be pursued through operational improvement programmes, such as total quality management, benchmarking, downsizing, value chain, and re-engineering.

Given the horrendous inefficiency in most Chinese industries, multinationals can compete against local enterprises if they can transfer their inherent strength in operational excellence to their ventures in China in a cost-effective way. In sugar production, some Western producers had formed joint ventures with local mills since restrictions for foreign participation were lifted in 1990. It was, however, no easy business because sugar was largely a commodity in China and local competition was fierce. Nevertheless, Western investors had kept improving their mills' efficiency by expanding their capacity, adopting more advanced equipment in key process areas and introducing tighter operating procedures. The time for these Western ventures to reap benefits came in December 1999 when the Chinese government decided to shut down some 150 small, loss-making local mills, i.e. 9 out of 14 sugar mills.

Excellence-based strategic advantage can be particularly pertinent to service industries where modern service and management methods cannot be easily copied by local competitors. Consider KFC. Noting KFC's success in China, many local restaurants began imitating KFC in 1990, with several kinds of fried chicken like "Ronghua Chicken" and "Xiangfei Chicken" soon appearing on the market. However, although it was easy to build the "hardware" of a fast food industry, i.e. the restaurant, the "software", i.e. service and management, could not be copied overnight. In contrast to KFC's high standard of hygiene including the cleanliness of the eating environment and the freshness of the food, local imitators could only maintain dismal standards. As a result, most local competitors had to turn to Chinese-style fast food, such as noodles, rice dishes and Chinese pancakes.

Inevitably and particularly in manufacturing, companies pursuing excellence-based advantage alone will soon face diminishing returns or even a price war as competitors imitate management techniques, new technologies, input improvements and customer services. Thus, unless an investor can establish a critical mass of businesses in the industry and thereby achieve economy of scale and a market leader position, there is a serious limit to how long it can profitably pursue excellence-based advantage. Whirlpool, for example, had to decide in late 1997 to shut down its refrigerator and air conditioner joint ventures barely nine months after they started commercial production. The main reason was competition from local companies, such as Haier and Kelon, which distinguished themselves from traditional state enterprises through investing in modern, usually imported production facilities, and employing modern marketing and service techniques, and from foreign companies through throwing in lower overheads.

Differentiation-Based Strategic Advantage

Differentiation means delivering a unique mix of value to customers through deliberately performing a set of activities that are different from rivals'. In a world where everyone is after your business, differentiation is the reason why your customers choose to buy from you instead of your competitors. It is thus the most advocated, understood, and widely pursued advantage.

Differentiation-based strategic advantage can be pursued through finer segmentation of the market and greater customisation of offerings along such dimensions as brand, access, design, functionality, reliability, speed, convenience, service and low price, which are not mutually exclusive and often overlap. For example, the successes of Coca-Cola and Pepsi in China have largely come from their brand recognition and nation-wide distribution. The combined billboards for Coca-Cola and Pepsi account for 92% of all billboards for carbonated drinks in Beijing, Shanghai and Guangzhou; both have built bottling plants in major cities throughout China.

Differentiation-based strategic advantage enables companies to command better control of their customers than excellence-based strategic advantage, and when the unique value is truly recognised and appreciated by customers, companies may even command a premium price. KFC and McDonald's have maintained growth in China through offering a unique, American, cultural experience that is valued by Chinese consumers. By any local standards, eating at KFC and McDonald's is not at all cheap, but Chinese consumers want to taste hamburgers, fried chickens and fries that do not exist in the Chinese food system. They also come to KFC and McDonald's to experience the atmosphere of equality and democracy, which is made possible by a limited menu, standardised food and predictable expenditure. This is in contrast to banquets at Chinese restaurants where people try to outdo one another by offering the most expensive dishes and alcoholic beverages in order to gain face. For yuppies that have higher incomes, eating at KFC and

McDonald's has become a way for them to participate in the global cultural system. Young couples like to take their children to KFC and McDonald's in order to expose them to American culture and help them learn a modern way of life.

Yet, the conventional wisdom that "where there is a will, there is always a way to differentiate" does not always lead to success. As companies try to differentiate their products or services from their rivals', it is possible for them to deliver something that is not what the customers really value. In addition, when products overly proliferate because manufacturers think they will sell more goods if they provide sizes, colours, shapes and flavours to suit every taste, dazed shoppers can be reduced to something approaching mental paralysis by the difficulty of deciding which to buy. And when this happens, exasperated consumers often react by buying the cheapest product or even nothing at all. This is exactly why several premium breweries like Foster, Guinness, Carlsberg and Bass have failed in China. Chinese beer drinkers were intrigued by so many different foreign beers but have stuck to their domestic brews, four or five times cheaper, because beer is not a traditional Chinese drink and Chinese consumers can hardly taste the subtle difference between premium and local beers. As for the social and status value in drinks, they prefer products like famous local Maotai Liquor or foreign Martell Cognac to "cheap" premium beers.

Alliance-Based Strategic Advantage

An alliance is a relationship that is entered into for mutual benefit by two or more parties having compatible or complementary business interests and goals. Depending upon the scope and nature of the relationship, an alliance can take many forms, including supplier partnership, customer alliance, licensing, technology transfer, original equipment manufacturer (OEM), co-operative venture and joint venture.

Companies establish different types of alliances with different types of players in order to pursue different types of strategic advantages. They may want to collaborate to cut the costs involved in traditional, transactional supplier–buyer relationships and to co-evolve. They may want to ally because they have potentially synergistic capabilities that allow them to cut the costs of differentiating themselves from competitors. They may want to co-operate to reduce the threat of future rivalry or to deny the resources of a partner to a competitor. They may want to band together in defence from an attack by another company. They may want to work together to develop an emerging market. Alliance-based strategic advantage can become a truly moving target as companies develop networks of alliances.

To solve its parts supply problem, Citroen's joint venture in Wuhan has brought its international suppliers, including Bundy International that makes fuel tubes, Pilkington that supplies windscreens, and Hutchinson that produces oil seals, to Wuhan to set up satellite joint ventures. Microsoft, on the other hand, has established customer alliances with more than 10,000 local companies, including software developers, equipment manufacturers and the giant telecom and financial sectors. To overcome its unfamiliarity with the China market, Whirlpool has entered into an OEM arrangement with Kelon, one of the leading Chinese white electrical goods makers, to supply washing machines that are marketed in China under the Kelon brand.

In 1984, Volkswagen established the Shanghai Volkswagen joint venture with the Shanghai Automotive Industry Corp. (SAIC) Group to assemble sedans, with SAIC being the sole sales agent for Shanghai Volkswagen. The joint venture has been ranked as the most successful foreign investment in China for many consecutive years since 1991. However, as foreign car makers rushed into China one after another, demanding a rapid response to changes in the market, Volkswagen established a new 50:50 joint venture with its Shanghai partner to handle the sales. Back in 1987, to prevent First Auto Works (FAW) from allying with other Western car makers, Volkswagen established the FAW–Volkswagen joint venture. But this move eventually led SAIC to establish its own separate joint venture with General Motors in 1997.

Despite the promised advantages, alliances inevitably involve risks and in some cases high risks. For an alliance to flourish and prosper, the mutual interest must be strong and lasting. You should not choose poor partners just to have partners because a bad alliance is worse than no alliance at all. Revpower, Peugeot, and Bass are only examples of many

joint ventures that are considered to have failed as a result of poor partner choice. Choosing the right partner is only the beginning. It is equally
important to know how to operate an alliance. An alliance works when
trust, sincere co-operation, perceived fairness, commitment to problem
resolution, a desire to learn as well as to teach, and, most important, a
mutual interest exist between the partners. If the mutual interest has
died, the problems of having a partner will quickly overcome the benefits and the alliance will struggle. In fact, when the mutual interest that
created the alliance fades, new mutual interest should be sought. And if
no mutual interest can be found and yet the alliance is continued, it can
become a black hole for management time and resources.

Innovation-Based Strategic Advantage

Innovation means creating a new market and then dominating it by
offering a tremendous leap in value. It is based on deep insights into
trends in technology, demographics, regulation and lifestyles that can
be harnessed to rewrite industry rules. Its pursuit requires a company to
develop and acquire new competencies and to push its products into the
realm of the unknown or untried. Often, its pursuit requires a company
to ally with players in other industries and even governmental agencies
in order to bring the new product or service to fruition. Above all, it
requires courage, creativity, and commitment.

In the late 1980s and early 1990s, with truly innovative pharmaceutical products that were non-existent in China, Xi'an–Janssen, Smith-
Kline Beecham and Bristol–Myers Squibb banked hefty profits and
achieved sales growth of more than 40% a year. Pfizer entered the China
market in 1993 by introducing its established products, including some
of its worldwide best-sellers, through its joint venture in Dalian. But the
US$58 million investment looked like a lame white elephant because
the established products had become very generic in China, competed
poorly on price, and faced fierce protectionist regulators. In 1995, Pfizer engineered a turnaround by changing to innovative drugs that were
fresh from its worldwide pipeline, with sales soaring to RMB200 million (US$24 million), a 50% increase over 1994. The Chinese govern-

ment subsequently named the Dalian joint venture as one of the best in China, with three Pfizer products receiving distinction awards.

More recently, to pursue innovation-based strategic advantage, multinationals have invested heavily in their R&D capability in China. Motorola, for example, has sought to regain its lost ground through investment in researching and developing innovative technologies and products since 1998. So far, the company has established over twenty-five R&D centres across China, with R&D expenditure reaching US$157 million. Joining forces with leading local companies, it developed China's first CDMA wireless telephone switches and 2.5 generation GSM handsets with high-speed Internet access functionality. To maximise its share of influence over the trajectory of the development of the third-generation technologies in China, Motorola established an R&D partnership with the Ministry of Information Industry. In 1999, Motorola launched its first Internet cell phone in China, the Motorola L2000WWW Internet series, which supported GSM, CDMA and Internet frequencies and WAP services, such as financial information, flight or train timetables, weather, traffic and geographic information. All existing Motorola products had also been upgraded to have a WAP capability. In 2000, Motorola regained the top spot in the Chinese mobile telephone market with a market share of nearly 36%.

Innovation of course carries its own risks, which were clearly shown in Microsoft's ambitious Venus project. In March 1999, Bill Gates announced the launch of "Venus", an operating platform that would allow Chinese electronics firms to combine a Web browser, a low-end PC and a video compact disc player in a single box. By connecting with an ordinary TV as a monitor, the product would target local consumers who could not afford a PC but wanted Internet access and also allowed them to view digital videodisks. To bring Venus to fruition, Microsoft allied with hardware manufacturers, application software developers, Internet service providers (ISP), and telecommunication operators. But when manufacturers began rolling out the product in January 2000, Chinese consumers seemed to snub set-top boxes because not many families could afford to get online, and for those who could, they were turning instead to the increasingly cheap PCs.

Thinking across Two Contrasting Civilisations

Given the challenges involved, joint ventures are now seen by many as hardly an ideal vehicle for business success, "anywhere in the world". Yet, if globalisation of business activities is rapidly becoming a reality, the principles for establishing and operating a successful Sino-Western joint venture – those of effectively working across two contrasting cultures – are rapidly becoming essentials of business success today and beyond. But the starting point is that you must think across two contrasting civilisations.

Taking a Higher Worldview through Combining a Western Things-oriented, Divided Worldview and a Chinese Human-centred, Integrated Worldview

Western and Chinese worldviews were both born 2,500 years ago but, despite their parallels, they were in sharp contrast with each other. Ancient Western philosophers like Plato and Aristotle strove to discover a natural explanation for the cosmos by means of observation and reasoning. Plato saw the world as being made of "things" governed by "Ideas"; Aristotle, on the other hand, introduced the notion of categories – things can be said "to be" in many ways. The Western mind, therefore, starts with the parts, breaks a complex matter into component parts, and then deals with them one by one, with an emphasis on logical analysis, one-pointedness and the search for prior, often absolute, truths that can govern subsequent practice.

By contrast, ancient Chinese philosophers like Confucius and Lao Tzu sought to find solutions to human problems and discovered that "Heaven and humanity are one" (*tianren heyi*), where "heaven" is more a description of the way the world is, rather than pointing beyond the world to some other reality. Confucius sensed that humans' behaviours are driven by their feelings for each other and proposed human-heartedness (*ren*) as the central virtue for mankind; Lao Tzu, on the other hand, considered that ultimate reality (*Tao*) can never be an object of reasoning and therefore advocated human harmony with the cosmos. The Chinese mind, therefore, starts with the whole, treats all things as inter-connected, and deals with them as a whole, with an emphasis on intuitive synthesis, all-inclusiveness and the mastery of wisdom (i.e. the "oneness of knowledge and practice" – *zhixing heyi*).

Due to the contrast between ancient Western and Chinese world-views, Westerners and the Chinese have taken very different historical courses. From the third to the thirteenth century, the Western mind's search for truth led to the rise and fall of the Christian worldview based on a *division* between the world and God, with events in the former controlled by the Will of the latter. Then, having suffered under the one universal, absolute truth, from the fourteenth to the nineteenth century, the Western mind began its search for individual truths, leading to the rise of the modern worldview based on emerging scientific disciplines. By contrast, the Chinese mind's pre-occupation with wisdom had en-sured philosophy, psychology, sociology and politics, all rolled into one, remained almost unchanged for 2,500 years, producing no religion or science as we have seen in the West.

Yet, during the twentieth century, the Western mind has discovered the Chinese *tianren heyi*: one cannot regard reality as a removed specta-tor against a fixed object; rather, one is always and necessarily engaged in reality, thereby at once transforming it while being transformed one-self. For example, quantum mechanics, the jewel in the crown of twen-tieth-century science, has revealed in an unexpected fashion that the nature described by physics is not nature in itself but man's relation to nature, i.e. nature as exposed to man's form of questioning. By the mid-twentieth century, the "side effects" of modern reason, ranging from the mechanisation of human beings and the stress of modern life to pollution and global warming, began pointing to the radical validity of the ancient Chinese human-centred, integrated worldview. But this was achieved following a 2,500-year trajectory, which of course saw other remarkable discoveries.

Thus nature, as it stands at the millennium, is not made up of parts within wholes but of wholes within wholes, and is constantly chang-ing. It can be much *better* understood if we combine the penetrating, conceptual vigour of the "masculine", Western mind and the embracing, intuitive power of the "feminine", Chinese mind. One of the most systematic examples of such a combination has been that of Western and Chinese medicine. With the invention of the microscope and the discovery of the cell, Western medicine is a discipline that is based on the philosophy that only what exists in the physical realm is real, and diagnoses and treats the effect that a disease state has on the body itself. It focuses on research and discovery of generic drugs that act upon the actual cells of the body.

By contrast, Chinese medicine is a discipline that looks at the body with analogies to nature and views symptoms as a manifestation of an imbalance in the whole body's system rather than attributing them to a malfunction of one of its parts or an isolated event. It emphasises the diagnosis of all the symptoms and experiences of the patient while taking into account the age, habits, physical and emotional traits and all other aspects of the individual as a whole. Its aim is to restore the internal balance of the body through the body's own internal systems, with the assistance of herbal remedies, acupuncture, massage, *qigong* exercise, nutrition and life-style prescriptions. It therefore offers each patient a safe and yet effective complement and sometimes even a powerful alternative to artificial chemicals that tend to have many potential dangers and side effects. It is now believed that the greatest strength of Western medicine is in its trauma care and therapies for acute problems, while Chinese medicine excels in the areas of chronic problems and preventive medicine.

Consider also the secret of Hong Kong's success. Back in 1923, Sun Yat-sen said: "How was it that foreigners, the Englishmen, could do so much as they have done with the barren rock of Hong Kong within 70 or 80 years, while in 4,000 years China had no place like Hong Kong?" By the early 1980s, with a leading financial market and a leading container port in the world, Hong Kong had become the most international city in the world. With robustness and vitality in one, Hong Kong's success had essentially been the result of a somewhat "forced marriage" between British legal conventions and administration expertise, and Chinese people. For the rule of law provided that security and majestic neutrality within which the best of Western and Chinese ideas and values could blend and flourish, business networks – often family/relative-based – could grow.

There are other fruitful examples. As early as the 18th century, *I Ching* inspired German mathematician Gottfried Wilhelm Leibniz to invent calculus. To Carl Gustav Jung, the rival of Sigmund Freud in psychology, *I Ching* was an explorer of the unconscious mind. Niels Bohr, Nobel Laureate for physics in 1922, was so deeply impressed by the ancient Chinese notion of polar opposites that when he was knighted in 1947 he chose the Chinese *Yin Yang* symbol for his coat-of-arms together with the inscription *Contraria sunt complementa* (Opposites are complementary). Japanese physicist Hideki Yukawa and Chinese physicists Yang Chen Ning and Lee Tsung Dao credit *I Ching* for helping them win the Nobel Prize for particle physics in 1949 and 1957 respectively because they consulted it in their research. In the classic best seller *The Tao of Physics* (1975), now available in more than two dozen editions around the world, Fritjof Capra has quoted extensively from *Tao Te Ching* and *I Ching* to explore the philosophical implications of modern physics.

According to British military historian B. H. Liddell Hart, had Sun Tzu's *The Art of War* been more widely read and accepted by World War I generals, much of the terrible slaughter of trench warfare could have been avoided. During the Persian Gulf War in 1990, in contrast to the Vietnam War in which the American administration regarded body counts as the measure of success and turned to theoretical physicists when President Johnson needed advice about warfare, *The Art of War* was one of the two books on President Bush's desk and also widely studied by US marines on the ground. By controlling the air both to follow Iraqi movements and to mask his own troops' movements, General Schwartzkopf fooled Saddam Hussein as to the location of his attack. Ultimately, it was the combination of strategies based on Sun Tzu's principles and the combat power of ground troops that gave the Coalition a stunning victory with extremely low casualties.

Although it was almost unknown in the West until the 20th century, Lao Tzu's *Tao Te Ching*, the wisest, most practical book ever written, is by now the most widely translated book in the world, aside from *The Bible*. *Tao Te Ching* looks at the basic predicament of being human and gives advice for living well and harmoniously. It teaches how to work for the good with least effort that comes from being in accord with reality, which applies equally well to the governing of a nation or the raising of a child.

But the significance of combining a Western things-oriented, divided worldview and a Chinese human-centred, integrated worldview goes far beyond the above examples. In January 1988, seventy-five or two-thirds of all Nobel Laureates gathered in Paris and made a manifesto, which began by asserting that if mankind was to continue to survive in the 21st century, it had to look back 2,500 years and absorb the wisdom of Confucius. Nowhere can this be more clearly seen than in the September 11 incident, which showed how much destruction the search of absolute truth without any human concern could do to mankind. Those who struck the World Trade Centre thought they had found the truth and they really believed it, as former US President Bill Clinton pointed out at the 2001 Richard Dimbleby Lecture. This is why they could choose to sacrifice their own life, not to mention take the lives of others.

When the incident happened, I was researching this book by reading some Confucian classics. Apart from the immediate feeling that the incident was a man-made tragedy, another feeling I had was that had these people had any chance to come into contact with the Confucian virtue of human-heartedness, they might not have acted as they did.

Thus, the challenge is to bridge the gap between truth and human-heartedness, and the most effective means of bridging this gap is business because it involves not only mutual benefits but also emotional, intellectual and even ideological interchanges.

Achieving Business Success through Combining Modern Western Management Excellence and Ancient Chinese Leadership Wisdom

Business, in its most primitive form, actually played a fundamental role in crystallising Western civilisation in the Mediterranean basin 2,500 years ago. Those who lived on the coast tended to look along it and outward across the sea, rather than behind them to their hinterland, and this made the spreading of ideas and techniques within the Mediterranean natural for enterprising peoples. But business had for over two millenniums been confined to exchanges of natural and agricultural materials until the advent of the Industrial Revolution in the eighteenth century. Apart from steam power and later the internal-combustion engine and electricity, the Industrial Revolution had been marked by the efficient production of industrial goods through organising work based on the principle of the *division* of labour, first articulated by Adam Smith in *The Wealth of Nations* in 1776. As part of the Western things-oriented, divided worldview, this principle increased productivity by orders of magnitude and has since been applied to almost every aspect of a company, including production and management, with the aim of reducing the cost of goods for the expanding mass markets.

Thus, for two centuries, business success in the West was almost synonymous with management excellence – improving efficiency while expanding capacity – because, deprived of material goods, customers were more than happy to buy whatever companies offered them. Meanwhile, business schools in the West focused on preparing students as specialists in functions like finance, marketing, operations and personnel; an MBA was equivalent to a collection of techniques for managing these functions. Even courses on strategy were dominated by analysis because it was easy to find material for analysis, and consequently straightforward to teach and comfortable to learn in a classroom.

However, by the early 1980s, Western companies began to realise that the rationalist model, i.e. the things-oriented, rules-driven, "corporate machine" they had relied on to achieve operational excellence, lacked flexibility to respond to external changes, such as increasing customer power, intensified competition, shortened product life cycles, and rapid technological development. Moreover, the idea of each company as a self-sufficient organisation with only transactional links with the outside world has since been rapidly dying because business success has increasingly been associated with staying close to customers, establishing long-term relationships with suppliers and forging alliances with competitors. To make matters worse, Western companies now have to confront all the above challenges in the context of globalisation driven by the lowering of trade barriers, the spread of de-regulation, and the plummeting cost of transport and communication. Over the past decade, foreign direct investment around the world has been growing four times as fast as world output and three times faster than world trade.

By the late twentieth century, it became widely accepted that human beings could not be treated as if they were just "things" or an "IQ" score, or even "skills" or "assets", because their emotions and value judgements are just as important. Indeed, underlying all the business challenges Western companies have to confront in the 21st century and beyond is the challenge of understanding human nature and capturing hearts and minds. The stakes are extremely high. Surveys put the success rate of alliances at about one in five and their life expectancy at about four years because of relationship problems; no leadership training programmes are as effective as an international assignment that significantly broadens one's people orientation, but most Western companies cannot guarantee jobs on return.

Yet, there is evidence that ancient Chinese wisdom is a source of inspiration for Western business people. Recognising that Western languages, with their subject-verb-object structure, shape straight-line perceptions, management guru Peter Senge called for a language made up of circles, which is important when people need to see beyond events and into the forces that shape change. But the Chinese language is based precisely on such a philosophy. This is also why *The Art of War* and *Tao Te Ching* have been widely interpreted for application to business. Even the popular movie *Wall Street*, a tale of corporate mergers and hostile takeovers, utilised Sun Tzu's wisdom in the battle of wits between Gordon Gekko, the film's villain, and the young hero Bud Fox.

In *Built to Last* (1994), a fixture on the *Business Week* best-seller list for more than five years with nearly one million copies sold worldwide, James Collins and Jerry Porras have used the Chinese *Yin Yang* symbol to represent the dualistic philosophy (one that is able to embrace two seemingly contradictory forces or ideas at the same time) of such highly visionary companies as GE, Boeing, Disney, HP and P&G. In *Good to Great* (2001), Collins again used the *Yin Yang* philosophy to develop his Level 5 leadership, which is equal to a duality of humility and will, and other business organisation concepts. IBM's "fit for the future" seminars introduce employees to *I Ching*. Andy Grove, former Chairman and CEO of Intel and "the best manager in the world" according to *Forbes* once commented to a Chinese fellow that his many ideas on running Intel were from Chinese philosophy. He also pointed out that the Chinese did not seem to attach enough importance to operational management.

Indeed, the few leading Chinese businesses with international competitiveness, such as Haier, which has grown from a small refrigerator factory in 1984 to the world's top sixth white household electrical appliances manufacturer with sales of US$7.3 billion in 2001, can attribute much of their success to embracing Western management. On 7 December 1999, Haier's CEO Zhang Ruimin was ranked twenty-sixth by *The Financial Times* on the list of the world's thirty most respected business leaders. Apart from habitually reading *Tao Te Ching* and *The Analects*, Zhang reads many Western management books. As such, he has absorbed advanced thoughts of both Western and Chinese civilisations to develop Haier's business philosophy and culture. For example, he sees that while the objective of a business is to maximise its long-term profitability, its aim is to harmonise with society and advance its evolution, and that a business produces not only products but also people. He also likened a business to a ball on a slope where, while it is important to bring individuals' initiatives into full play, fundamental management is essential to stopping the ball from rolling down. Recognising Haier's achievement, Harvard Business School in 1998 invited Zhang to its MBA class to discuss its philosophy and culture.

Of course, in this increasingly "messy" business world, the "new economic superpower" stands out – the overseas Chinese, whose businesses exhibit all the characteristics that Western companies lack, such as "responsiveness" and "flexibility". They can be big or small, local or regional according to need, using their ready-made, "trust"-based network of allies to dart in and out of markets quickly. Consider Li Ka-shing, one of the best examples of Chinese entrepreneurs, to whose offer another Chinese businessman once responded within fifteen minutes to enter into a joint venture. Li's father, a teacher, moved his family to Hong Kong in 1940. He died two years later when Li was only 13. After some hard work in factories, Li struck out on his own at 24, starting a plastic flowers business. In 1958, he began buying property. In 1972, Li took his main company, Cheung Kong, public. Today he controls companies worth over 10% of Hong Kong's total stock market value.

Back in the early 1960s, Li keenly sensed the complementarity as well as the differences between Western and Chinese cultures. He said: "I like reading books on philosophy. I think that some Confucian thoughts, such as keeping one's word, being loyal to one's friends and being willing to forgive others, are invaluable. But Confucian thoughts are weak in enterprise. Western thoughts are rules-based and enterprising. It is most effective to employ a combination of Confucian and Western thoughts." Li therefore strove to avoid Chinese family-style business administration by using Western managers, such as Erwin Leissner and Paul Lyons, while he concentrated on the making of crucial decisions. He said that with respect to business administration, it was better to acquire Western scientific management knowledge, but with respect to self-cultivation and dealing with people, it was better to learn ancient Chinese philosophical thoughts. He sent his two sons to America for higher education but also taught them to embrace Chinese wisdom, such as respecting human feelings and knowing when to compromise and when to stay low.

Noting the outstanding success of the overseas Chinese, Peter Drucker appealed in 1995: "Will *The Secrets of Chinese Management* be the title of the management best-seller of the year 2005?" I would conclude that, in short, the secret lies in **combining modern Western management excellence and ancient Chinese leadership wisdom**. And through examining Sino-Western joint ventures that are an engagement of 2,500 years of almost oppositely developed Chinese and Western civilisations, this book has shown how to.

Indeed, history has come full circle: after 2,500 years of exploration, the West finds that the solutions to its business problems reside in ancient Chinese agricultural civilisation. But *The China Executive* has been as much about "how to think" as it has been about "what to do". For, just like the fact that to ultimately have a successful family you must first have a family mindset, to ultimately have a successful ness, you must first have a global mindset. And a global imply an elevated, enlarged mindset that seeks to combine of the Western mindset and those of the Eastern mindset.

INDEX